The
PERFECT
PUNTER

The
PERFECT
PUNTER

A year of losing everything
and trying to win it all back

DAVE FARRAR

BLOOMSBURY
LONDON · BERLIN · NEW YORK · SYDNEY

To the memory of Tony Cooper

Published in the UK in 2012 by
John Wisden & Co
An imprint of Bloomsbury Publishing Plc
50 Bedford Square, London WC1B 3DP
www.bloomsbury.com
www.wisden.com

Copyright © Dave Farrar 2012

ISBN 978 1 4081 4081 9

He shook his head. 'I saw you lighting a candle. Come here.'

'I like candles, they're pretty.'

He ran his hands through her hair: 'You like their flicker. You like their transience. I understand.'

'There's something you should know about me,' she said, 'I'm a bit of an arsonist. Not serious. I wasn't going to burn down the church. But I am turned on by flame.'

He laughed and kissed her face: 'Hush,' he said, 'hush my love.'

In the morning he woke to twin realisations. The first was that she had left him. The second was that his sheets were on fire.

The Finkler Question, Howard Jacobson

CHAPTER ONE

She's where it begins, so I suppose you'll want to know what she looks like. All that I can see, every morning when I wake up and think that she's there, is curls and kindness and warmth and the colour red and a smile with a gap in it. And for that flicker of an eyelid my heart leaps at the thought of her. And then she's not there. And that's all that you're getting.

She hated me gambling, but I don't think that's why she left. I don't know because she never told me, but what she did was so considered and so precisely timed, that it couldn't have been the gambling. That would have been a storm down the road in tracksuit bottoms and no make-up, disappear for an hour and then a shaky warning on return. But she walked out when I wasn't there, and left me four lines on a piece of paper. And in case you're wondering, because people always ask, the lines were: 'I'm leaving. I'm sorry. Don't call me. I'm not coming back.' And then she signed her name. All of those times that real life seems like a bad movie, bundled together and scratched onto the back of a London Underground map.

In the midst of the shock, the pain, the terrible emptiness, I needed something to blame, and it couldn't have been me, so I blamed the gambling. If I hadn't been so selfish, if I'd realised that she wasn't as understanding as she said she was, if I'd known that she was just being kind and patient, but never happy, then maybe I'd have had the answers, maybe I'd still have her, and maybe I wouldn't be standing here holding a torn piece from her diary. Her diary has lines of poetry, books she had to read, CD ideas and birthday reminders. Mine has a profit and loss column, a sporting calendar and little else.

When something like that happens, and when you have no reason to cling onto, you need something to blame. I was blind to any other cause, and so I blamed the gambling. It was what had got me into this mess, and so it was gambling that would get me out, as I thought that it had so often in the past. It was time to make my deal with the devil, my Faustian apology. I'd get punting out of my system, and then I'd win her back. I'd bet like a demon, I'd double my usual stakes, and I'd win a small fortune. And then I'd take her on holiday, buy her a house, give her the things that I thought she wanted, and everything would be all right. It wouldn't take long, and then I'd be done with betting and happy with her. Writing this down for the first time makes me realise how wrong headed it was, and if I could type with one finger while covering my eyes in shame and embarrassment, trust me I would. But back then, it seemed like the perfect idea, the solution to everything, a few moments in time that would make things go back to the way they were. I just chose the wrong time, the worst time.

I don't think I'm addicted to gambling. I know how that sounds, because I've seen the look on people's faces when I say it. I've always gambled a lot, and sometimes it costs me money, but then my gambler's logic goes that hobbies and interests cost money. Even when I've had a bad year, I still have friends who'd spend more on a new car or a skiing holiday than I would ever lose at a race meeting, and so that's always been the convenient rationale. I hate cars, I can't ski and I enjoy punting. Plotting a bet and standing by the winning post and watching months of research and bundles of instinct mean that you've predicted the winner of a particular race, a football match, a golf tournament, is one of the best feelings that anyone could ever have. And over the years, I haven't been bad. There've been shocking days, but I still remember Rooster Booster in the Champion Hurdle, Justin Leonard at the Open, and Superior Premium in my favourite race, the Stewards' Cup, back in 1998. There was even the 100-1 shot Norton's Coin, for pennies, in the Cheltenham Gold Cup when I was still a student, when the woman who ran my halls of residence gave me a tip out of the side of her mouth, and when £200 was an awful lot of money. The memories are way better than the financial gain, and it's gambling for fun, rather than profit. But there's always just enough success to make you come back for more. Just enough to make you believe that you could make a go of doing it properly for a month. My first English teacher was an Alexander Pope fanatic, and so I learned poem after poem by heart: 'A little learning is a dangerous thing.' I'd learned, but never listened.

Because everything that I touched went wrong. Horses were beaten a short head, or fell at the last, or ran their worst race of the season when they were carrying my money. Late chances were missed, putts didn't drop, and I found my betting accounts down by more than they'd ever been and I started to panic. After a few months of carnage, she seemed even further away than she had been at the start of the year, and I had to at least break even. We were a few months down the line and I'd already lost half of the sum that I'd set aside for this period that was supposed to change my life and win her back. And so I started to chase my losses. And chasing is the worst thing that you can do, and the closest to out and out insanity that I've ever felt. Or rather not felt. Because I lost all feeling for what I was doing, all sense of the worth of things, and I started to bet on anything, to take prices which were far too short, because I wanted to guarantee a winner, or backed outsiders in the hope of having a big win, the kind of booming win that I now needed to make back what I'd lost. And short price, long price, they all lost. I was King Midas's hopeless younger brother, and I was running out of time.

I'd started out with a sensible staking plan, a level headed idea of how things should be approached, and how adversity should be dealt with, and that was out of the window before I knew it. You start out wanting money to chase a dream, and end up with no sense of what money is anymore. Your confidence is shot, and without confidence, you really can't gamble.

The darkness at the heart of every addiction is knowing that what you're doing is harmful, but being powerless to stop yourself doing it. Ask the alcoholic about his last drink of the night, the user about their erratic journey at four in the morning. And because I was hurt, and lonely, and in need of a blazing light at the end of a long tunnel, all that I wanted to do was win, and get back on an even keel. I dreamt of the day that I could look at my betting account and just see a zero there. No profit, no loss, just break-even would do. And I told myself that when I got to that point, I'd be finished with gambling forever. The downward spiral started with Superbowl night, when a former drug dealer from Florida threw me a big bundle of despair. Superbowl night, of all nights.

You see I'd met her on Superbowl night four years earlier. In Kilburn, in a dirty bar with a late licence and a TV screen. I only go out in Kilburn because my friend Sean lives there. Sean is an eternal optimist, and has to be. He's one of the nicest human beings that you could ever meet, but he's had a bit of bad luck with women down the years and so the optimism can be misplaced. He has a line in conversation which veers from the history of Bolton Wanderers to the economic policies of Hugo Chavez. He's the Che Guevara of the Reebok Stadium, and as a friend, he's priceless, but as a wing-man, usually a disaster. It was him who spotted her first. As I cheered on the Carolina Panthers against the New England Patriots (I'd backed the Panthers, and they lost, of course), he stalked the bar, bored several people out of their wits, before finding the only other person in there who wasn't glued to the game. They got talking, he came over and told me that he was 'in, son' (he calls everyone 'son', even girls) and then, during the half-time show, I went over to join them, Justin Timberlake showed Janet Jackson's nipple to the world, and Emma laughed. And, at that moment, I knew that I'd do anything for her, would build my life around her, if only she'd let me. I was hooked.

So, to my Superbowl experience four years later, on a drab night in Rome of all places. I was there for work, and that day at the end of January 2009 is still burned on my mind in Technicolor. It was a week after she'd left and was supposed to be the start of the gambling spree that would win her back. For a fortnight I'd loved, along with most of America, the story of Kurt Warner, the Arizona Cardinals' quarterback, who had dragged his team back from position after impossible position to somehow get them to the big game. Warner is the same age as me, and is the kind of man that I'd like to be, but am nowhere near. Honest, funny, self deprecating, and exceptional at what he does. I like letting my heroes carry my money, and so the Cardinals to win the Superbowl against the hot favourites the Pittsburgh Steelers had to be the bet. And I was optimistic. The life changing series of bets that would make me rich and get her back was about to start. The Cardinals were 4-1, far too big a price given the frequency of Superbowl upsets over the years. A friend of mine, a hugely successful American Football punter, had backed them big. And I wanted to do likewise. So I went to an internet cafe in Largo Argentina, looked at my gambling account, saw the money that I'd put in there to start this journey, and whacked it all on the Cardinals. I'd let Warner do the rest, and I'd be up and running.

This was proper money, and the most reckless that I'd been, and as I sat down at the nightmarish bar full of American students where we watched the match, I sipped my fizzy beer, and knew that if Arizona won and I walked out of the bar with a big profit, then I was on my way. I'd be in profit, I'd have momentum, and the stars would align themselves until Emma came back. I even felt that fate was involved, that Warner was a hero, he even looked like a handsome version of me, and it would happen. And when you start to believe in that kind of nonsense is when you should know that you're in way too deep. The Steelers led until the fourth quarter, the Cardinals weren't at the races, and I'd given up on the money. And then Warner drove his team downfield, conjured two fabulous touchdowns, and took them to the brink of a win, to a 23-20 lead with 35 seconds left. I was counting my money, and the biggest win of my gambling life was within touching distance.

And then a man called Santonio Holmes, who sold crack on the streets of Miami as a kid and who knows a thing or two about addiction, plucked a pass out of the air and won the game for the Steelers. Just like that. A leap and a twist and an amazing grasp at a very different kind of redemption, as mine flew out of the window. The commentators raved about one of the greatest plays in Superbowl history, and even though I knew they were right, my ears were ringing and my head felt like it was about to explode.

It's hard to describe how black your heart gets and how heavy your head weighs when you lose like that. It's an overused phrase, but in gambling, it really is the hope that kills you. I was surrounded by cheering Steelers fans, a few of whom had a thing or two to say to me as I'd been cheering on the Cardinals. It was time to get out and I trudged back to my hotel in a ferociously appropriate rainstorm knowing that the money was gone, and that now, after the first step of the journey that was supposed to change my life, I had nothing. No money, no her. In my mind, I was finished.

Except of course, I wasn't. In trying to start with some momentum, I'd lost my entire pot on the first bet that I'd had. So I transferred the same amount again into my punting account and started again, this time with my confidence on the wane and my vision a little more hazy. It wasn't the last time that I'd have to do some replenishing over the next six months, and I went through that first part of the sporting calendar in a blur. The Cheltenham Festival in March was a nightmare, a place where I'd always been successful turned into a steady stream of losers. That was followed by what I thought was a good outside shout on the Australian Neil Robertson to win the World Snooker Championship in Sheffield. He was undervalued in my opinion, and played fantastically to reach a semi-final in which he fell well behind, and then fought back to level at 14 frames all. Then he faded, and with him went my latest bit of hope.

I took a bit of time off, and then chose to wade in again, this time with a could not lose bet on Rafael Nadal to win the French Open at odds on. And he lost. His knees were betraying him and he fell to a first ever defeat at Roland Garros. The man who beat him, Robin Soderling, didn't even have the decency to go on and win the tournament, losing to Roger Federer in the final. The French Cup had always been kind to me, and so that was next on this whistlestop nightmare. In the final, I really fancied Rennes to beat Guingamp, couldn't really see how they could lose, and when Rennes took the lead with 20 minutes to go I thought that the slump had finally been arrested. And then Guingamp scored, and scored again, and I was beaten again. And so the irrational spree went, via a Serie A game here or there, and a bet on Phil Mickleson to win the US Open (he came second) and Lee Westwood to win the Open (he came third). Those two golf bets would normally have paid out, as I'd always bet each way on golf, but of course, in this frame of mind it was win only. Somewhere in between I decided that the undefeated Ruslan Chagaev might have enough to cause a shock against Wladimir Klitschko (he didn't) and that was the beginning of the end. In the end I lost count of how bad it had got, and felt like I was beaten. It was easy enough in the end to stop gambling as I didn't really have too much left to gamble with, and so I was able to come out blinking into the sunshine on the other side.

I had to stop behaving like an addict, and that wasn't hard. The basis of my mad six months had been emotion, had been desperation, and I knew that things had got as bad as they could. I decided that I would never gamble again, and would earn back every penny that I'd lost before I ever placed another bet. I'm lucky enough to do a job that pays well and, being freelance, I was able to work just about every day for the next four months to try and build up my bank balance.

In between those two losing golf bets, I'd realised that things couldn't get much worse, and so I'd taken myself to Vegas, via Los Angeles. If you're wondering how I paid for it, well it was already booked, and most bookies don't take airline tickets. Looking back now, I think that this was the beginning of the end of the nightmare. I'd never been to Vegas before, but I wasn't really going there to gamble. It was therapy before I truly realised that I needed it, and it was the best thing that I could have done. If you have an ounce of common sense left in you, then nowhere are the lessons clearer than in Vegas.

Somehow I knew that as I watched people overloading their senses with bet after bet then I might learn how valuable discipline could be. I stopped in Los Angeles on the way, and my choice of arrival date made life feel even stranger, even more like I was sleep-walking. Michael Jackson had died 24 hours earlier, and the place had turned several times on its axis. The crazies swarmed to Hollywood Boulevard, and the usual inhabitants were overrun. That included the lookalikes, all but one at least. On any run of the mill day in the middle of the summer, you can pay five dollars and get your photo taken with Elvis and Marilyn, with Barney and Shrek, and with two

Playboy bunnies to whom I seriously considered proposing. They'd all made their excuses and left, knowing that the queue to the Jackson star would be tacky, but maybe not *that* tacky. And yet one lookalike had stayed. And Bernard was making money: Bernard had decided that there was a game to be played as they poured out of the subway station to stare at a star on the sidewalk. Bernard is a Michael Jackson impersonator, and the day after his hero and meal ticket breathed his last, Bernard went to work, and to hell with those who thought it was in bad taste: 'people can say what they want, they can say that I shouldn't be here, they can shout and scream at me, but I ain't exploiting no one, I'm on my own train, and not on nobody else's.'

I admired Bernard just a little bit, as he danced and moved and picked up his five dollars a time. Because people did pay to have their photo taken with him, and even took some solace from what he was doing. As he moonwalked and mugged his way past the Chinese Theater, he must have earned enough to cover two months' worth of slow days, and on the subway home Elvis and Marilyn cursed their luck that they'd died so very long ago.

I thought of Bernard's road less travelled a lot when I was in Vegas, and realised that going against the supposed wisdom of the crowd really has to be the first rule of gambling. All steaming heat and false hope, Vegas is the place where people are scared of missing a trick, and where a rumour can become reality in the blink of an eye. If you hear that there's a party with free drinks at a club on the strip, then half an hour later you'll be standing with a martini in your hand and an eye full of female skin, and if word goes round the Sports Book at the Hilton that there's a good thing running at Churchill Downs then it will be backed off the boards. There's not too much room above the noise to hear the beat of a different drummer, and I realised that the cacophony which overpowers common sense in a casino, is exactly the same noise which had filled my head in January, and which had drowned me.

But if you can turn the volume down, Vegas is the perfect place to think about punting. Value isn't a concept in this town, it's all about luck, and if you ever needed a lesson that gambling is about a lot of hard work, a dash of science, a knowledge of numbers, and as little luck as possible, then that lesson is on offer everywhere, but only if you go against the crowd, the people who pretend to know something. It's not just about getting lucky, about your numbers coming up, about some warped sense of destiny: card counters and really good poker players aside, if you do the opposite of what everyone does in Vegas, then you're somewhere near the right track. I needed these lessons if I was to have any chance of winning back my money.

In the Paris casino, complete with rude waiters to give it that final dash of reality, I sat at a roulette table and saw a man in a pink suit, playing with pink chips, drop a couple of grand in five minutes, all playing the number 17, which he told us was his lucky number. He then played red and black and dropped four thousand more. And all the while he told the girl he was with that he knew exactly what he was doing. And when a guy sat down on the other side of the table and started to get lucky, the man in the pink suit jumped on the train and played the new numbers. And watched 17 come up twice, and dropped thousands more. Everywhere I went, the herd mentality was on view, and it got me thinking about the times that I'd fallen into that trap. An overreaction to football team news, jumping on a horse when the price has plummeted, convincing myself that I know something when all that I really know is the way that the crowd is moving.

The lesson that Vegas reinforces is that you have to thoroughly understand what you're betting on, and to use your knowledge to get an edge on the crowd to have any chance of making a go of gambling. Ignore the crowds or push against them. And make up your own mind. I could tell you many other stories about Vegas, about dead-eyed girls at four in the morning, and desperate people risking more than they have, but you'll have heard them all, and I'd got the only one that I wanted. Because the oddest thing about the town that is all about gambling is that it also produces the worst gamblers: the people with systems, the ones that feel lucky, the kind with too much money who lose what I had every single month. Because in Vegas the town will always beat you. Just look at the place, who do you really think pays for it?

When I got home I felt different. I started to watch sport again as I had done as a child, loving it for what it was, and not needing to bet on it to get a buzz. I never heard from Emma, and wasn't that interested in other girls, but somehow I felt cured, and oddly liberated by losing my money. It was said of the writer and wit Willie Donaldson that he only started enjoying life when his bad investments and worse habits freed him of the burden of his inheritance, and I started to realise what that meant. I was enjoying things for their own sake, and not because some greater good might arrive. I skated over the fact that Willie lived out his final years as a penniless crack addict and I started to get up early, and learn how to be properly fulfilled. Walking, swimming, smiling at people who I didn't know. This was the way forward. This was the way to be happy. And if she didn't want to be part of it, then she was the one who was missing out.

So as summer turned into autumn I was content. I wish I could say that I met a girl, one of those impossible beauties in print dresses that I always want to talk to, but somehow never can. I wish I could tell you that I was swept away in a new love affair and that my escape was somehow complete. But that would be a lie, and all the while, behind my happiness, there was something that wouldn't go away. Now that my head was right, and the darkness had gone and the pain was only just discernible, the loss of all of that money still weighed on me. I thought about how much people who actually work for a living earn, and how long it would take them to save what I had lost. And thoughts like that bring guilt, and guilt weighs you down, and with that heaviness in your heart you know that there's something else that you need to do to make everything right, to restore equilibrium, and to move on, and I'm sure that you know what I'm going to say next.

Because I started to wonder whether I could win the money back. I could accept the material loss to a point, but not the fact that punting had beaten me. The last thing that I wanted to do was have another bet, and yet I knew that the only way I could get it out of my system for good was to go in again, one last time, but this time do it properly, this time get it right. I'm competitive like that, and after all I hope that I'm a reasonably intelligent person, I do understand gambling, and there are plenty of people who punt successfully for a living. There had to be a way to learn how to be the perfect punter. This sounds as deluded as my previous plan, and seemed reckless and doomed to failure, but I couldn't get out of my head the idea that there must be a way of learning a skill that has so many unspoken rules, and so many potholes. If you could pick up some of one, and avoid most of the other, why couldn't you do it? I'd need the discipline to play at the right time, and I'd have to spend much more time on research than I'd ever done, but I was determined to give it a go.

And I was ready. I wasn't jumping on anybody else's train, I wasn't going to wear a pink suit, and I was sick and tired of being sick and tired of losing. I had to learn the courage of my convictions, and make sure that those convictions were as well thought out as they could possibly be. I wanted to need as little luck as possible, and I would need the help of anyone I could find. I was nearly ready to give myself the green light, and to go in once again, but this time to do it properly.

And to make the whole thing more cathartic, to finally try and get rid of that feeling that sport had beaten me, I'd only punt on the events on which I'd lost. I liked the idea of going back down the same well-worn route, the one which had just about broken me, and this time be the one in control. And control had to be at the centre of the new approach. Previously, I'd been a million miles away from the action, throwing darts in the dark at a board without a bullseye. So this time I'd visit each event that had cost me, and really get to know it. You can do your stats on a football match, on a horse race, and that will sometimes be enough, but nothing beats being there, and soaking up the atmosphere, letting your eyes and ears help you come to the right conclusion. So the bedrock of my attempt to claw back what I'd lost wouldn't be some financial whizz-kid approach, some City boy master class in how to gamble, but it would be about getting to the root of every single sporting event that I was going to chuck my money at. So much nonsense is talked about the process of gambling, that there's a danger of thinking about it too much. If I could properly analyse and truly understand every single event that I bet on, then I would be in prime position to make money. And what I imagined to be a gambling odyssey would actually become a sporting one. There'd be no more watching the Superbowl on the TV and guessing. If I was going to have a bet on it, then first I would have to visit Tampa, or New England, or Miami, or wherever the hell it was going to be played, and properly try to understand just what was going to unfold.

If it didn't work, then I was done with gambling, but I hoped to at least rediscover my love of sport for sport's sake, as well as the ability to predict how things might play out, and then get on with the rest of my life. Knowledge, pure knowledge, travel and hard work would be the keys, as I tried to turn myself into some cold-eyed punter who didn't feel the pressure, a Rahm Emanuel of the racecourse.

Before I committed myself, I felt that I needed a couple of trial journeys, which would at least give me a notion that this more forensic approach, this sporting approach, could work, and so, without staking any money, I fell back on my favourite football league, my old familiar, and scoured the Serie A calendar for something suitable. A friend of mine had told me over the summer that he felt Palermo would be making a big challenge for a European place that season and that their new coach Walter Zenga would try to do it by playing energetic, attacking football and taking a risk or two. My ears pricked up at this, because entertaining Italian teams are as valuable as boring German ones when you're betting on how many goals there'll be in a given game. The general perception of Italy is that not many goals are scored, and that every game in Germany finishes 6-3, and you'll often find value bets if you oppose the general consensus that Italian games will be low scoring and ones in Germany full of goals. What you need is a team whose profile hasn't really become known, and one which doesn't receive a heap of media coverage outside its own country. Palermo seemed to fit the bill. So I picked a Wednesday night game against a Roma team which certainly wouldn't go to Sicily and play for a 0-0 draw, and this would be my test case.

I made my way from the airport into town, on one of the slowest trains imaginable, and found myself blinking in the tatty, dusty central square where the locals look at you as if they can't believe that you've made the effort to come all this way. This was it. If the next two days worked, and I could translate them into profit on the night of the game, then it wouldn't definitively prove anything, but I would know, just for myself, that I was onto something.

Palermo is the only football team in Europe that wears pink as its number one colour, and maybe that's the reason that you don't sense the presence of the club in the town itself. It's one thing to see a group of burly tough guys waddling to the stadium on a match day swathed in fetching pastels, quite another for them to dress that way in their everyday lives. With a little investigation, though, fans aren't hard to find, and my first port of call was Giuseppe, an old friend who had supported Palermo all of his life, and who promised to take me as close to the heart of his club as he could. I needed to talk to people who had watched every game this season, and it was vital that they had no real idea of the bet that I was intending to place. I wanted them to tell me things, not simply confirm them just to make me feel welcome. The question: 'How do you think the match will play out on Wednesday?' is far more likely to get an honest and accurate answer than: 'I think there'll be goals on Wednesday. Do you?' And so it was that on the terrace of a hotel with an impossibly perfect view of a mountain I could talk to a roofer called Carlo, a pizza chef (I'm not making this up, I promise) called Gianni, and a man called Andrea who knows a lot about his team, but who I never quite managed to pin down, career wise. In Sicily, it's sometimes better not to ask too many questions.

They were bemused by my being there, but flattered that I wanted to know what they knew, and there is a fundamental truth, one on which I was relying heavily, that every football fan loves talking about their own team. None of them were convinced by Zenga, feeling that somehow he was at the club to better himself, rather than try to achieve something for Palermo. But they all said that they admired the kind of football that he was trying to play, and that they felt that the team would at least be worth watching this season. Zenga was playing 4-3-3, with the heavily tattooed and richly talented Fabrizio Miccoli playing in between two Uruguayans, the effeminate Edinson Cavani and the speedy and powerful Abel Hernandez. Miccoli had been brilliant in every game, Cavani inconsistent but occasionally outstanding, and Hernandez, a new player, looked like a real find. Those three, the fans agreed with some feeling, would get goals. But Palermo's problem in their eyes was that they'd concede too many to be able to mount a solid challenge for the top four. The Dane Simon Kjaer was excellent, but was surrounded by defenders who were either honest and cumbersome, or not brave enough. The view was that the defence needed more protection, and that playing 4-3-3 would expose their limitations. With Roma coming on Wednesday, Palermo would more than likely score, but it would be a miracle if they kept a clean sheet.

I asked the three for predictions, and Carlo the roofer went for 2-2, Gianni the chef for a 2-1 defeat and, after a lengthy pause, the inscrutable Andrea for a Palermo win by a 3-1 scoreline, a prediction which was greeted by respectful snorts of derision from the other two.

I realise that there's a danger of reading too much into the views of fans, as they're often spiked with either loyalty, or bitterness at the coach, or hopeless optimism. But the right kind of questions had, I felt, given me a picture of the team painted by those who knew it best. And at every bar I visited, every hotel reception, restaurant or shop I asked the same questions, looking to try and establish some kind of universal opinion about the match, the wisdom of the crowd. I pulled a string or two to go and watch the team train on Tuesday, and was impressed by the brightness and optimism of the players, and the tempo at which they were passing the ball. They looked to me as if they would try to catch Roma by surprise, and to overwhelm them with sheer energy. For a man who had come to Sicily feeling that this was a game which would produce goals, everything that I watched reinforced that idea. Zenga's news conference was characteristically chaotic, and when he was asked what his team's approach would be, the man who looked just as long haired and flamboyant as he had when he was Italian national goalkeeper smiled and said: 'We won't beat Roma by sitting back and letting *them* play.' I was onto something.

The final pieces of this jigsaw were the conditions on the day of the game. A monsoon hit Sicily, and with water sluicing through the streets there was a big question about whether the match would even take place. At four in the afternoon, just under five hours ahead of kick-off, I'd pretty much given up on finding any more dry clothes in my suitcase, and on having a game to watch that night. The last two days would have been in vain, and the potentially frustrating nature of this journey would have been hammered home. But then the rain stopped, and as I sat on the bus to the Renzo Barbera, a stadium which is an awkward distance outside of the city centre, a rainbow appeared above it. I was tempted to read this as a sign, but told myself that this was the kind of thing I had done in my previous gambling life, and that the new me, the wannabe perfect punter, was going to be all about cold-headed logic and not emotion. So with the rainbow to the back of my mind, I grabbed a coffee, complete with pink sugar sachet, and went out to see what damage the rain had done to the pitch.

It looked perfect, and a word with a groundsman confirmed that the rain had been a help not a hindrance, that there was no standing water and that the ball would move quickly across it. He added that it would be a very difficult pitch on which to defend, and that both Miccoli and Roma's iconic centre forward Francesco Totti could well have field days. Just as he mentioned their names, I saw Miccoli and Totti, two players united by the burden of being creative geniuses in an often stultifying league, chatting together on the pitch, laughing and smiling. They looked relaxed, and I think they agreed with the groundsman that it could be their night.

So I was in exactly the position that I'd hoped. Scores of gamblers around the world would be betting on this game and, while many of them would have done a lot of research, would know how many goals Palermo and Roma averaged per game, how well both teams performed when certain players were in and out of the team, none would be in the position that I was. Standing next to the pitch, having had the game and the conditions put into context by fans, by the coach, by the groundsman, and by the looks on the faces of both Miccoli and Totti. This was an experiment, and so I didn't have a bet, but I knew that this would be a maximum stake on there being at least 3 goals in the game (over 2.5 goals in gambling parlance) and a smaller, but still considerable stake on there being at least 4 (over 3.5). The next 90 minutes would define whether this journey to try and get ahead of the game, to literally chase my losses, and to try and become the perfect punter was on, or off. I felt like the next part of my life was at stake, and as the memory of Emma drifted further and further into the past, I knew that the next 90 minutes, and whatever followed, would be for me, and for no one else. There were ten minutes to go until kick-off, the rain started to lash down again, but too late to affect the pitch, and a bolt of lightning flashed over the mountains in the distance. I'd never been better prepared to place a bet, and I sensed that this was the way that it should be for the next year. The stage was set, and as the lightning flashed again, I was ready for anything.

CHAPTER TWO

The game in Palermo finished 3-3, and could have been 6-3 either way. There was even an added pictorial flourish: as Francesco Totti slammed home the equalising penalty two minutes from time a fork of lightning streaked across the mountain which overlooks the Renzo Barbera. 'It's just coincidence,' I muttered to myself, 'it's not a sign.' I walked away from the stadium not really noticing my wet trouser legs and just about ruined shoes and regretted not having a bet, but realised that this would be the start of a journey to a few more. There'd been a moment in the tunnel after the match when the Palermo manager Walter Zenga and Totti, two old friends and rivals, had stopped to talk to each other. They were smiling, and neither seemed too bothered that their team had dropped a couple of points. There was a hug and a 'good match Francesco, good match Walter' and then they were off. It was as if they knew. Not the kind of 'knew' that is often associated with Italian football, more a sense of the inevitable. Games like this always have goals, and players and managers know it. It's just a shame that punters don't. The closer you get to the action, though, the more chance that you've got.

I thought that proving a result to myself would be enough, but I still knew that the events which had started off my meltdown, the NFL Playoffs in America, were a couple of months away, and so I had time to set my sights, and try another experiment. I worked as a commentator at the Ryder Cup, and didn't want to abuse the trust of my closeness to the players by punting on the outcome of every match, but I felt that it was OK to surmise. As I got my second soaking of this putative mission, it was hard to keep any kind of focus.

The three days that became four of the Ryder Cup were wonderful in many ways. The rain absolutely pelted down on that first Friday, and the fairways weren't just covered in water, they had streams running down them, the drainage system a mini torrent alongside. I was so bored, sitting in a temporary broadcast studio and waiting for things to get going again, that I decided to go for a walk around the course. I was accompanied by the former European Tour player John Hawksworth, one of the sport's great characters, who simply jammed a rolled up fag into the corner of his mouth, turned up his collar and said: 'Come on son, let's go and see how bad it is.'

And it was terrible. The wet weather gear that I'd got for Christmas a couple of years ago, and which I'd packed quite smugly, knowing that it would keep me dry, was rendered useless in the space of five minutes as the rain drove sideways, and Hawksworth's fag went out. There was an unforgettable spirit among the fans who we spoke to, huddled against the side of grandstands or jammed under enormous umbrellas, but there was at the same time a feeling that the event couldn't possibly be completed. The rain was too powerful, the course too unprotected, the time of year too unkind. The greenkeepers and broom pushers, the organisers and forecasters will never get enough credit for what happened over the days to come. And Europe were good, they were very good. The players were lifted by a magnificent crowd, but they also seemed to deal better with the rain delays, and realise when the moment, and ultimately the match, could be seized. This was British sports fans at their best, determined and dogged, and not to be put off by a bit of rain.

I learnt a lot from Hawksworth as we walked the course that Friday. We were ankle deep in mud and in the mood to chat, and he told me a little about what life had been like as a professional golfer. He had been an absurdly talented amateur, good enough to play in the 1985 Walker Cup, the amateur Ryder Cup, alongside Colin Montgomerie. While Montgomerie soared as a professional though, winning eight European Orders of Merit, Hawksworth struggled, and I was fascinated to know why. Montgomerie is perceived to have underachieved in his career because he never won a major championship, but Hawksworth would have given anything for that kind of underachievement. And, as so often, it's the sportsmen who didn't make it who can tell you more than those who did. Hawksworth is funny, and self-deprecating, and can be seen as spiky by those who don't know him, but he taught me a lot about the mental struggles that golfers go through on that walk in the rain.

Once you become a tour professional, then day-by-day and week-by-week you're simply trying to make the game work for you. You want to win tournaments, you want to contend, and to do that you have to do your job. Hawksworth remembers Montgomerie as a pretty negative character in their amateur days, self-critical and never able to see the light, and yet he ruefully reflected, as we dodged another mini lake on the fairway, that 'something must have changed in him when he turned professional'. The problem, as always with a sport that is so technical and in the mind, is that what one player does can't be bottled and handed to another for them to get the benefit. That's why there's an industry of sports psychologists and putting coaches and swing gurus and personal trainers that follow every golf tour, trying to find a way for the players to make it work.

Hawksworth says that he never felt any pressure once he was in contention for a tournament, the pressure began for him at the start of the event, trying to *get* into contention in the first place. Do that for too long without breaking through and you'll feel like you need help. You'll think for hours before a round, you'll spend too long on every shot, and a game that you had played with such ease for the whole of your life will suddenly become very difficult. There's no easy answer when you're not entirely sure of the question. Hawksworth never found a way for his talent to take him to the place that he deserved, but he was happy in the end to emerge from the experience of being a pro with his sanity intact, and to sum up the frustration and the madness of the life that golfers lead, he told me the story of the day that finally changed him, that turned him into a positive thinker. He went to see a hypnotherapist in Blackpool, a recommendation from a friend, and was forced to confront every demon and doubt that had engulfed him. He'd dreaded the session, but found that talking about his frustrations allowed him to deal with them, and as he left a nondescript house on a suburban street, he closed the gate and emitted what he describes as a primeval roar, yelling to the heavens and vowing that from that moment on he would change. It went on for a while, and as he stopped, he turned and saw a woman who was out walking her dog staring at him. As ever with him, a serious and life enhancing tale ends up with you doubled up in laughter.

It was tempting to get my gambling frustrations out, and if I fancied a primeval roar, then Celtic Manor in the wind and the rain was definitely the place. But I decided that it was probably better not to look like a nutter, and walked on, and in, towards the warm.

With Friday just about a washout, the Ryder Cup organisers announced a change in format on Saturday and Sunday, with the intention still to try and complete the event by the end of the weekend. The different formats used in this unique event can be confusing, and so it's worth remembering that the players contest fourballs, in which all four players play a ball and the best score wins the hole. Then they play foursomes, which is one ball per team and alternate shots, and ultimately singles, which is man against man and a fight to the death and all that. Fourballs tend to be fascinating but tortuously slow, foursomes thrilling and hard to predict, and singles in turn either dramatic or one-sided.

The way that the Ryder Cup normally works is that four fourball matches are followed by four foursomes matches on the first day, that format is reversed on the second day, and the singles finish things off on the third. That means that a captain can technically use the same eight players on the opening two days, and then only use the four weakest members of his team on the third. That rarely happens in these days of higher golfing standards, but the hastily cobbled together format change at Celtic Manor, devised by Colin Montgomerie, meant that every single player would have a crucial role. And that's really how it ought to be.

Once the four fourball matches which had been left over from Friday had been completed, the two teams would play six foursomes followed by six more fourballs, before the singles on Monday. It meant that as soon as the players had finished one lot of matches, they would turn straight round and go out and play another, and this flurry of action, two days' worth crammed into just over half that time, would decide the Cup. And the foundations for Europe's win were laid on that Saturday evening, when Lee Westwood and Luke Donald led an extraordinary performance, and Europe took convincing leads in every one of the six foursomes matches. The USA team had gone into that third session of matches with a 6-4 lead, but as the light faded and the crowd got noisier, the European players were inspired. Turned out as they were in designer rain gear, which looked great, but wasn't waterproof, I don't think the USA players ever quite came to terms with the delays, with being cold and stiff, and then having to play brutal matchplay golf.

The strangest moment of the day was the sight of Steve Stricker being offered a greasy chip greenside by one of the on-course commentators, and accepting. 'Sure,' he said, 'what are they? Kinda fat fries?' He dunked a couple in ketchup, and munched away, anything to warm him up and make him feel at home, but he and his playing partner Tiger Woods were soon done for, swept aside by Donald and Westwood. And for all that they fought hard on a dryer and warmer Monday, and won the singles, the USA couldn't pull it back. The European team and its captain Colin Montgomerie received a lot of justifiable praise for the way that they won the Cup, but cold analysis of the facts afterwards showed that, of four sessions of intense golf, the USA had won three. The fact that Europe won those fourballs, the ones that started on that strange Saturday evening, by 5½ points to ½, was what put the gloss on their performance and led to them winning the Cup. You couldn't say that Montgomerie was lucky, but you could reasonably say that the USA were unlucky.

Amid all of the euphoria of Saturday and Sunday though, I didn't feel that every member of the European team was playing well. It was more a case of eight or nine players producing sensational golf, and carrying the team along. That, after all, is the point of a team, and what makes the Ryder Cup such a unique event in such a self-obsessed sport. The way that the format works should be perfect for a gambler who is prepared to do some research. In a strokeplay event, a player's level of performance is there to see in black and white on a scorecard at the end of a day's play. Sure, there'll be times when someone gets lucky, and shoots a better score than they deserve, and the reverse can be true as well, as Lee Westwood proved in just about every major championship of 2011, but more often than not, the best player over four days wins in strokeplay. In matchplay, particularly in the fourball format, it's possible to be carried by a partner to a win, and go into a singles match on the final day having officially scored a few points for the team without having played well.

After following them around for a while, I felt that two big members of the European team were undercooked. Martin Kaymer, the apparently super cool German who had kept his nerve better than anyone to win the USPGA Championship that August, had performed sporadically and nowhere near his own high standards. Some players seem to be inspired by the team format, and thrive off the buzz of competition, having a team room to bond in and your mates to cheer you on. Ian Poulter is the obvious example of that, while Kaymer seems quiet and calculating, and happier to plough his own furrow. A nice guy, but better as an individual than as part of a team. Kaymer had won 2½ points on the previous two days, and ostensibly had performed well, but the statistics proved that he hadn't been at his best.

The other player I had my eye on was Padraig Harrington, a man who had played brilliantly to win three major championships back in 2007-8, but who had continued to tinker with his game, and now gave the impression on the tee of a slightly fussy uncle putting up shelves. Harrington had worked hard before those major wins with a coach called Bob Torrance, father of Sam, on being able to fly the ball higher through the air, something that comes naturally to American players who aren't brought up, like Harrington, on windy links courses in Ireland. The hard work was rewarded with the Irishman's third major championship, the USPGA at Oakland Hills in Michigan, and at that point he had seemed certain to become one of the best two or three players in the world. But having tinkered to get somewhere, Harrington felt the need to fiddle again, and, to many experienced eyes, he started to overthink his game. One former European tour professional likened it to a normal person putting food into their mouth with a fork. It's something that we've all done hundreds of thousands of times, but if we start to think about what it is that we're actually doing as the fork is in mid-air, then we'll miss once in a while. What should be natural becomes anything but, and so it was with Harrington's swing. Grooved and second nature since he was a boy, and now fraught and self-conscious. There's nothing wrong in theory with trying to be a perfectionist, but not if it takes away your golfer's instinct.

Harrington was in just that position, and watching him play with Ross Fisher on the Saturday and Sunday had been torture. He had lost accuracy with his driver, and Celtic Manor was playing long. To win a match here you needed to be driving well. When I saw Harrington hoick a couple of drives way to the left on the 12th hole, and saw Fisher produce a birdie to win the hole, it summed up the feeling of the day. Harrington was desperate to make a contribution to the team, but he was struggling badly while his partner flourished. After he and Fisher had won their point on Sunday afternoon, Harrington was a livewire presence around the greens. Sitting next to a bunker on the 17th, and watching Francesco Molinari line up a tricky putt, I saw Harrington tiptoe over to Montgomerie and whisper to him that he knew the line of the putt as he'd missed it earlier and he feared that Molinari was about to make the same mistake. Montgomerie looked a little confused and said: 'Shall I tell him?' Harrington nodded and so Montgomerie quietly made his way onto the green and whispered the line of the putt into Molinari's ear. He missed, but the whole incident painted Harrington as a man who knew that he wasn't making much of a contribution, but was desperate to help the team out. A good man, just one who wasn't playing well, and, in betting terms, one who had to be taken on.

Having watched the Irishman spray the ball wide of so many fairways, and knowing just how important driving was on this course, I asked a few of the ex-players who were working around the course just how he could get his driving right for the singles matches. They spoke in that way that golfers do, always hoping that they can find a way to make things click, but knowing that the answer is nearly always hard work and timing. Keep practicing, and it will come. So the verdict was that Harrington would go to the driving range that night and hope that things would come together, then work again in the morning and do the same thing, maybe throwing in a call to a psychologist who could try and find a way to make things work. That sounded a bit vague to me, and so I asked again what were the chances of that actually happening, of everything suddenly clicking into place. The ex-pros shrugged their shoulders, talked again about hope, and I realised that Harrington was looking for a miracle.

In my mind, whoever he played in the singles would have a great chance of beating him. So all there was to do was wait and see who he would have to play. I hoped on that Sunday night as we waited for the singles draw that Harrington wouldn't be up against one of the big American players, a superstar like Woods or Mickelson who would start as a heavy favourite anyway, and completely nullify any benefit that my strong opinions about Harrington had given me. I was praying for Jeff Overton, the young rookie from Indiana, who had played wonderfully for two days but hadn't quite got the credit that he deserved. Harrington would more than likely be odds on to beat him, and Overton would have a massive chance.

In the end, Harrington was drawn to play Zach Johnson. I wasn't too disappointed. Johnson is another of those unflashy players who tends to be undervalued, a God-fearing man who hides behind sunglasses and who was still a long way from being a household name, despite winning the US Masters back in 2007. He was 7-4 to beat Harrington, and, after being selected as a wild card by the USA captain Corey Pavin, had played well enough in the Ryder Cup so far to make that an attractive price. So that was my second theoretical bet, the second part of proving to myself that I could make the next six months work – Palermo part two. Kaymer pulled Dustin Johnson out of the hat, but having seen Johnson implode in that summer's US Open, and then suffer a mental lapse in the USPGA, I couldn't put my faith in him against the German. And so the bet was Zach Johnson to beat Harrington. Again, no money involved, but what a conman would call a convincer.

I didn't watch a ball that Harrington or Zach Johnson hit on that Monday. I was out on the course, watched Kaymer get into trouble early on against Dustin Johnson and cursed myself for not opposing the German, and then went off to follow Tiger Woods against Francesco Molinari. The Johnson v Harrington match was the penultimate one, preceding the Graeme McDowell v Hunter Mahan pairing that would ultimately decide the Cup. I only had the occasional scoreboard to help me watch the Irishman's progress. Early on, as Molinari took a lead against Woods, I felt like I'd cracked it. Johnson was two up on Harrington after just two holes, and I had visions of him romping to a win by a gigantic margin, with all of my theories about Harrington's lack of accuracy and confidence being proved right. As Woods started to fight back in spectacular fashion against Molinari, and I became absorbed in that match, I lost sight of Johnson v Harrington, but then spotted a leaderboard which told me that the American was now five up and was going to win easily.

Johnson *did* win, and yet that didn't tell the whole story. After the American had gone two up after two holes, Harrington fought back to level the match, only for Johnson to streak clear again. Eventually, they shook hands on the 16th green, with Johnson three up, but a closer analysis of the scoring told me that I'd been lucky, and wrong to write off Harrington so dismissively. The Irishman had opened with two bogeys, and lost those holes, probably causing a few who were watching to raise their eyebrows and wonder whether he'd ever get his mojo back. He dug deep, and showed the kind of spirit that you have to have deep in your soul to be a multiple major champion by birdying two of the next three holes to level the match up. And from then on, it wasn't a case of Harrington falling apart, which was the basis of my bet, but of Johnson playing unbelievable golf. He won five of the next eight holes but did so in 6 under par, and blitz of five birdies and an eagle that no other European on the course could have coped with. Johnson took 44 strokes to play holes 1–13, and only Tiger Woods, in frightening form, was better over the same stretch, taking 43. Harrington hadn't played particularly well, but would have beaten a few of the Americans that day. I'd struck lucky, however, in picking Johnson. He may not have grabbed the headlines on that Monday, but played at a level that only Woods could match. He would have beaten anyone. Kaymer *did* fall apart, losing 6 and 5 to Dustin Johnson, and so it turned out that the Johnson double would have paid out. For now, though, I was happy that Zach had given me another theoretical win, even though Dustin had passed me by.

I always try and take something out of every sporting event that I watch, and think about bets for the future. I interviewed Woods after his stellar performance, and, as well as being surprisingly gracious (surprising because of all the stories I'd heard), I got the impression that he felt he was coming back to his best. When I suggested that the player that we had seen that afternoon was something approaching the old Tiger, I thought that I might get a glare or even a punch in the face, but he just smiled that smile and said that, yeah, he felt better than he had in ages. I would be backing him to win the US Masters next spring, and I would also keep an eye on Rickie Fowler, who had looked like a scared kid as the event started, and yet had managed to birdie the final four holes under immense pressure on the final day to get the half point against Eduardo Molinari that very nearly kept the Ryder Cup on the other side of the Atlantic. Fowler clearly had a steel which wasn't apparent when you looked at the baby face, the tan and the outlandish clothes. He would surely win a major one day, possibly the following year. Lee Westwood was looking like the best player on either team and I also wondered about Poulter. If he played in major championships like he did in Ryder Cups then he would have won one by now, probably a US Open or an Open. Poulter had cost me a lot of money in his career so far, as I'd always been convinced that he would make that breakthrough. As I watched him celebrate on the 18th green with his mates he seemed in his element, and maybe that's him: destined to be a great matchplayer, a wonderful pressure putter, and a great team man without ever quite having the discipline over four days to win a major championship. I hope I'm wrong, as I've always thought there's a nice bloke hidden behind the peacock clothes. But I'd desert him for now. I also felt that Harrington was becoming a lost cause (he hasn't won an event since), and that Kaymer might be starting to go backwards (he won the following week). I realised that lazy suppositions would get me nowhere.

There's a picture frozen in my mind from those celebrations on the 18th green on that remarkable Monday night. Poulter and Westwood, Ross Fisher and Donald, were all in great form, smiling for the cameras and obliging to every interviewer. The Molinari brothers sat proudly with an Italian flag, and Kaymer stood and smiled. And through a spray of champagne, I can remember the three Northern Irishman, Graeme McDowell, Rory McIlroy and the non-playing vice captain Darren Clarke, arms round each other in celebration. One had already won a major, one surely would, and one must have been standing there wondering what might have been. All three of those men would have an enormous impact on my efforts to win my money back over the next year. But for now, I'll leave them frozen in celebration, friends at different stages of their lives, all with no idea what was about to happen to them.

CHAPTER THREE

It's a funny habit, gambling, a strange addiction. If you're an alcoholic or drug user then there's an obvious physical deterioration and a lack of focus which, however slowly, will indicate that all is not well. You'll turn up late for work and be a dick to your friends, and so you're there to be saved, if there's saving to be done. You can't escape any addiction before you've worked it out for yourself, and so the private humiliations pile up. In the spectacular story of his alcoholism, *Dry*, Augusten Burroughs talks of not feeling anxiety 'until you have carried a plastic trash bag stuffed with a few hundred beer bottles down the stairs in the middle of the night, trying not to make a sound.' Addiction is an essentially private torture, and the skill of the addict is lasting for as long as possible with as few people as possible realising that anything is wrong. Burroughs' few hundred beer bottles are a gambler's ability to go to work the day after a spectacular loss, still able to buy a lunchtime sandwich, still able to hold a conversation about sport, even the event that has cost him the night before.

Because most people take drugs of some sort (and yes, I'm including alcohol) they have a natural empathy with anyone who's fallen foul of them, feel like they can understand what it must be like when you end up wanting to deaden all of your nerve endings. And that empathy helps a non-alcoholic, say, to at least feel that they understand alcoholism. A close friend of mine told me this year that she had been going to AA and that she'd had a problem for many years and that all of the times that she was throwing back shots with me when it seemed like fun she was feeding this monster that would eventually take her over. The agony and shame in her eyes as she told me the real story, her inside story, of the last ten years made me feel desperate for her, and the look of pride when she told me how many days she'd been clean made me happy. But a large part of me, as her one-time drinking partner made me think: 'shit, that could have been/still could be me'. We understand the drinking, but can't quite comprehend the final slide, the thing that makes you lose control completely. The vodka on the breakfast cornflakes; the sleeping in a shelter on the seafront.

I went to a couple of meetings during the course of this process. One, with a friend, was an AA meeting, and I sat in silence and was just there to try and help. There's a mixture of desperation and hope, and with that comes a humbling sense of support. As long as the hope outweighs the desperation then you have a chance. At the Gamblers Anonymous meeting I went to, this time for myself, the balance was the same, between desperate people and the hope that they could move forward, but there was an added feeling that no one outside the room really gets it. No matter how bad you are at the process itself, no matter if it's online poker or horses or fruit machines or lottery tickets, only a gambler understands a gambler. It comes back to the empathy thing. If you've had a drink, then you're less likely to judge an alcoholic. If you've had a bet, you're less likely to judge a gambler. And more people have had a drink than have had a bet. So the empathy, and therefore, sympathy pool is smaller. I'm not asking for sympathy, just interested that there is none. If you're going to gamble, be prepared for a whole world of sneering from those who don't get it, and for the constant application of a series of rules that apply to your subsection of society, and yours alone. Take the following two conversations, which are played out in workplaces all over the world every single Monday morning. Conversations between people who have what they would describe as the odd flutter, and people who, well, take it more seriously and are in a bit deeper:

'So Dave/John/Julia, how was the racing at the weekend? Any winners?'

'No, I had a bit of bad luck early on, and tried to get it back on the last, but Chris Catlin got boxed in on the rail and the horse finished second. One of those days.'

'So how much did you lose?'

(At this point, you want to say that it's none of their business and that you haven't asked them how much *they* spent on Friday while they were trying to grope the new girl in accounts over a last desperate round of tequilas. But you tell yourself that you're not like that, and the thought stays inside, and instead you take a bit off the real amount and say, with what you imagine to be a shrug which is both generous and world weary at the same time):

'Oh, I don't know, about a hundred quid.'

'Ah,' comes the response, 'that's why you'll never see a poor bookie.'

The last statement is usually accompanied by a knowing smile and a sense of certainty which you could undermine by telling the story of how much independent bookies actually struggle, and how the fact that they're still prepared to stand on the rails at Cheltenham and take a proper bet is actually something to be admired rather than taken for granted, but you'd only make yourself angrier and so you smile, say something you presume to be pithy, and walk away.

And then there's the second conversation:

'So Dave/John/Julia, how was the racing at the weekend? Make any money?'

'Yeah, it was brilliant actually. Backed three winners, and me and some mates got the placepot up too. Had a great day, champagne at the end to celebrate and everything, it was excellent.'

'Really? How much did you win?'

(At this point you still think that it's none of their business, but you know that you're going to tell them, and so you think of the real figure and inflate it, and you say):

'I don't know, a grand and a half?'

And with that you get a knowing smile, followed by, so the whole office can hear:

'Drinks are on you then!'

So gambling is a habit to be milked when it's working and patronised when it's not, and I can't think of any other pastime to which the same set of social rules apply. A pitying presumption that what you're doing is stupid, and yet an active desire to join in the fun when it works out. Most people *think* that gamblers can't win; we pretty much *know* that we can't, but we enjoy the ride, and we wake up every morning with that hope, that feeling that today could be the day. And the fact that the wider world doesn't understand makes us all the keener to be successful, and to refuse to play to its rules. Punters aren't self consciously in a gang, like rugby players or Cliff Richard fans, but they can spot each other a mile away and there'll be a nod, a moment of respect. I always remember Ian McGeechan's speech to the British Lions in that DVD that a certain kind of person always recommends: 'All it will be between you is a look. No words. Just a look. And it will say everything.'

Well, it's the same with gamblers. After a bad day at Cheltenham, a good day elsewhere, a casual conversation in a pub, a reaction during a sporting event – we can always spot each other. It's not the same look that McGeechan is talking about in his spectacular call to arms. That's about pride and inspiration and a job to do. It's the same reason behind the look though. Something in common that no one else will understand. The look that punters share is all about fear, and self-loathing, and worst of all, hope. Always hope.

I spent a long time looking for a gambling parable that I could cut out and keep. A source of strength that I could keep in my wallet and that would remind me of just how absurd it all is. An Australian girl that I knew in Paris, a drinking partner and a brilliant philosopher on late night walks home, told me once that whenever she was feeling that the world was against her, or that things really weren't adding up, she would look up at the stars and imagine that they had formed into a large mouth. And then she imagined the mouth opening up and emitting the biggest belly laugh that you've ever heard. 'Dave,' she would say, 'if you can look up and believe that the whole sky is laughing at you, then you'll realise that you're fucked anyway, and so you'll soon put your real life in perspective.' She had a way with words, did Annie, and also the habit of saying things at four in the morning that still made sense the next day.

The thing that I found, that turns my sky into a belly laugh, that I keep in my wallet, and which stays there all the time, long after the money has gone, is a story from an American racetrack, one that features in Jon Bradshaw's brilliant gambling book from the 1970s, *Fast Company*. And it'll do for me:

'A gambler arrives at one of the Eastern tracks a few years ago with $5 in his pocket. He was a familiar figure at the course in his rumpled suit and scuffed shoes, a punter down on his luck of late. In the first race of the afternoon he bet the $5 on the second favourite and the horse came in paying $30. In the second race he bet the $30 on a long shot which went off at 12 to 1. The horse won easily and the gambler collected $390. For the remainder of that afternoon, in each successive race, the gambler bet his total winnings on some previously selected choice. By the sixth race, he had amassed $4,000, and he placed it all on the nose of a 3 to 1 shot. The horse, a tip from one of his friends in the paddock, came from behind to beat the favourite in a photo finish. The gambler now had

$16,000 in his pocket. In the final race of the day he bet the lot on the heavy favourite. The race began, and the favourite, taking an early lead, held it into the top of the home straight. At this point, the horse was more than a length in the lead but, tiring, she was beaten on the line by a short head. The gambler was broke. Buttoning his rumpled suit, he shuffled slowly along the track. At the main entrance he was hailed by an old acquaintance, who asked how he had fared that afternoon. Lighting a cigarette, the gambler shrugged and said, "Not bad, not bad. I lost five dollars."'

The reason that I love this story so much is that it reminds me how impossible it is to try and stay steadily ahead of the game when you're a punter, and also of the unceasing optimism that we all share when we're setting off for a day's racing, or trying to plot a way through a Saturday afternoon of sport. There's a similar parable in rather more rarified surroundings, which sits at the start of Franz Kafka's nightmare of a novel, *The Trial*. A man arrives from the country and wants access to a thing called 'the law', and in front of him sits a door and a gatekeeper. He asks to go in, and the gatekeeper tells him that there are a series of gates, and that he will only be allowed in if he gets past every gatekeeper, but never explains how this is possible. The man bribes the gatekeeper, who accepts his money, but only does so, he tells him: 'so you do not feel that you have failed to do anything.' After many years, the man starts to fade, and the parable reaches its end:

'Finally his eyesight grows weak, and he does not know whether things are really darker around him or whether his eyes are merely deceiving him. But he recognises now in the darkness an illumination which breaks inextinguishably out of the gateway to the law. Now he no longer has much time to live. Before his death he gathers in his head all his experiences of the entire time up into one question which he has not yet put to the gatekeeper. He waves to him, since he can no longer lift up his stiffening body. The gatekeeper has to bend way down to him, for the great difference has changed things considerably to the disadvantage of the man. "What do you still want to know now?" asks the gatekeeper. "You are insatiable." "Everyone strives after the law," says the man, "so how is it that in these many years no one except me has requested entry?" The gatekeeper sees that the man is already dying and, in order to reach his diminishing sense of hearing, he shouts at him, "Here no one else can gain entry, since this entrance was assigned only to you. I'm going now to close it.'"

I'm not going to launch into some deconstruction of what Kafka meant by 'the law', or how that parable influences the rest of the novel. I'm not going to do that, mainly because I can't, but I can tell you that those words sum up pretty well what it feels like to be a gambler. Whatever your timeframe, you're always searching for a way through. And it has to be your own way, probably one that, in all of its subtlety, is only open to you. Whether it's over a football season, a golf tournament, or a day's racing, there are a series of things that will happen and you have to predict them. You don't have to go through just the one door, as you can decide what you bet on. And you can use as many tools as you like. There are no gatekeepers to bribe, but it's easy to get the feeling that everyone else knows something that you don't, and that the secret of making it all click, about getting punting to work, is always going to remain just out of reach. That illumination that Kafka mentions in the parable is what we're always looking for, and my greatest fear is that one day I'll be lying there in the bed by the door in the local hospital and wondering whether I ever really got anywhere near the light. I'll lose the will to live, and then as I'm fading, everything will suddenly be illuminated. And when I think that, I think that I should probably give up punting.

I'd be interested to know what your reaction is as you read this. Some of you might see me as a bit self pitying, others as deluded and defensive, and the odd one of you might feel sorry for me, though I'm not holding my breath. But if you think that you're not in some way involved in this, then I've got news for you. I can guarantee that you're a gambler. You may feel that the £2 each way that you have every year on the Grand National doesn't really count, and you'd probably be right, but that's not what I'm talking about. If the financial crash of the last few years taught us anything, it's that we're at the mercy of gamblers, and therefore are gamblers ourselves. Having an ISA, a pension, even a mortgage, is no less of a gamble than giving ten grand to a mate who's good at betting on the Bundesliga and paying him commission to bet for you. And I have mates who know a lot about the Bundesliga who I'd trust a whole lot more than some faceless weasel in the City who is interested in his bank balance, his cocaine habit and his penis. For years, we've all seen investments in the stock market as sure fire: solid things that will appreciate over a period of time. That hasn't looked so true in the last five years, and even though the stock market will probably end up being a good investment again, that's only because you have good gamblers looking after your money. Don't kid yourself that 'speculation' means anything other than gambling.

For a pastime which so labours against negative imagery, it's amazing how widespread gambling is. Despite years of refurbishments and publicity campaigns, most people still think of a bookies as somewhere dirty and to be avoided, and would never dream of going inside to have a tenner on the 2.50 at Bangor. And yet tens of millions of people do the National Lottery every week and watch Nick Knowles mug his way through a life-changing quiz. A significant part of the population keep Noel Edmonds in shirts by gluing themselves to his mid-afternoon gambling fest *Deal or No Deal*. It may not involve laying out money, but it proves a fascination for the process of gambling. Choosing those boxes involves exactly the same mental process that sports gamblers go through every day. You might not want to admit it, but it's true. And remember those innocent old days of *Bullseye*? When the couple who'd won had six terrible prizes in the bank and had to decide whether to risk them all against the likelihood of ending up with a caravan? What was the word that the audience merrily screamed at the contestants? '*Gamble*.' I could go on. *Million Pound Drop*, *Who Wants to be a Millionaire*, they are all fundamentally about a bit of knowledge and a lot of gambling. A friend and I tried to get a TV show about gambling commissioned last year. About the process, and the effects, and how it permeated society. And we got nowhere. 'Ofcom don't like gambling shows,' we were frequently told, 'we don't go anywhere near them.' You couldn't make it up.

I'm not trying to bludgeon you into admitting you're something that you're not, because fundamentally I messed up and got in too deep and you didn't. I am saying, however, that you're far more of a gambler than you think, and far closer to the madness than you may believe.

All of the gambling mediums that I mention above involve differing degrees of luck, and I was doing my best to take luck out of the equation as much as I could. Of course, you can plan all that you want, and get plenty right, but ultimately, as you try to plot your way to success, you're at the mercy of fate, providence, caprice, whatever you want to call it. The trick is to try and remove as much of that as you can, be as sure as you can, and the difference between a brilliant professional gambler and a hopeless amateur is the level at which you're always sure of what you're going to do next and why. That was what I lost in my six months of madness. I was on such a bad run that all I was looking for was a winner, at any price and on pretty much any event. The question that I had to ask myself throughout this process was whether I was able to become someone who could be that clear minded, that ruthless and disciplined, that good at gambling.

So as the start of my six-month plan drew nearer, I needed to work out an approach, and that would start with a staking plan. Many professional gamblers will tell you that working out how much you should place on each bet is every bit as important as the bets themselves. It sounds insane if you don't punt regularly, but it's absolutely right. You can back ten winners and a loser in a single week, but if you have a bigger bet on the loser than on any of the winners there's still a chance that you'll end up down on those ten bets. The tale of the gambler at the racetrack that I have in my wallet is perfect proof of that, and the good financial analysts who know about the important intricacies of spreading risk when you have a portfolio of stocks and shares will back that theory up too, as will the old wife who was first to say: 'don't put all your eggs in one basket.'

Just read the financial pages every Sunday and look at the advice and the headlines. They'll talk about turning a profit and making things pay, and taking a punt and yet those pages are regarded as something that sensible dads all around the country read in order to make their nest egg a little bigger, and when you say that you're a gambler you become some kind of outcast. That's because there are so many layers and such a lack of knowledge of what actually happens in the stock market. The fact that it's gambling remains hidden.

I'd always gambled pretty arrogantly, presuming that somehow I had an instinct for how much I should put on each bet, but the first thing that you learn about people who do it more professionally is that they approach their betting, most of them anyway, forensically. A record is kept of every single bet that they have placed, and notes are even made of the mistakes that went along with the losing bets, and the clear application of logic that worked when they won. The system of how much they place on each bet differs from gambler to gambler, but they all have one.

The most popular is the points system, which allows you to grade your stake for each bet that you have. For a small stakes punter, a point might be a pound, for a big hitter, it might be a hundred thousand pounds, but the system remains the same. The points range from one to ten, with one being your smallest bet and ten your biggest, and you judge the number of points that you stake on how much you fancy the bet in question and, to a certain extent, on the price. You're unlikely to have a ten point bet on a 20-1 shot, for example, as your capital will be quickly eroded if too many of those lose. You'll stick a point or two on the longer shots, and leave the eight, nine and ten point bets for shorter priced favourites that you feel can't lose. Most telephone tipping lines operate on a points system, so that they can be used by anyone, whatever their actual stake. And so many people go this way, that it's probably the best system.

Not everyone uses the points system, though. In his book *A Bloody Good Winner*, the professional gambler Dave Nevison says that he is likely to have the same stake on a horse, whatever the price. So unlike most people who'd have, say, £20 on a 20-1 shot and £200 on an even money shot, he'll put the same stake on both. His logic goes that, when a big priced winner comes in, then he should really be able to celebrate. All I can say is that I wish I had his balls.

I knew that I needed a system and that one that I liked the look of was one which had been mentioned by Kevin Pullein in the *Racing Post*. The *Post* is the source of pretty much all knowledge for most punters, and has always been my favourite newspaper. Pullein is one of its star columnists: a maverick, a thinker, who acts as a gently cajoling wise man. I know a lot of people who criticise the tips that he gives, as they're invariably low key and rarely focus on the major event of the day. But he is a man worth listening to, and he has clearly worked out that steering clear of the major events of the day is the best way to make a profit. If you're reading this, and are disappointed that it's not the guide to gambling that you thought it was, then do yourself a favour and find everything that Pullein has written. The man talks more sense than everyone I know put together on the subject of gambling. His suggestion of a staking plan went like this. Every bet that you place should be to win the same amount. If, like me, you don't have the internal accounting skills of a City whizz-kid, then it's not a bad place to start. So, with apologies to Pullein, I nicked his system. Every bet that I'd place on this six-month journey would be to win two grand. The good thing about the idea is that it's easy to keep track of, but much more importantly it gives you an instant understanding of price and value.

Value is one of the most commonly used words in the gambling world, and the fundamental principle is sound. It was best explained to me by a friend who used a supermarket analogy: 'If a pint of milk costs 50p, then you wouldn't go into a supermarket and spend £2 on it, would you?' He said. I suggested that you might if there was a milk shortage, to which replied: 'Fuck off Dave, you know what I mean.' I did, and if you apply the same logic to betting, then you should only take a price which is bigger than you think it should be, which is 'value'. In effect, you should always be looking to pay 25p for a pint of milk.

And the system that I was going to use allows you to monitor that. You get an idea of the chances of something happening and know what stake you'll have to place to win two grand. If it's a 20-1 shot, you'll be placing a hundred quid, an even money shot will cost you two grand. There can still be value at odds on, but knowing that you'll be staking, say, four thousand pounds to win two, will force you to look into the price, and properly work out the probability of your selection winning. And that was a discipline that I knew I needed. It's not for everyone, but you have to find a system that fits the way that your brain works. That's what I hadn't done when everything went wrong, and what I was determined to do now.

One more thing happened to me before I set off for the USA on my first leg of trying to win everything back. I was at a fortieth birthday party, and was being insulted by a bloke who seemed to know my friend, but hadn't been sent an invitation. He was, in short, a dick, and I was getting into that 'one more word, sonny' territory, when a beautiful girl came and stood next to me. That kind of thing doesn't happen to me, at least it isn't meant to, and so I carried on staring at the guy and ignored her. She was out of my league and I was only going to make a fool of myself by talking to her. In retrospect, I thought a lot about this natural lack of self-confidence. Maybe the sort of people who make good gamblers are the ones who turn around and talk to girls in situations like that. Maybe that's all I need to know. My natural instinct is to be an insult avoider, a low-risk character, a shocking punter. Anyway, the guy was getting the message when suddenly I felt a tap on my shoulder. It was the girl, who said: 'Can you keep standing there please, I'm hiding from my boyfriend.' The sentence was a double-edged sword, as the mention of a boyfriend instantly (well, unless you're a young Frank Worthington) erased the prospect of any hope, and yet hinted at a need and an intimacy. So I listened, and smiled, and said, in my most reassuring voice: 'Sure.'

She wanted to talk, and what followed was a story of addiction, and of doubt, and of a wedding that she hoped for, and a boyfriend who she loved dearly but who was a hopeless alcoholic. She was hiding from him because he was drunk, and she hated it when he got like this. And as I struggled with my initial reactions of fear (I didn't need a drunk bloke thinking that I was cracking onto his girlfriend) and anger (the dick was still staring at me) and disbelief (how could someone even *think* about running the risk of losing a girl like this?), she looked me straight in the eye and asked me if I was addicted to anything. It was a perfectly natural question, given the position that she was in and given the subject matter that was flying through her head, but when I thought about if afterwards, I wondered whether she had seen something in me. Whether, in the same way that one punter can spot another, a victim of addiction can spot a potential addict.

So I stuttered a bit and said that I liked a bet, but scientifically rather than recklessly, and she said is that possible and I said of course it is and she said I don't think it is and I know a bit about betting as I like horse racing and I thought god, she's more perfect than I thought and she said don't you love the thrill of having a big priced winner and I said of course I do and she said you must be addicted to it then and I thought god maybe she's right and maybe my head is just as messed up as the boyfriend I could now see whirligigging his way around the bar falling into people and a long way from dangerous. And then I paused for breath and said: 'Maybe I am, maybe you're right.' And she said: 'You've got to stop. Look at him. If it gives you a buzz then it's got to stop.'

She got to me, and I remember walking home clutching her phone number and determined to inject more sense into the way that I was punting. I thought again about the need for a staking plan and how controlled it would feel. Just the kind of thing of which this bar room angel would approve, and so that would be me for the foreseeable future. Feeling controlled, whether I won or lost, and somehow proving to myself that I wasn't an addict. On the brink of being one, but not quite. Drunk and a bit too chatty, not falling over and glassy-eyed and desperate.

A year later, I signed up to an internet messaging service that gave you a 'status report' for anyone who bothered to fill it in. It was then that I realised I still had her number in my phone, despite never ringing it, never finding out how her story had ended. Her one line description of herself said, 'married, with one child.' And for some reason that made me happy. I like to think that she remembers our conversation as well as I do, but I bet that she doesn't.

So my sensible staking plan was borrowed from Kevin Pullein, and then sealed by an encounter with a girl who I'd never see again. I like to think that I'd unwittingly latched on to something that worked for me, but it's equally probable that I didn't really know what I was doing. I like it, though. If you struggle for self-control, then it has a ring of sense to it. The very fact of every bet that you place being to win the same amount means that you're adding control to your punting via a system, rather than relying on your mood. Of course, you still need to be in the right mood to implement the system, but we'll cross that bridge when we come to it. So that would be the plan for this trawl back through the sporting events that nearly finished me off. Every bet that I'd place would be to win a set amount, and I'd stick to that. I'd try and win two grand per bet, and see where that left me at the end of the summer. Every bet would be texted to my friend Dan Roebuck, the former *Guardian* betting columnist, who would act as a profit and loss column and make sure that nothing was invented. Having established that I had a chance, now it was time to get serious. To head stateside, and confront the sporting event that had started it all.

CHAPTER FOUR

As a gawky kid who'd just started being a teenager, I fell in love with American football. It seemed so otherworldly, and what had been a tiny world looked a whole lot bigger. Mick Luckhurst, a tall man with dubious hair and a lisp, would appear on Channel 4 and drawl for a few minutes through his perfect teeth, and the 13-year-old me would be transported to places like Denver, and Cleveland, and Dallas. Places that I'd barely heard of, and that I'd surely never go to. Commentators like Dick Enberg and Merle Olsen would talk about plays, and the get go, and linebackers and touchdowns, and for those hours on a Sunday I'd be in another world. If the sport had been played in England, or Holland, or somewhere more prosaic, I don't think it would have found an audience. It wasn't just the game that we fell for, it was the glamour of location, the mannered presentation, the sense of otherness.

I may not have made any real money so far, but Palermo and Padraig Harrington had given me confidence. It seemed like there really was something in this plan to travel around watching sport up close and hammering my demons. And there's nothing like confidence in a gambler, and so I headed across the Atlantic with head held high, and heart beating fast.

Confidence is a curious thing. If you've never had a bet, then you probably think that it's a terrible trait. You'll think of lines that you've heard a million times in movies or a certain kind of television programme. A Willy Loman clone in an old raincoat and a bashed fedora will beg for a final line of credit from the bad guy and say: 'Please give me the money. It's a sure thing. It can't lose and when it wins I can pay back everything I owe.' Willy is at the bottom of a river within five minutes and you, the non-gamblers, can sit and mutter that old line about there being no such thing as a sure thing. But confidence isn't about thinking that you have a sure thing, it's about knowing that you're in the right frame of mind to do the *right* thing. And you're more likely to do that if you're coming off the back of a big win. Yes, there's a danger of overconfidence, but if you can control that then you're onto something.

Before setting out at the start of the year, I surveyed one hundred people who consider themselves to be serious gamblers, pros and amateurs alike, and asked them to list the three words which best describe them when they're gambling well, when they're on a roll and making money. The two most common words by a long way were confidence and balance, and interestingly enough, only one person said the word that the non-gambler would think was number one. 'Luck' was noticeable by its absence. So, with thanks to Padraig Harrington's driving and Fabrizio Miccoli's finishing, I headed to the NFL playoffs with the feeling that I could win, even that I *would* win, and the only hope that I had was that the next six months would all feel like this.

January 2011 wasn't the cleverest time to go to the East Coast of the USA. New York had just been hit by its worst storms in 60 years, and the mayor Michael Bloomberg was being pilloried for his failure to deal with the clinging snow which glued the traffic together and mashed pair upon pair of thousand dollar shoes. It was funny to see the inbuilt sense of entitlement that New Yorkers seem to carry around being so disturbed by the weather. A balding man bawled at a taxi driver that: 'I need to get there. What do you mean I can't? What do you mean the road's closed? Because of snow?' I overheard a group of dainty Russian students who were drinking coffee in the Trump Tower and loudly comparing iPhone covers. One of them said: 'I want one of those blue ones like you have but I have to get across town to get it and it's so truly sad that I'll have to wait until the snow clears before I can.' Truly sad. An iPhone without a cover. Poor her. On the same weekend, the shootings in Arizona were all over the news, as was the story of suspect packages, possibly containing anthrax, being discovered in a post office. The way that life simply went on in the city, with normal worries and far from unusual desires, was extraordinary.

The New York Jets were in the playoffs and the city was buzzing with the prospect of their trip down the road to the Indianapolis Colts. The Jets are a blue-collar team, with an attitude and a sense of dramatic failure that makes them easy to love, but hard to trust. The Jets are coached by a gigantic man called Rex Ryan, a fellow who knows how to fill out an XXL sweater and who tells the press where to go but doesn't appear to mean it, and who had recently been involved in a scandal surrounding an internet video. Ryan had been caught on camera sucking the toes of his wife although why anyone wanted to watch him do it was another thing. He'd gone red, got suitably angry and then laughed it off. And now he was talking his team up against the Colts. Aside from the presence of my nemesis Santonio Holmes in their team, I didn't really care about the Jets. My plan was to catch the train about 100 miles south to Philadelphia, to watch a man who knew as much as Holmes about trouble and redemption.

Michael Vick is one of the most naturally gifted quarterbacks ever to play in the National Football League. Vick has a quicksilver arm which can throw a football onto a tiny target 60 yards away, and do so by propelling a ball that weighs 15 ounces, and is 11 inches long, at roughly 65 miles per hour. Pick up a bag of flour and then imagine hurling it at the speed that you drive down the dual carriageway and you'll have an idea. And then imagine throwing it half the length of a football pitch and landing it into a washing up bowl. Michael Vick is by no means the quickest or most accurate passer to play the game: that honour would go to someone like Dan Marino of the 1980s Miami Dolphins or more recently Brett Favre, notably of Green Bay. But Michael Vick isn't just about throwing. He can run 40 yards in 4.3 seconds and his dancing feet make him elusive: a tackle shrugger, a hit avoider. If it was decided on natural ability alone, then Michael Vick would be one of the most lauded and respected athletes in the USA. The problem is that most of the country thinks that Michael Vick is an asshole.

Vick didn't kill anyone, although he may ruefully reflect now that he'd be less of a pariah if he had. In 2007, a widespread investigation into animal cruelty led to Vick being revealed as one of the organisers of a dog fighting syndicate called the Bad Newz kennels. So brutal was the treatment of the animals that were bred purely to fight that injured dogs were routinely executed: hanged, drowned, electrocuted. Vick went to prison claiming that his trust had been abused by childhood friends and that he had barely been involved. In 2009, the former Atlanta quarterback was released and now here he was in Philadelphia, after an extraordinary season, hoping to take the Eagles all the way to the Superbowl and make himself famous for football again. He knew that he'd blown his chances of ever being an icon, and that all he could hope for now was to be remembered as a deeply flawed, and very good, football player. He was guaranteed to forever be the subject of documentaries, and now he was in control of whether or not they'd have a happy ending.

In the first week of January, the post-season playoffs are big news. The NFL's system of deciding who will be its champion is near perfect in comparison with the clunky mechanisms that exist in other sports. Thirty-two teams play sixteen regular season games, and, based on a win and loss ratio, the twelve best go into the playoffs. From then on, winner stays in and loser goes home, regardless of how well a team has played in the previous four months. It's brutal, and one bad performance can throw away sixteen excellent ones. If it seems unfair, then fans of the sport will tell you that it's the only way to decide who are real champions, who really deserves to be given a Superbowl ring, an absurdly chunky piece of jewellery that's the most prized possession in American sport.

The four teams with the best records get a bye to what are effectively the quarter-finals, and that means that the other eight must play each other in what are known as the Wild Card games. The whole playoffs experience is about brinkmanship, but never more so than on this weekend, where desperation mingles with the sense of a second chance. And they frequently provide upsets. They're nearly always about the spirit of a team on the day and a tactical plan rather than some easy to work out equation, and that makes them perfect for betting. You can find a reason to take the favourites on, and you can come out on top. The Eagles against the Packers looked like being the closest fought game in the best atmosphere, and so I went to Philadelphia looking for a bet.

Michael Vick's Philadelphia Eagles would play a Green Bay Packers team led by an understated quarterback called Aaron Rodgers. I have a habit of referring to him as Anton Rodgers, and the temptation was made all the greater after a disturbing incident in a New York sauna a couple of days before the Eagles v Packers match. Not quite the kind of disturbing incident that you might be thinking of, so please read on.

I walked in wearing a pair of shorts but without a towel, and a tall man who bore more than a passing resemblance to the English character actor informed me in a reedy, robotic voice that: 'towels were compulsory, absolutely mandatory.' I resisted the urge to make a comment and obligingly returned with a towel. And I found him stretched out on his back, towelless and tool out. Rather than wait and risk detecting the beginnings of an erection (in him, not me) I retreated to the cold and spent the rest of the day talking about the Green Bay quarterback 'Anton, sorry, Aaron Rodgers'. As the football player's fame grew throughout January, the sauna memories slowly subsided.

The four wild card games are played, two a day, over an amazing sporting weekend. Two massive college matches bookend the first weekend of the NFL playoffs, and I was invited to watch the Cotton

Bowl on Friday night in a New York bar by a girl with whom I once shared an embarrassing clinch in a Parisian nightclub. She was all bleached blonde hair and flip-flops and her college team, LSU, was playing Texas. They won, I think, but the potential awkwardness of the evening put me off and meant that I spent my evening working on stats and trying to pick a bet for Sunday in Philadelphia.

There's a website called sportsims.net which simulates games 10,000 times to predict an eventual result, and they decided that the Eagles would win the match 58.7 per cent of the time, and that their closest idea of the correct score in the match was 31-17. On the purely statistical analysis that a website like this is entirely reliant upon, that wasn't an unfair conclusion, but if betting was about simply following stats then we'd all be millionaires, and I'd never have got myself into the mess that I did. So it was time to look deeper.

The Eagles against the Packers would be the final game of the Wild Card weekend, and so that gave me two Saturday games to watch, and a Sunday one to have half an eye on, and try and come to a conclusion. And if you ever needed a day to open your eyes, then Saturday was the one. The Seattle Seahawks went into their match against the reigning champions, the New Orleans Saints, as one of the biggest underdogs in playoff history. They'd lost more games than they'd won in the regular season and, in the week leading up to the game, experts piled in with their opinion that the Seahawks' qualification for the post-season was just a statistical quirk, a failure of the system that showed that it was flawed. And the beauty of that lunatic day in Seattle was that, while one set of journalists was trying to devise a way that the system could be ironed out, another group was watching one of the biggest upsets in the history of the NFL.

The Seahawks did everything right, and a Saints team, which clearly felt that they had a right to win, did pretty much everything wrong. The outsiders led early on, the champions fought back, but then a running back called Marshawn Lynch produced a golden, never to be forgotten, moment. He bounced off eight defenders in total, he ran for 67 yards, he scored an incredible touchdown, and the Seahawks had produced a shock for the ages. After the game, the same experts who had lined up to deride their presence in the playoffs spoke of their indefatigable spirit and the force of will of the Seattle crowd. None of them had mentioned it before, and that series of events neatly sums up where the world of the gambler and the world of a particular kind of journalist part ways. One has to decide why something might happen before it happens. The other always has the benefit of hindsight. Although there was something in the theory that the Seahawks' fans had contributed to their win: John Vidale, the director of the Pacific Northwest Seismic Network, reported that a monitoring station which is 100 yards west of the Seahawks' ground registered seismic activity during Lynch's winning run. The earth moved that night if you were a Seattle fan.

A result like the Seahawks' victory gives you confidence. If outsiders as rank as that can win, then surely the Packers could find a way to beat Philadelphia in what was a far closer match up. The Packers, after all, had Rodgers, and the Eagles' defence had given up an average of 23.6 points per game during the season due to lapses in concentration and poor tactics. No team had ever reached the Superbowl with a defensive record as bad as that and yet we were expected to believe that somehow the Eagles could use home advantage and find a way to stop the Packers. I would travel to

Philadelphia on Sunday morning with every intention of backing Green Bay to win.

The need for gambling lessons throughout this process had always struck me as important. The idea that somehow someone who had punted like an idiot could suddenly think about things and then become the king of the world is ridiculous, and there's always the chance of a relapse or two along the way. It's why I went to Vegas and why, the day before my trip to Philadelphia, I headed to Aqueduct racecourse in New York, a place to which I'd linked many times from a radio studio, but never visited. And the 'Big A' has lessons aplenty.

Aqueduct is about an hour and a half away from Manhattan by train, but considerably further in terms of downward mobility. When I asked the fey indie drummer wannabe who was working as a concierge in my hotel how I should get there he looked at me as if I'd just done a poo in reception. The best that he could manage was to throw at me the alphabet soup of the New York subway system. A, B, C, all lines could lead to Aqueduct if I wanted them to, so in the end I walked out of the hotel, and asked someone who looked like they might know. And I grabbed the A train, went past Brooklyn, and wandered to a racetrack that likes to make itself hard to find. This is no Ascot, it's not even a Wolverhampton or a Kempton Park. As you cross back over the train tracks and make your way to the entrance in the snow, you become aware of just how desperate the place is.

Everyone seemed to have something wrong with them: a limp, a stutter, a twitch, and as the single file of punters crossed the waste ground that leads to the racecourse, you knew that we were all dreaming. It's that feeling that most gamblers have on a Saturday.

There's a fresh race card in front of you. This could be the day, the life-changer. And yet the sense of how frequently those dreams turn to dust hung in the air over those train tracks. This was a place to watch, never one in which to win.

The racecourse at Aqueduct is the kind of place where the very act of smoking a cigar gives you a distinguished air. This isn't a place where people come to have fun. They're here to try and make money, try and change their lives, service an addiction. The New York Racing Association had recently launched a laudable publicity campaign to try and persuade more Manhattanites to come racing, but the sad truth is that those people who'd decided to try it stood out and felt awkward. It's hard to merrily wander along and explain life to a small child when on one side a man in a brown hat is singing a song about icicles, and on the other someone is yelling the word 'cock' over and over again. It's a sporting venue that exists on TV and on the radio, one that you can bet on from afar. It's a name, not a place to visit.

I decided to hang around, though, because I had an interest. The night before I was walking through downtown Manhattan when I saw a sign for a fortune-teller. I did that thing that you do when you're in a foreign city and your mood is good and I thought that I'd try something different. Some people get their teeth whitened; others learn how to windsurf. I, of course, had to see if you really could see into the future. If I could nail that, then my gambling life would be the least of my worries. So I walked down some stairs, pushed open a curtain, and found myself in a room that looked like a London mini cab office. Shabby walls, battered sofa, small window with a grille. I stood awkwardly for about five minutes and was on my way out when I bumped into a woman who was wearing a veil. 'Sorry,' she said, 'I didn't hear you come in.' So she could predict the future but she couldn't tell if someone had walked into her shop. It wasn't promising.

She grabbed my hand and took me into a back room, and before I knew it I was having my palm read, largely against my will. I'll skate over much of what she told me as I'm sure that you'll have heard it before: I loved someone, well yes, so do most people. That love was unrequited. Slight risk on her part, but I was on my own, so the odds were with her. I liked sport, I was wearing a shirt with the word 'football' on it, but I don't play it so much, I'm overweight. It went on like this until she suddenly grasped my hand and said: 'I see a raven, a dark raven'. Now, I'm no expert in these matters but I immediately thought of Tarot cards and images and portents and stuttered: 'That doesn't sound very good.' She smiled and told me that it was whatever that I wanted to make it. I then sought reassurance, like a hypochondriac sitting with a family doctor, and checked and double-checked that it didn't mean I was going to die tomorrow. She reassured me and started to usher me out of the door. After looking very much like her only customer of the day, she was now getting rid of me. I'd bored a fortune-teller into submission.

You forget things pretty quickly in the noise and madness of Manhattan and so, apart from being slightly frustrated that I'd wasted my money on a psychic, I'd woken up and hopped on the train to Aqueduct and forgotten all about it. Until I opened the racecard. And there, staring at me, leaping from the page, was the name of a fancied horse that was running in the first race. Moon Raven. Unbelievable. My fingers tightened around the edge of the paper and I was pretty sure that the man sitting next to me who'd been whistling 'My

Darling Clementine' stopped for a moment in the style of a pianist in a Wild West bar. Jesus Christ, Moon Raven. For a while I pretended to be a proper gambler. I checked out the other runners, looked at Moon Raven's previous runs, but even if the guy picking the tips for that afternoon's racing had told me that the horse had lost a leg in training I was still backing it. I hadn't come to Aqueduct for a proper bet, I hadn't come for this to be part of the journey, but Moon Raven had fallen into my lap, and I started to pace around. The paper said that the extra distance could work for him today, the race was off at 1.38, and I was hooked. The last time I went racing in the USA, I was struck by just how good the bare fact analysis was. What the predictor guy in the paper or the programme said tended to be pretty near the mark, and that angle that you look for in most sporting events maybe was less important. And the guy in the paper liked Moon Raven. So, with the stars aligned, maybe it did come down to fate, with a bit of luck thrown in.

I got there an hour before racing and listened to the mixture of world-weariness and hopeless optimism that washes around a place like that. Aqueduct seems so small scale that one of the jockeys in the first race was having a shouted conversation with a friend that he'd spotted in the crowd. That was fun to listen to until it was drowned out by a man who walked down to the side of the racecourse, stood next to me, and shouted: 'All the way with this. It's the *one* horse in this race. They gotta handicap dese fuckin' things, and dey fucked up here. I'm tellin' ya, this is a tip all da way from Oklahoma.'

They stood for the National Anthem before racing began, and it was an act of surprising tenderness. These racegoers were battered and broken, and I imagined that many of them had served their country. For the moments that it took the flag to be slowly levered to the top of the pole the place had a dignity, and a silence. The misfits' party had a purpose.

And then the bedlam began. As that confidence thing washed over me again, I had a pretty big bet on Moon Raven, and watched it lumber down to post, crawl out of the starting stalls, and lope apologetically home in about eighth. If there was one lesson to take out of Aqueduct, it was one that I should have known already – there's no such thing as fate when you have a bet. All those times that you go racing and you like a name, or you have a feeling, and the horse comes in. Well done to you. Enjoy the win. And then try and remember all of the times that you liked a name or you had a feeling and the horse didn't win. And you can't. Because you don't remember the unremarkable moments, only the seemingly incredible ones. But the unremarkable is far more common. If Moon Raven had won then it would have been an extraordinary coincidence, yet a coincidence all the same. After slipping back into my old gambling habits so readily, it was good to get a sharp reminder. Aqueduct had served its purpose.

So, a Sunday, and the very early train to Philadelphia to see if fate would fall for Michael Vick. The newspapers were full of the Jets' win against the Colts the previous night, with a last-minute field goal kicked by Nick Folk. A headline writer's dream, I thought, and the first paper that I read obliged with 'FOLK HERO' shouting out from the back page.

Philadelphia had suffered its coldest December for a decade, and the snow had fallen there too. The city felt like it was beyond freezing, and the accompaniment of a ferocious wind had left the streets pretty much empty that Sunday morning. The wind seemed certain to play its part in the game that night. Before that, though, I decided to go for a walk to the one place that 'any sports fan simply has to go when they're in Philadelphia.' I know that because I read it in a guidebook.

That's why I found myself at 10 a.m. with a snowstorm burning my ears, facing the Philadelphia Museum of Art, with 72 steps in front of me. You'll all know why they're famous, as I'm sure that you'll all have seen *Rocky*, but here's the thing that you maybe didn't know. The whole scene is a con, running up the steps is about as difficult as eating a piece of cheese. In the short time that I was there, I saw children bound up it, an emphysematic old man take it in his stride, and brilliantly, a group of students get to the top while carrying a set of speakers which were blaring out the film's theme tune. Local joggers include the steps as part of their routines, and if you prize that scene as something which represents the ultimate challenge, some unattainable goal, then I suggest that you never go there. I opted to light a fag before sauntering up backwards. The funny looks were worth it.

At the top of the steps, and looking back down Benjamin Franklin Parkway to Logan Circle, you got a sense of just how strong the wind was. And I thought again about the game. The Lincoln Financial Field where the Eagles play may not be in the centre of the city, but it isn't far, and the wind would blow just as powerfully there as it was doing here. The Parkway is decorated with the flags of every major country, and they were blowing like crazy. I had gone to Philly fancying the Packers to turn over the favourites, but the wind was making another bet leap out at me. I stopped those locals who had dared to go outside and asked them if they thought that it would carry on blowing like this. Most of them stared and me and mouthed a word or two before scurrying away, but two old guys stayed and talked, and told me that it would get stronger if anything, and that these were the kind of days on which locals stayed inside and that 'only the crazies' stayed out. I looked at them, they looked at me, crazies all of us, and we went our separate ways.

Wind can make a mess of sport, and make us a profit too. In their analysis of the relationship between English and Italian football, Gianluca Vialli and Gabriele Marcotti devote a section to discussion of the wind and how it affects the conditioning and training of footballers in windy countries. The points they're making may be about a different sport, but they seemed relevant that afternoon in Philadelphia:

> 'The wind affects everything. You can be the most technical
> footballer in the world – you can be Zidane or Maradona
> rolled into one – but if a fierce wind is blowing, you won't
> be able to do any meaningful work with the ball in the air,
> whether it's volleying practice, heading or keepy-uppy. Even
> any kind of passing over ten or twenty feet becomes pointless
> when it's windy.'

The game started at 5.30, but that's not the time that you arrive if you're a fan of a team like the Philadelphia Eagles. South American football supporters get to games several hours early so that they can put up flags, smoke copious amounts of weed, fight, and sing themselves to a standstill. American Football fans have tailgating. I always thought of this practice as something romantic and charming, involving up and coming bands and pretty girls, with fans providing a messy backdrop.

The kind of place where Andrew McCarthy would do something sickly sweet and stupid in a brat pack movie. But tailgating at the Eagles v Packers game consisted of big men with beards carrying massive crates of lager from truck to truck, table to table, and drinking it. There were bands and there were girls, but they were to be swayed to and leered at, and I wondered how I could be so naive. The Eagles' supporters have a reputation for a kind of aggressive masculinity, one which is best summed up in the *Bury Me in My Jersey*, memoir of a more thoughtful Eagles' fan called Tom McAllister, who writes about the numerous message boards on which supporters communicate as:

> '... an exaggerated version of locker room bravado. Every post featuring a picture of a woman is guaranteed, within ten minutes, to elicit one specific response. "I'd hit it." Of course, the poster wouldn't just have sex with "it", he would hit it, because even when he's being intimate, it's violent and painful, and he's totally in charge, as a real man would be – and as the Eagles would be. It's a locker room atmosphere without the checks and balances of the locker room.'

The Eagles' fans, with all of their bare-chested machismo, clearly fancied it. This was a team which had been reinvigorated by Vick, and which believed that it had the X-Factor that you need to win the Superbowl. They'd challenged in recent seasons, but the coach Andy Reid always seemed sensible, rather than inspired, small and chubby and bespectacled, the kind of character actor who turns up as a janitor or a head waiter in *Curb Your Enthusiasm*, and is the butt of a joke for a scene or two. Only two coaches in the history of the NFL had won more matches as a coach without ever winning a Superbowl. Reid had guided the Eagles to the playoffs in nine of his twelve seasons in charge, but only once had they reached the Superbowl, in 2004, when they went down bravely against the star-studded New England Patriots. You couldn't criticise the consistency of Reid's teams, but there was a feeling that he was steady and a little uninspired. As Bob Ford wrote in the *Philadelphia Enquirer*, 'Reid has built an impressive edifice of success, but he has never been able to add a penthouse to the structure.'

With Vick firing, though, this Eagles team had its millionaire and its game breaker, as well as Reid's usual solid structure. His go-to man was a wide receiver called DeSean Jackson, a wild kid whose sporting instinct gives him the ability to look as if he's moving quicker than anyone else on the field. Jackson's job is to run downfield and get himself into enough space for Vick to find him with that quicksilver arm, and then use his blistering speed to burn off would-be tacklers and take himself into the end zone. Jackson is one of the most outwardly emotional sportsmen in the world, a crazy celebrator of a touchdown and a wild remonstrator if a pass didn't reach him as he wished. It was Vick who seemed able to keep Jackson calm enough to perform to his best. The reformed wild child knowing more about what made the younger man tick than anyone else on the team.

Because of Vick's ability to zip passes into their intended target, and Jackson's to catch them, the Eagles had the look of a flashy team, one which scored a lot of points, and conceded them too. The third key member of their offense was a kid who used to practice moves in any crowded place that he could find, who'd deliberately bump into people in crowded shopping malls and airports, who would use the bustle of everyday life to work out the physics of movement. If quarterbacks and wide receivers are the most obvious stars of American Football, it's the running backs that tend to win you matches, and Le Sean McCoy had shown that he was a winner. Moody, a practical joker, an annoying presence in the locker room, he was also a player who could change direction with a flick of his ankle and who could bounce off the soles of his feet like a basketball player. His job was to carry the ball forward, to gain yards for his team, to give Vick an option, and to set up scoring positions. And the Green Bay Packers knew that if they allowed the Eagles' holy trinity to perform, then they would be out of the playoffs.

That's the battle at the heart of American Football, and the reason that it so fascinates those who have loved the game all their lives, alienating those who don't understand it. The sport is highly tactical, so much so that each team is broken up into individual sub teams. Put simply, the offense have to gain yards and put points on the board, the defense have to try and stop them, and then it's the job of the special teams to do something, well, special. Within each of those battles there are thousands of different plays, pre-worked movements which each set of co-ordinators use to try and find a way to win their individual battle. It's a kind of ballet for big guys, each game broken down into key battles that must be won.

So it was Vick, Jackson and McCoy against a Packers' defence led by the giant Clay Matthews. Matthews had been at the University of Southern California during the time that stars like Will Ferrell and Snoop Doggy Dogg would turn up to practice, although the player didn't much care for celebrity. In fact Matthews admits that he 'doesn't have many friends'. He just wants to play football, and it's hard to play defense and be popular. In Philadelphia, he taunted Vick all the way through the match: saying he was coming after him and that he was going to get him.

A strange twist to the story was that Vick owed Green Bay a favour. He had started the season as the number two choice at quarterback, and only got his starting chance when Reid's preferred choice Kevin Kolb had suffered concussion at the hand of the Green Bay defence in the first match of the season. Green Bay had won a close game 27-20, and Vick had never looked back.

The Eagles had carried all before them for much of the season, but in the final month there was a sense that other teams had started to work them out, and that the blitz worked against Vick. The quarterback blitz is when the defensive players, rather than defending the ball, head for the quarterback, the kingpin, trying to stop him throwing it, and duff him up in the process. The Packers had already produced 47 quarterback sacks during the season. The Eagles would have to rely on Vick's mobility to get them out of trouble, both with his ability to scramble and to throw what are known as screen passes, simple, and out wide, and away from trouble. Green Bay would be blitzing, you could be certain of that.

At a casual glance, all roads in Philadelphia seemed to lead to a high-scoring game. The Eagles had broken their points scoring record in the regular season, with 439, and that meant that they could boast the second best offense in the league, with only the all star Superbowl favourites New England Patriots scoring more. And the Eagles were weak defensively, even more so because of injuries, and Reid knew that they were likely to concede points, and so the only way for them to win would be in a game with a whole heap of points. And that's where the wind would come in. Because producing a high-scoring game full of drama and incident is one thing. Producing it in the wind is something else altogether.

The flags at either end of Lincoln Financial Field were blowing as strongly as the ones on Benjamin Franklin had been earlier. The mechanics of the stadium are interesting, as one end, the one in front of which I had a strange seat in a sloping press box, is open in both corners, and so the wind blows in from either side, creating swirls and eddies at that end of the field. At the other end of the stadium, the one with the line of flags, one side was open, and this meant that the direction of the wind was almost impossible to predict. American football players are pretty smart and adaptable, and I knew both quarterbacks would be capable of throwing passes, but there was no question of high-sided stands protecting the playing area, and Vick and Rodgers being surrounded by calmness. They would be buffeted, and would find getting into a rhythm extremely difficult. As I watched the two sets of players warming up and Vick throwing a pass or two, the movement seemed staccato, and not much was going to hand.

I still fancied the Packers to cause an upset, but for all of his human failings I think that Vick is an incredible athlete, and fundamentally I decided that I couldn't bet against him. This might seem like lazy logic, but there is a list of sportsmen who I religiously refuse to bet against. Maybe it's because they've cost me money in the past, maybe there's something about their inscrutable will to win, perhaps it's because I think they're better than me. It's illogical, but sometimes as a gambler instinct has to overtake logic, and my list is an example. It includes people as different as the Sussex batsman Murray

Goodwin and the England rugby coach Martin Johnson, and Michael Vick is on it too.

What was more interesting than trying to predict the winner, though, was the points line. It had been set at 46.5, which means that you get a price of 10-11 on the game featuring under 46.5 points, and the same price if the match went over that mark. The pre-match feeling that this would be high scoring was easy to fall into, but it didn't seem to tally with the reality of what was in front of me. I managed to get pitchside, by playing the tourist and convincing a security guard that I was after a photo opportunity, and down there it was close to freezing and blowing a gale. You could sit in front of your television at home and expect this to be free flowing and high scoring, but it would be a lot harder to get the ball moving than it looked.

The points line seemed to be so high because of a perception based on the way the Eagles might play. The Eagles were top of the NFL in passing plays of 40 yards or more, with 15. In your mind's eye you picture American football as a game of long passes, of dramatic completions, and yet the bare statistics tell you that it doesn't happen that often. It's a highlights DVD, and in 16 matches during the season it only happened 15 times. In addition to that, the Packers had only produced three games all season which had gone over 50 points, the previous week beating the Bears 10-3. Earlier in the season, in far better weather and with fresher minds and legs, this match-up had finished 27-20, *just* over the line.

There were other reasons for opposing the feeling that there'd be a lot of points. Philadelphia had played eight times this season at home and only four times had the matches gone over that 46.5

points line, but maybe most importantly only once had they blown the line, when they won 34-24 v Houston. The other three times that it had happened the matches had been 0.5, 1.5, and 2.5 points over the line, away from home, in less tricky venues, where the Eagles had scored heavily.

The other reason for favouring the points bet over an outright punt on the Packers was that, in conditions like this, a team's running game was vital. And the Packers were hopeless at running. It was Rodgers who had got them this far with his ability to throw the right pass at the right time, both short and long. But there's an old dictum in American football, which goes that you have to pass to score and that you have to run to win. Only one of the Packers' running backs had managed to run for more than 100 yards in a single match all season. However, it is possible to manipulate the ball downfield with less risky throws, and that's what the Packers had done so well all season so far. John Kuhn, the massive full back whose terrace chant had become as recognisable as Luke Donald's (go on, you can work it out), looked like he'd be a vital man for them.

As the kick-off approached, and the noise became deafening, I had my eyes on those flags at the end of the stadium, away to my left. For a time they'd stopped fluttering, and I feared that the wind had dropped and that conditions had suddenly become perfect for throwing the ball and producing a high scoring game. I started to have real doubts about the under 46.5 points bet, for all the logic that had gone into it, but then, after taking a rest, the swirling and eddying wind picked up again and I knew that the conditions were on my side. I watched the Philadelphia Eagles' kicker David Akers, one of the best around, and he was struggling desperately in practice. He missed three field goal attempts in a row and looked up at the posts in confusion. This was a man who was used to kicking at this stadium, and even he was struggling. And, if there were any lingering doubts, that was the sight that made up my mind. Under 46.5 points at 10-11 was the call. Even though it's not usually my kind of call.

One of the most common mistakes that anyone new to betting makes is, in spread betting parlance, to buy rather than sell. Spread betting can seem hard to understand to someone who has never tried it, but the principle is pretty simple. For each sporting event, the bookmakers set an estimate of what they think will happen in that event. So, in a football match between two evenly matched teams, the goals spread might be 2.3 to 2.5. If you buy, then you'll be in profit once there are three goals in the game, and will make more money for each subsequent goal. The risk you take is that, if the game finishes 0-0, then you will lose 2.5 times your original stake. So, let's say that you buy goals for £100 a point. If the game finishes 2-2, then you'll win £150. If it finishes 0-0, then you'll lose £250. And most people's inclination is to buy, which is only human. When you watch a sporting event, you want things to happen, and want to make money by watching those things happen. No one, apart from perhaps the BBC commentator Alan Green, sits down to watch a football match and wants it to be terrible, and therein lies the problem if you're having a bet. Because to sell goals, or corners, or goalscorers' shirt numbers, or any of the other plentiful markets on offer, is to sit and hope that nothing happens. I'll admit that I am, by inclination, a buyer rather than a seller, an optimist and not a realist. And yet now, there I was, fulfilling a lifelong ambition and waiting for a playoff game to start, and I wanted it, in the local vernacular, to suck. My bet wasn't a spread bet, it was an all-in win or lose. Under 46.5 points and I'd win two grand, anything over and I'd dropped my cash. The next three hours would be torture.

I try and deal with these kinds of bets by calling them Harold Steptoe bets. Imagine the screwed up face of Wilfred Bramble and then apply it to everything that happens before, during and after the match. It's a coping mechanism that works for me, but I don't think that it endeared me to the inhabitants of the Philadelphia Eagles' press box. So, when the guy next to me, a pleasingly optimistic looking man with an open face, heard my accent and said: 'So, you're over from England? Looking forward to the game?' I scowled a little and said: 'Well, yes, but I think it'll be a disappointment.'

I stayed in Steptoe mode all the way through the first half, cheering to myself when a pass went astray and muttering when Vick or Rodgers did anything good. Rodgers threw a touchdown pass in each of the first two quarters, and all that the Eagles could manage in reply was a field goal. So at half-time the under 46.5 points bet was looking good, with only 17 points on the board. The Packers had controlled things well, and shut the crowd up, and the biggest surprise of all was that they had found a running game. A young player called James Starks had already run for over 50 yards, absorbing hits and finding gaps, and his performance allowed Rodgers the ability to make gradual gains, nothing flashy, and work his team downfield. The game had been a little dull, as myself and my alter ego wished, and Vick had seen his opportunities limited. He'd made the best of them, completing seven of his twelve passes, but it was a long way from fireworks. My favourite moment of the half had been in the last minute, when Rodgers threw a perfectly weighted pass to

James Jones, who was wide open and waiting to stroll into the end zone to make the score a worrying 21-3. And he dropped it. Steptoe did a little toothless dance, and 14-3 it was.

At this point, I was happy with the bet that I'd placed, but frustrated that I hadn't backed the Packers, who'd been a pre-match 13-8 and who'd really responded to the pressure. They'd stopped Vick, the friendless Clay Matthews had been immense in defense, and Rodgers was proving what a friend of mine had told me a couple of years earlier. That one day this guy would take the Packers to a Superbowl. The 12-1 that had been available before the playoffs about the Packers winning this season's championship was looking pretty big now.

Vick, though, is a superstar for a reason, and the third quarter would prove excruciating. You should never take anything for granted in sport, and I of all people should know that, but at half-time I considered my points bet to be just about won. The two teams would need to produce 30 points in the second half for it to lose, and it just hadn't felt like that kind of game. And then suddenly it did.

Vick drove the Eagles down the field after just a minute of the second half and threw a lightning pass, which was caught to reduce the deficit to four points, at 14-10. Then, six minutes later, after an expert drive downfield, Rodgers responded with short pass after short pass, run after run, building momentum until he, too, threw a touchdown pass. There was still over 20 minutes left in the game, and suddenly it was 21-10 – 16 more points and I'd had it. And it was turning into a classic.

The thing in my favour at this point was the clock, just about the only thing. As any of you who've watched even a confusing five minutes of American football will have realised, the clock is far more important and tightly controlled in this sport than it is in our version of football. The best way to stop it is to throw passes out wide and get the receiver out of bounds. That's what you do when you're behind in a game and need every second available. The best way to run it down is to run the ball, and that way, as long as the runner stays in bounds, the clock continues to tick. And Rodgers, with an 11-point lead, knew that. The Eagles couldn't find a way through for the rest of that third quarter, and when the Packers got the ball, Rodgers moved it expertly, risk free and clock ticking. He was sitting on the lead, and suddenly the points bet was back on – 21-10 with 15 minutes to go.

In the fourth quarter, the wind played its part. The Eagles had carried the ball forward, had come agonisingly close to scoring a touchdown, and had finally been forced to kick a field goal, to take three points and regroup. The ever-reliable Akers stepped up to do something that he does many times every day of his life. And he missed it. He had misjudged the wind, just as he'd been doing in practice, and even though it was only three points, somehow it rattled the Eagles, quietened the fans, made them start to realise that it wouldn't be their day. Akers has missed only one of his last 20 field goals in post-season. Now, after an earlier aberration, he had missed two in this game, both at crucial times. When his coach was asked afterwards how he felt that the misses had affected the result, his assessment was brutally short: 'We can all count,' grumbled Reid.

Now Green Bay got the ball and once again Rodgers ran down the clock. Starks, the rookie who had only run for 101 yards all season up until this point, was having the game of his life, carrying the ball forward and watching the time tick. He would end up with 123 yards in an out-of-nowhere performance, and he was by far and away the biggest reason that I was winning the bet.

When Vick did get a chance, he showed his incredible athleticism. He was, ironically enough, a wounded animal and he scrambled and threw and finally got into the end zone to make the score 21-16 with just over four minutes to go. That was 37 points and ten more would lose me the bet. Steptoe was scowling once again. More clock running down meant that I started to feel as though the points line was as safe as it could be, and now I could sit and watch this match as a sport. Vick was trying to conjure a show-stopping comeback, and no matter how much he was hurting, he was brilliant. The man may have behaved like a coward earlier in his life, but now that he had woken up he showed that on the sports field he was a hero. He had hurt an ankle badly, and a member of the Philadelphia staff tried to take away his helmet to stop him from continuing, but Vick would have none of it, and went back out and drove his team downfield. With 1.45 to play, the Eagles were still down 21-16 and De Sean Jackson caught a pass from Vick and they marched down towards the line. Rodgers watched on and could do nothing. Vick was completing passes, taking risks, and found himself with a shot at redemption, on the Green Bay 27-yard line.

So it had come to this. The Eagles needed a touchdown to produce a win from nowhere, and they had 38 seconds to do it. Vick knew that he had a couple of chances to produce the winning moment, but he tried to take the first one. He decided that it was now or never, looked up and saw that his get-out man Jackson was covered. Then he turned and tried to throw a pass to a less reliable player in Riley Cooper, but this time the ball came out of his hand wrong, his arm jarred at a slight angle, and the ball was short of its target, caught by a Green Bay player and that was the end of that. Vick admitted afterwards that greed had got the better of him, but still rounded up enough sporting swagger to say: 'Hey, at least I went down swinging.'

After the match was over, and the Eagles were out, something strange happened. I found myself in Andy Reid's press conference, which was suitably downbeat and desperate and, afterwards, I saw the local journalists filing through a door behind the dais from which Reid had been speaking. I followed, and suddenly found myself inside the locker room of the Eagles. I was sure that I'd seen pictures of interviews being done inside locker rooms in American sports, but knowing it and accepting the reality were two different things. There I was, surrounded by benches and discarded rolls of tape, and disappointment. The Eagles' players were filing around, either on the way to the showers or frozen in agonised poses, and my heart was in my mouth. I couldn't believe that I was standing there. I know that it's not very journalistic to admit that, and I'm a bit more cynical and world weary when I get up close to football, but this was American football, this was the world that I'd always wanted to come to as a kid, and suddenly, after going through a small and unpromising door, here I was.

I told myself to play it cool, and make out that I belonged, and thought that I was carrying it off when a gigantic hand slapped down on my right shoulder. I turned round and was faced by a security guard who was big enough to have played in the game. 'Who the hell are you?' He said, clearly realising that I wasn't a local. I went for my usual tactic of an absurdly posh English accent, which often works in

America, and said, for some reason invoking the name of the publishers of this book. 'Erm, I'm from Bloomsbury.' This irritated bear looked confused and said: 'Well, who are you interviewin'?' I had the chance, the choice of any number of grunts, of irrelevant players, of guys who teammates hadn't even heard of, and I would be home free. Name one of them and he would let me go, and at least spend a little longer in this thrilling environment. And I said, and I still don't know why, 'I'm here to interview Michael Vick.' My feet barely touched the ground, and I was out, not just of the locker room, but of the stadium, before I knew what was happening.

In the bits of the press conferences that I'd managed to hear, Rodgers got the praise, although he was decent enough to say that 'in all my time in the sport, I never saw a football player win a match all by himself.' I was wrong to underestimate him, but was satisfied that I had refused to bet against Vick. He had taken his team to the brink of a win, and just come up short. I felt that both teams had struggled to cope with the wind, and that I'd been right to allow the conditions to play in my favour. Akers, in particular, had messed up and it was his two missed field goals at important times that had sealed my winning bet. There was part of me, as I walked away through the rain and past the guy at the subway station selling a perplexing variety of drugs, that delighted in Akers' misfortune.

Back in England the following week came the real truth about Akers and the wind, the heartbreaking pay-off. Akers had found out not long before the game that his six-year-old daughter Hailey had been diagnosed with a tumour. The kicker had kept things private as he didn't want to unsettle anyone in the build-up, but his wife Erika was in the stands for the game against the Packers and she said that she 'could tell he was doing his job. But I knew that he wasn't there.' Akers had been missing those kicks in practice beforehand because he was thinking about his daughter, not because of the wind. And he had failed under pressure in the game because he's a human being, and not a sporting automaton. I'd thought that I was so clever, seeing the way that the wind was blowing and calling the result, and yet none of it had anything to do with that. It was down to a man who was worried about his little girl. Ashamed, I moved on.

CHAPTER FIVE

One thing is clear in my mind. In black and white and for the record. When I go, whether it's of over-excitement at trading the final stages of a major golf tournament, watching a favourite get beaten on the line, or kicked to death by a bunch of angry Italian football fans, then there's only one time and place that I want my ashes scattering. Just after the gates have opened, in Festival week, in front of the main grandstand on the final furlong of Cheltenham racecourse. Nowhere am I ever happier. Sitting in the just broken emptiness, watching the strings of horses exercise as the sun rises above Cleeve Hill in the distance and the morning mist starts to burn away. It's a place of possibilities. You can sit there on one of the benches, pretty much alone, and read your *Racing Post* or your Timeform card or whatever tool that you might use, and you can revel in the silence, and the anticipated noise. You know that, quiet though it is at 10 a.m., in four hours it will be swamped with people, and humming with noise and opinion. As a human being, the place has always been a thrill, the best week of any year. As a punter, I've had some happy memories and some absolute disasters. But I always come back. As we all do, all of us who are lucky to know just how great it is.

There's nowhere better than Cheltenham in March, and that's why my 2009 performance here, the low point of my Emma-inspired slump, hurt so much. I only ever want good memories of Cheltenham, but that year I managed to accumulate some terrible ones. If you're in the wrong frame of mind, and have lost focus and discipline, then the quick turnover of races can be brutal. You fancy something, it loses, and so you feel the need to go straight back in and get your betting day going. And then the next thing loses. And the next. You get the picture? Over the course of the week there are 27 races to get wrong, and if you're determined to have a bet on each of them, then that can add up to an awful lot of money. It's a hard course to get right as a gambler, a real punting challenge. And you need a great deal of focus and a little bit of luck. Betting here should be all about discipline, and planning, about course knowledge and about awareness of what has happened before and how it will affect the future. It's not a place to turn up and behave like a drunk after midnight at a wedding.

Before you run a mile, and deprive yourselves of the biggest thrill in sport, I should make it clear that if you turn up casually to have a fun day out then the Cheltenham Festival is always great. Six or seven bets a day, maybe following your instinct, maybe a tip that you got the night before, maybe listening to Pricewise in the *Racing Post*. You'll have a bet, and you'll maybe have a bit of luck, but as long as you keep stakes low then it won't break you. For the average punter who comes along with a planned budget and determination to have a good time then there's no danger. It's when you go to the Festival with a sense that you can make it seriously work for you that you can get in trouble. Big trouble. I'd come close to madness the previous year, and was dead set on doing the opposite.

So this year I was all about discipline and preparation, and I thought that Cheltenham might be an interesting object lesson in whether I could get myself into as perfect a frame of mind as possible to have a bet. Remember the thing about confidence and balance being the two most important things for any punter to have on their side? Well, I wondered if you could try to manufacture those states of mind. People in all walks of life use techniques which allow them to cope, which help them get better, and so why shouldn't punters do it too? And I knew the feeling that I was looking for, the one that the punters that I surveyed had marked down as the one that you want. I call it the opposite of pissed. Let me explain.

It's common knowledge in the gambling world, and simple logic outside it, that you should never bet when you're drunk or when you have a hangover. The reasons for that seem pretty obvious, but they bear closer inspection. Alcohol impairs your senses, and too much of it makes you wake up feeling terrible. Like you've been punched in the head, like you've been locked in a sauna, like a dog has slept in your mouth. Most of you will have been there. But I don't think that it's any of those physical effects that lie behind the reasons that you shouldn't gamble in that state. It's the mental games that alcohol plays which make it the most dangerous accompaniment to a trip to the bookmakers or an online gambling account. Alcohol is an instant stimulant, and then a gradual depressant, and both of those states of mind are deadly. The most obvious one is the stimulation: you get drunk at a racecourse and you think 'Whey hey, I'm going to be a millionaire!' The amount that you lose will be entirely dependent on how much that you had in your wallet before racing, and, on top of that, how much your equally pissed mates will lend you. But the aftermath is more interesting, and what was biting me at Cheltenham. Because the varying degrees of depression that hit you when you're hungover are a gambling nightmare. Not because they make you negative, but for the opposite reason. You feel terrible, and so you want something to make you feel better. If drink is normally your thing, then it will be the hair of the dog. If you're an eater, then comfort food and chocolate cake will be loaded up until you feel stodgy, and sated, and somehow better. If you're a punter, then that feeling of wanting to lift yourself up will make you gamble in a way that you believe will change your life and make everything better. So you sit and eat ice cream with a fork and punt the Brazilian football at 1 a.m. And guess what? You don't win very often.

So if being drunk or hungover is the worst thing, then surely there's another way? Clear headed, sharp, and able to make good decisions. The opposite of pissed. I knew that Cheltenham had the potential to wipe me out, as it had done once already, and so I set about trying to find a way to stop it happening again. Other than not having a bet, of course, and that was never going to happen.

The following couple of paragraphs are going to sound like, for want of a better phrase, complete bollocks. But they're not as bad as they could have been. I got through an awful lot of self-help books with relentlessly optimistic titles, all of which struck me as aimed at people who had no idea how to be happy. I'd already had a brush with something approaching astrology at the fortune-teller's in New York, and while I'm sure that there are many of these books that have helped people out, I'm equally certain that there are plenty which simply confirm feelings which any ordinary person has, just like astrology. So, as you may read in your star sign that 'you've had a bad month, so now you feel that something special is round the corner,' you read in a self-help book that 'you may not feel it now, but I'm telling you that you can be anything that you want.' All of this struck me as distinctly unhelpful, particularly the suggestion in one book that before each day started I should imagine myself sitting in a big office with a view of Central Park and I should tell myself at the top of my voice that I'm special, and this is going to be my day. I was tempted, in a try-anything sense, but somehow I resisted. Walking around the parade ring at Cheltenham screaming, 'I'm special and this is going to be my day,' would more than likely lead to me watching the racing from a hospital bed. I would need a less obvious way of getting myself ready. So I went down a couple of roads that I never thought I'd travel, just to see if they'd work. When you'd messed up like I had, anything had to be worth a go.

My logic went that the mental stems from the physical, and with the words 'balance' and 'confidence' ringing in my ears I found a few things that I thought might help. And that's why, on a cold day at the end of February, the scents of lemon and lime burnt my nostrils and I found myself face-to-face with a pensioner in lycra. I was lying on my front, my arms were stretched behind me and it was a small, slightly too warm studio. We were both there for a reason and we were both fully clothed, so any puerile snickering should stop right here.

The lemon and lime is easy to explain. I have a friend who's an aromatherapist and I asked her if there was anything she could recommend that could increase focus and make me think more clearly. She gave me these citrus essential oils, and so I bought one of those slightly embarrassing new-age oil burners and sat down and waited for something to happen. I'd read somewhere that a few Hollywood stars drank lemon juice first thing in the morning to help cleanse them, and I could see how that might logically extend to the brain. Then I remembered a magazine article in which Francis Rossi of Status Quo said that he started every day with a glass of lemon juice. I was following advice on equilibrium from a man with little or no septum. Brilliant.

The studio and the pensioner were to do with Pilates. Friends of mine had raved about how going to classes and stretching had done wonders for their bad backs and their outlook on life and so I gave that a go as well, and it made me feel better. A month later, of course, on the same day that I was sitting at the Crucible Theatre watching John Higgins playing a World Snooker semi-final, the practice of Pilates would get its biggest ever boost because of Pippa Middleton's backside. There was clearly something to it.

Now, at this point, I appreciate that you've bought a book about gambling and sport and you find yourself reading a chapter which is ostensibly about Cheltenham but which has turned into something entirely different. We'll be onto the horses in a moment, I promise. Pilates definitely works, and I've now become the kind of convert who waxes lyrical about the practice at every opportunity. In short, the kind of person I would have *hated* a couple of years ago. There's no need to go into the details here, but suffice to say that it makes you feel energised and gives you a focus for the rest of the day. The Pilates ethos is all about the way that breathing and the control of your core muscles can increase your flexibility but also the sharpness of your mind and your sense of balance. It can be a bit dull, and in the wrong mood the classes seem to last forever, but whenever I've done it early in the morning then I've punted really well later that day. If you're sceptical, and I bet that you are, then do me a favour and try one thing. Next time that you have a big day coming up, whether it's gambling or something else, and you want to prepare properly, either stand up or sit up straight in your chair (it's better to lie down but I'm not expecting you to go that far just yet) and breathe in and out several times really deeply. As Joe Pilates (yes, that was his real name) said: 'Squeeze out your lungs as you would wring a wet towel dry.'

When you've done that a few times, start focusing like mad on your stomach muscles, and, as you breathe out, pull them in tightly while still standing or sitting straight. Just those muscles, and nothing else. Keep them pulled in, and keep breathing in and out deeply. Stop when you feel like it, or when the muscles start to feel uncomfortable, and then walk around for a couple of minutes to loosen up. That, in a massively simple nutshell, is the basis of the whole practice. And it's amazing how muscles send messages to your mind and you start to feel balanced and ready. Alternatively, laugh it off and dismiss me as a pretentious dick. In gambling as in life, the choice is yours. For my Cheltenham though, with so many chances of going off the rails, I would be accompanied by a strange stretchy band and a job lot of lemon and lime oil.

The weeks before the Festival are always taken up with anticipation. The National Hunt Racing season starts in September, and from that point on you're looking for clues as to what might happen in March. At the turn of the year, you know that you're only three months away, and you flick through the prices in the *Racing Post* on a daily basis, and even if they don't change they offer you a chance to anticipate. The same names had been towards the top of markets for months: the likes of Imperial Commander, the reigning Gold Cup champion; Big Buck's, the World Hurdle king; Binocular in the Champion Hurdle. On a good day you'll have some clear thoughts, and on a bad one the names will leap off the page and tumble into your mind, where they'll just be names, with no form and no logic, there to swim around and confuse you, to stand as questions and not answers. There's a huge amount of joy in simply being at Cheltenham, but the anticipation provides a thrill of a different kind.

You'll see that AP McCoy is 8-1 to be Top Festival Jockey and wonder if he can overcome Ruby Walsh and his book of rides, and see 6-1 being offered about Willie Mullins being top trainer, and think out loud that if Ireland have a good Festival, then that could look a huge price come next Friday. And then there are the individual races. They'll just look like black and white to most people, but a riot of colour to a Cheltenham lover. So many questions which have built up throughout the season, even throughout the year, and there's the knowledge that they'll all be played out from 2 p.m. next Tuesday. Cue Card is 9-4 for the opening race of the Festival, and surely has to be opposed, and you wonder about Medermit in the Arkle at 3-1, with Alan King's yard having come back to form. Quevega seems to be ridiculously short at even money for the Mares' Hurdle, but then who can possibly beat her, and how can Oscar Whisky be 12-1 for the Champion Hurdle? And that's just Tuesday.

I knew that I had no chance of finishing the Festival in profit if I had a bet in every race, and so, after the oils and the stretching, that was my first promise to myself. I would pick out a handful of races, five at most, and try and become as expert in them as possible, getting my stakes right and finding a winner or two. I knew that I'd start with the Champion Hurdle, which has always been a favourite of mine and which looked fabulously competitive this year. And already I was thinking back to something that had happened the previous year. On the Wednesday of the Festival, I was wandering near the Guinness Village early in the afternoon, carrying a microphone and feeling self-conscious, when a short, friendly man with black hair walked up to me and said in a Scouse accent: 'Peddlers Cross will win the next race.' No hellos, no formality, just a bare statement. I wasn't even sure that he was talking to me and so I said, with exaggerated politeness: 'I beg your pardon?' In slightly more staccato fashion, which emphasised his Scouseness, he said, as if talking to an idiot: 'Peddlers. Cross. Will win. The next. Race.' There was a part of me, the romantic part, that just wanted to say thank you, stroll off, and have the entire contents of my wallet on the Donald McCain-trained Peddlers Cross to win the next race, which was a Novice Hurdle referred to as the Neptune. The previous year had taught me the danger of impulses, though, and so I thought that I should dig at least a little deeper. 'Why would that be then?' I said. The man replied that he had spoken to the trainer that morning and that there was a great deal of confidence in the camp, and he had done his homework and just had a feeling that the horse would win. A feeling that today was the day for the big one. And so he had placed a massive bet on Peddlers Cross and was encouraging me to do the same.

I love people like this, admired his confidence and his guts, and wished him luck, punter to punter. He shook my hand and finally introduced himself. 'Phil Williams is the name,' he said smiling, 'don't forget who gave you the tip.' I walked off and emptied my wallet, and chucked the contents on Peddlers Cross. It was always inevitable, but I felt like I'd delayed it at least, for half a minute. I got 8-1, and then watched in wonder as the horse hit the front and battled up the hill to win. I collected my money, and knew that Peddlers Cross, and the conversation, would always have a special place in my heart. I'll never know if Phil really knew something, or whether he was punting on instinct or a really good judge, but I'm sure that he was telling the truth about having a sizeable bet. He was filled with the right kind of nervous energy, and I know that feeling. The last that I saw of Phil that Wednesday was on his way out of the racecourse, just before six, when everything starts to wind down. He didn't see me at first, so I could watch him on his way out, swaying gently from side to side, and singing in that same scouse accent: 'I see birds in the sky, red roses toooooooo, I see them bloooooooo, for me and yooooooooooo. And I think to myself, what a wonderful weeeeeerld.' I caught up with him and shook his hand. 'We did it,' he said, the smile cracking his face. 'We did it.'

Peddlers Cross was back again this year and was right at the heart of my plans for the opening day. Having won as a novice the previous year, the horse was back for the Champion Hurdle, and the race this year looked to be a classic. Up until the previous Saturday, the hot favourite had been last year's winner Binocular, but the horse had been pulled out dramatically because of an illegal substance that had been found in its system. This mirrored the situation from the Festival last year, when Binocular had seemed an unlikely runner in the race up until the days before, a fact that had put punters off. And then he had won impressively. I could fill a whole chapter with the comments that I've heard from disgruntled gamblers about Binocular, but that's a different story for a different day. Now that the favourite was out, the race looked wide open, with Peddlers Cross third in the market, behind the two new market leaders, Menorah and Hurricane Fly, two horses with very different profiles who divided opinion.

Menorah is trained in Somerset by Phillip Hobbs, and the horse had done nothing wrong and had already won at Cheltenham twice this season. Menorah had also taken the Supreme Novices' Hurdle at the Festival last year, and had looked better with each run. And there was no reason to believe that the horse wouldn't improve again. Hurricane Fly is from Ireland, a horse who had been talked about more than almost any other over the last few years, and yet had never been to Cheltenham, with injury always preventing the horse from making the journey. Hurricane Fly was trained by one of the greats, Willie Mullins, and the word was that he was supremely confident, and yet given the particular challenge of Cheltenham, I couldn't see how such confidence was justified. There was an added breeding quirk that Hurricane Fly had been sired by Montjeu, the great French flat horse, whose progeny hadn't won a race at Cheltenham in over 30 attempts. I couldn't understand why Mullins, who had previously expressed doubts about his horse's temperament when under pressure, could suddenly be so confident.

Plenty of experts were suggesting that Hurricane Fly was a sure thing, and I was tempted to jump on the bandwagon, as there's no feeling like the one of being part of a racecourse gamble, but my head was telling me that I had to leave Hurricane Fly alone, and if he won, then applaud him, and deal with the fact that he hadn't carried my money. Letting a horse that you like win a race, and ignoring him because of the price, is something that you have to get used to as a gambler.

I'd become a bit obsessed with trends in the build-up to this year's Festival. Not in a fashion sense, as the only trend that you'll see at Cheltenham is a penchant for wearing bright tweed and massive brogues. I'm talking about trends in a horse sense, patterns which are repeated year after year. A friend of mine had banged on at me for years about the idea that what has happened in a particular race in previous years is by far and away the best guide to what might take place in the latest renewal. Ironically enough, sticking with trends often means that you avoid the more fashionable horses, and ignore what is seemingly relevant, discarding up-to-date information while slavishly following specific statistics.

There's an admirable book published every year before the Festival, written by a brilliant devotee of racing called Paul Jones, in which he identifies each statistic on a certain race that you, the punter, should regard as relevant. It's a great read for a jump-racing fan, but probably not one to lend to a disinterested partner. It takes a while to get your head around using trends, as they are strictly factual and logical and seem to largely take opinion and the naked eye out of the equation. I was trying to cover every base in the Champion Hurdle though, and so I waded in.

The two stats that jumped out from Jones' book were that 23 of the last 27 winners of the Champion Hurdle had won the last time that they'd been on a racecourse, and that 16 of the last 22 winners had won at Cheltenham before. Both of these statistics confirmed two basic principles that plenty of non-racing experts could confirm.

The horse should be in good form, and should like running at the track. The second of those two bare facts encouraged me to disregard Hurricane Fly, but the problem was that the last two winners of the race, Punjabi and Binocular, had never won here either, so, although I had faithfully planned to follow the trends, I still had my doubts.

Another strong trend was the one that said that the last 16 winners of the race had already run in that calendar year. Many argued that this was far more relevant in the days when yards didn't give horses as much intensive fitness training, and rather than being kept super-fit at home, horses would need to go to the racecourse for a tune-up. With trainers these days having costly all-weather gallops, and bundles of kit to keep a horse fit, then surely it didn't matter when the horse actually ran in a real race. If it was so irrelevant, I wondered, why had it been proved true for the last 16 years?

This trend was further complicated by the damage that had been done by the weather to the winter racing schedule. Horses that would have had a run had not been risked, and so perhaps extraordinary circumstances meant that we should ignore this pattern as well. If we believed it though, it counted heavily against Menorah, who hadn't run since December. The other negative that I had against the Hobbs horse was the reaction that there'd been to the burst of acceleration that Menorah had shown to beat two talented younger horses, Cue Card and Silviniaco Conti, at Cheltenham in December. I like trusting my eyes, and I was standing at the final hurdle that day, where the apparent burst came. I thought that it looked good on television, but up close, the two younger horses had both faded badly, worse that it looked from a TV picture, and by simply keeping going Menorah had looked to have quickened up considerably, a bit like a sprinting athlete overtaking two tired ones at the end of a marathon. I wondered if Menorah might not have the finishing burst to win a Champion Hurdle.

The other key trend is that winners tend to be aged between six and eight years old, and if you put all of those statistics together, then you were left with a shortlist that consisted of my old friend Peddlers Cross and Nicky Henderson's horse Oscar Whisky.

The process described in the paragraphs above isn't particularly sexy, as you might have noticed, and I apologise for making you wade through it. But that, in essence, is my point about the madness of Cheltenham. I've described a tiny fraction of the process involved in trying to pick the winner of one race. Now imagine doing that 27 times, the same level of research for every race. It's almost impossible unless you're superhuman. And I'm barely human. That's why it's about discipline and money in pocket and focusing on a limited number of races.

The day before the Festival, a friend and I had walked the course that would be used for the Champion Hurdle, to try and get an idea of what was facing the horses and jockeys, when the atmosphere would hit them and when they'd enjoy the strange solitude that's always there on the racecourse, although hard to find in this particular week. The first two days of racing during the Festival take place on the Old Course, the inner of the two that are available to the Clerk of the Course, Simon Claisse. Claisse had started to water the course the week before the Festival, which is always a difficult juggling act, and the operation was continuing. The job of the Clerk of the Course is to make sure that the ground is safe enough, and that means with enough give to make the conditions safe for racing. If he doesn't water, there's no rain, and the ground is so hard that horses are injured, then he's criticised. If he waters, and it rains, and the ground is too soft as a result, then he's criticised even more. It's a thankless balancing act, and one that he does with grace and wit.

As we walked the course in the sunshine, there were sprinklers to dodge. If you've never been out and experienced what a racecourse is like underfoot, you'd be surprised by how rough the ground can be. When you watch from the stands or on television, you think that the green swathe might be a toughened up billiard table, but in reality it's more like a well manicured field. If you didn't already realise how tough a horse has to be to win at Cheltenham, then walking just 50 yards of the course is an education.

There are only eight hurdles for the horses to clear in the Champion, and that's why it's a race in which pace and judgement, as well as toughness, have always been key. Jumping may not seem to be important, as the obstacles are so much smaller than fences – a less obvious distraction – and yet the horses' movement has to remain balanced and fluent, and a missed stride over a hurdle or a bad landing at the wrong time can cost you the race. The aim for the jockeys is to skim over the obstacles, as low as possible without making significant contact, and so momentum continues and the chance of winning remains constant.

There's always talk of tactical speed in these big hurdle races, and despite using the phrase myself on many occasions, I never quite knew what it meant. But out on the course you do. As the field starts to bowl down the destabilising hill before the final turn then the jockeys have to get their horse in a position to win, and with the pace in the Champion always furious, that means that their horse has to have the speed to get them into contention, maybe correcting a positional mistake that they've made. And then, after they've turned left for a final time they face the Cheltenham Hill. So much has been spoken and written about the hill that, when you stand at the bottom of it, you expect the north face of the Eiger, but it seems gentler than that, nothing more than a slight incline. Any Cheltenham regular knows, though, that the hill can find you out as stamina drains and the legs get weary. Horses have looked certain winners jumping the last fence or hurdle and then they've started to tread water. You can take a risk if you like, but you have to be as certain as you can that any horse you back at Cheltenham can get up the hill.

After walking the course, I bumped into Simon Claisse, scurrying around and making sure that everything was in place for the following day. He asked how the course had looked and I made the mistake of saying that it was great but I was surprised how rutted it was in places. The minute that I'd opened my mouth I regretted my choice of words. I was talking from a layman's position, and was trying to describe my surprise at how unlike a billiard table it was. Claisse looked at me through his glasses and said: 'Rutted? Where is it rutted? Can you take me out and show me?' I swiftly backtracked and said that, no, there weren't tyre marks or anything like that, it was just that I'd been surprised at how uneven the course was in places, how the camber around some of the turns caught me by surprise, that I knew nothing and I'm sure that it was in perfect condition. Claisse said: 'But you said rutted. There must have been a reason for that.'

He was worried that he'd missed something on the eve of the Festival, and even though he seemed to accept my stumbling explanation, I'm sure that he went out one more time that evening and checked for ruts. I like to think that maybe I helped and that he discovered something that made the course even better on that extra journey. But I doubt it.

It was time to leave the people at the course to do what they're good at, and for me to make a decision. For all that there wasn't a rut in sight, I'd been taken by how hard the race was, and with the quality of the field meaning that the pace was likely to be strong, I was sure that the horse which won would have to be fast and tough. That meant that with the help of the trends and a close inspection of the course, my shortlist was down to three. Peddlers Cross and Oscar Whisky, both of whom would want a test of stamina but could be caught out in a dawdling race which turned into a sprint, and Hurricane Fly, who had won over 2 miles and 4 furlongs and wouldn't be at all inconvenienced by a fast race. Even though he'd never run at the course, I still couldn't put a line through his name. I was taking on Menorah, and running the risk that he would improve and be good enough to win, but felt that my rather haphazard December judgement still held true.

All the way through that Tuesday morning, I bumped into people I respected who told me that Hurricane Fly would win. The most convincing was Martin Kelly, the journalist and TV pundit, who was out on a birthday bash with friends and who had clearly had a big bet on Hurricane Fly. Martin is someone whose judgement I respect, but in the end I had to make a decision. I would take the risk against Hurricane Fly turning up and winning at his first try around Cheltenham, and I would back Peddlers Cross to win at 9-2. I was so confident about the statistical lines that I'd put through the rest of the field that I backed up that bet with a £50 straight forecast on Peddlers

Cross to finish first and Oscar Whisky second. Decision made after a lot of hard work, and I was ready for the race.

As I was making my way down to the course to watch, I saw Phil Williams, the hero from last year. I asked him if he'd had a bet on the Champion and he said: 'Stupid question, don't you remember last year?' He was on Peddlers Cross again, and somehow that made me feel better.

What followed was a vintage Champion Hurdle, which to my surprise developed much as I'd expected. Peddlers Cross had a pace-maker, his stablemate Overturn, who made sure that there was pace in the race, and after a breathless gallop, the race started in earnest as they approached that final turn, where they would see the hill looming in front of them. Peddlers Cross, Oscar Whisky and Menorah were in good positions throughout, with Menorah jumping expertly, and travelling fluently. The Peddlers Cross plan was working to perfection, with Overturn continuing to lead them through and Peddlers Cross waiting to hit the front and try and break their hearts. And he did. He surged past Overturn as they jumped the third last flight and Oscar Whisky came through to join him. My selections were first and second and with Menorah starting to crack and no other horse looking threatening from my viewpoint, I was getting excited.

And then I saw him. Really saw him. The blue colours of Hurricane Fly were starting to cut through the field and Ruby Walsh, his jockey, had barely moved a muscle. He didn't look that inconvenienced by Cheltenham. As the front two battled, Hurricane Fly loomed up on the outside. The Irish horse jumped into the lead at the last hurdle, and Peddlers Cross showed what a brave horse he is by battling back and turning it into a fight up the hill. But Hurricane Fly had it convincingly in the end, and my first bet of the Festival was done. And yet strangely I felt a little strengthened by what had happened. By sitting down and spending more time than I'd ever done on a race I had narrowed the field down to three, and had discounted one horse simply because there was a doubt in my mind about his price and his familiarity with Cheltenham. And he had won, leaving my two selections second and third. If Hurricane Fly hadn't performed, then I would have had the winner, and the forecast of first and second in the correct order. I'd ended with nothing, but somehow didn't feel as stupid as I had at Cheltenham two years earlier.

Hurricane Fly's win was part of a treble on that Tuesday for Ruby Walsh, a man who had been laid up with a broken leg for much of the winter, and who had woken up on the Saturday before the Festival not having ridden a winner for four months. Mon Parrain did the job for him at Sandown, and by the end of Cheltenham Week he would be top jockey there once again, a punter's favourite. The relationship between gamblers and jockeys is an interesting one, far more than the frequently used throwaway line about jockeys making bad tipsters.

Jockeys are often spoken about like automatons by punters, machines that somehow have to do the same job every day and always do it perfectly, particularly when the money is down. They will occasionally have a nightmare, and, of course, the better jockeys are the ones who make the fewest mistakes. But, rather than criticise when things don't work out, we should be amazed by their consistency, and the fact that they're only noticed when things go wrong. In a race that is run at such a serious pace, the judgement of the jockeys is crucial. I'd never say that you should go racing and back everything that's ridden by the two greats of the sport, Tony McCoy and Ruby Walsh, but if you do one thing that you know about the two of them is that your horse is certain to have a good chance of winning. That isn't always the case. The previous year, I'd backed a horse called Carlito Brigante, one of my favourites, to win the Triumph Hurdle, and I'd spent the rest of the week complaining to friends about the ride that he got from a normally reliable Irish jockey called Davy Russell. Russell had never previously given me cause for concern, but I felt that in that Triumph Hurdle he had allowed the leaders to get too far in front and had asked Carlito Brigante for an effort way too late. The horse had responded and charged up the hill to finish fourth. Carlito had done nothing wrong, but hadn't been given the chance to win.

He was back, Carlito Brigante, on the Wednesday, running in the Coral Cup, the mad, impossible to pick, 28-runner handicap that's fun to watch but a nightmare to bet on. The image of my favourite horse charging up the hill into fourth the previous year was burned into my memory, and I felt that a horse which had been good enough to finish an unlucky fourth in the Triumph Hurdle shouldn't really be 16-1 to win a lesser race the following year. The Coral Cup is a handicap, and so Carlito would have to carry more weight than most of the field because of his class, but he hadn't performed particularly well that season and so I felt that the handicapper may have got it wrong. This was a horse that would be lit up by being back here, could carry the weight, and he would carry my money. This was nowhere near as scientific as my first bet, but it came from the right place: from what I'd seen before, and from what I thought might happen that afternoon. My only doubt was how much I *wanted* the horse to win. He's such a favourite of mine, for all of the illogical reasons that any of us fall in love with horses, that I wondered if I was backing him through logic or sentiment. The truth was that it was probably a bit of both.

Some friends came to Cheltenham that day, and, despite knowing me, they still asked for any tips that I might have, and I was so worried about the sentiment side of things that I told them that I was backing Carlito Brigante for the Coral Cup, but didn't necessarily think that they should, as I was probably just being soppy. I did warn them that I'd come and watch the race with them and that I'd cry if he won. And he did, easily. And much though I tried to hide it, I kept up my end of the bargain. I was up and running, and determined to give Thursday a miss, saving myself for what was my bet of the meeting. One that came about almost by accident, after a rainy Saturday in Surrey.

A couple of weeks earlier, I'd travelled to Kempton Park for a lesson in paddock picking from a man who knows more than most about the subject, David Cleary. David works for Timeform, and is an unobtrusive presence on a racecourse, never one to shout his opinions from the rooftops, just calmly state them and see where they lead. And he is an expert in watching horses parade before a race, and working out from that how they might run both on that day and in the future. I realise that there's something ridiculous about trying to learn an art as subtle as that in a day, but what I was after were pointers, something that might make me feel less stupid when I watched the chinstrokers and whisperers applying their horse sense to the Cheltenham parade. The first race of the afternoon was the Adonis Hurdle, and David made the point to me that the art of paddock picking has become less important over the years. In the old days, when horses didn't really have fitness regimes at home, it was possible to pick out a runner that had a belly, particularly early on in the season, and discount it because of that. Now, most of the horses carried a certain level of fitness, although races like this one, featuring inexperienced horses, interested him, as you had the chance to see just how a lightly raced horse might take to racing.

The Adonis Hurdle is a very good race in its own right, but that can also have major significance as a final pointer to Cheltenham, although that wasn't the reason I was there. As we watched them walk around on a rainy afternoon, David said that all of the runners were looking settled and calm, apart from one. He told me, kindly, that my eye was as good as his and that all his trained eye was looking for could be picked up by my untrained one. How is the horse moving? Does it have a long stride? Does it look healthy and happy? The process is a lot more complicated than this, but David said that those were the key things to look for. So I watched them parade, and tried to pretend to myself that I had any idea but was at least reassured by the thought that I knew what to look for, if not how to find it.

After we'd watched them, David asked me what I thought, and I said that I thought the Nicky Henderson-trained Molotof looked like a tough horse and seemed well, and David didn't disagree. I gave myself a pat on the back and then David qualified his initial comment by following up with: 'They all looked well really. Well, apart from one. I wouldn't be backing the number 10. He looked on his toes as if he wouldn't enjoy racing today at all. Very immature looking horse.' I thought back to the way that they'd looked as they'd walked around and remembered that one horse had seemed a little edgy, rearing up on occasion, and seeming unsettled. But I wasn't sure what to make of that. On previous occasions, I've seen a horse look a little fiery before a race and then been told dismissively by someone in the know that 'he's just showing off.' I couldn't tell the difference between nerves and showing off, and I had a long way to go.

David and I went our separate ways to watch the Adonis, him to make copious notes and me to cheer on Molotof, and yet the Henderson horse was well beaten by one trained by Paul Nicholls and having its first run over hurdles. And one that was wearing the number 12. David smiled when he met again and said sheepishly: 'Well, I did tell you that it was an inexact science.' The horse was called Zarkandar, and my first thought was that if he had run that well here when he was edgy and on his toes, then how good might he be when he's in a more relaxed frame of mind. David laughed and said: 'I know why you might think that, but we may discover come the end of Zarkandar's career that he only runs well when he's on his toes, and when he's relaxed he doesn't perform. Your version of events is the likelier, but by no means certain. That's why I carry a notebook.'

Zarkandar would go to the Triumph Hurdle at Cheltenham, and that evening I couldn't get him out of my head. He was a four-year-old, was nervous at his new surroundings, and had surely used up a lot of energy with his behaviour in the parade ring. He was from a top stable, and Paul Nicholls and his team would surely be able to find a way to help him cope. Earplugs had worked on Hurricane Fly after all, why shouldn't something similar happen here? Soldatino had won this race the previous year and had gone on to take the Triumph, and after clocking a decent time at Kempton there was no reason why Zarkandar couldn't do likewise. The experiences from that day at Kempton would be taken forward to the Friday of Cheltenham.

The morning of the Triumph Hurdle was taken up with talk of the Cheltenham Gold Cup, which isn't just the feature race of the Friday but of the whole meeting. The big question was whether the potential new star of steeplechasing, Long Run, could topple the previous year's winner Imperial Commander, the torch carrier for the older generation. I was looking forward to the Gold Cup, and had a fancy for the Irish horse Kempes, but all of my attention was on the Triumph. In the spirit of the new calm and collected Cheltenham me, I had a plan. I would look to support Zarkandar at 9-1, but I would send a friend of mine who is an expert horsewoman to the parade ring to take a look at him and see how he was taking to the crowd. If he looked calm and purposeful, then he would have to be the bet, given what we had seen at Kempton. A rumour was going around the course that the Paul Nicholls team fancied Zarkandar's stable-mate Sam Winner, but these kinds of rumours should be ignored in my experience. You or I could start a rumour at a racecourse if so inclined, and if the horse wasn't right then Nicholls wouldn't run it. From listening to him speak at a corporate event the week before the Festival, as well as reading his Betfair column, I got the impression that the Nicholls' team felt that Zarkandar was potentially very special, and that no risks would be taken with the horse. There was, after all, always next season.

Zarkandar's pedigree is built for speed, but not necessarily for winning races at Cheltenham. He had been born to the same mother as Zarkava, the filly which had brilliantly won one of flat racing's biggest prizes, the Prix de l'Arc de Triomphe, a couple of years earlier, and so it was odd that he should be tried over hurdles at all. The run at Kempton had been the first in which he'd been required to run over obstacles, and he had coped well, despite his the antics beforehand. The horse's behaviour had been even worse when he had first arrived in the Nicholls' yard, but being gelded calmed him down, as it probably would me, and if his temperament was right here, then he clearly had a major chance.

Half an hour before the race, I sent my friend down to the parade ring to take a look at him, and what she told me was perfect. In the pre-parade ring, the smaller and more sheltered area where the horses prepare before a race, he had once again seemed a little edgy, but she had noticed his stride lengthen as he went around the jockeys' weighing room and into the main parade ring, and he was a picture of calmness as he strolled around. I thought of all of the energy that he must have saved compared to the performance at Kempton, I thought again about the speed that his breeding had given him, and rushed off to back him. Zarkandar would have the potential to turn this into a stellar week. It was then that I realised the difference made to my mindset by the staking plan I was following. In the old days I would have piled all the profit from the Carlito Brigante win onto Zarkandar, but I was determined to show discipline and not risk throwing it all away, no matter how confident I was.

Zarkandar was brilliant, though still looking a little inexperienced and losing his position as the horses moved towards that final turn. But as the field started up the hill he had so much raw pace that his jockey Daryl Jacob was able to sit still and allow the horse to get himself back in contention. Zarkandar flew up it and won pretty easily. That was the best moment of this whole process, as I don't think that I ever doubted him. What I'd seen at Kempton, both before and during the race, had been translated into a breathtaking performance.

Zarkandar will run in the Champion Hurdle next season, and racing against Hurricane Fly will possibly be the highlight of the week.

For all my punting success though, there was no question about the highlight of this Cheltenham week. The wonder of the place, the way that history leaves its handprint, was summed up by a Gold Cup for the ages. The young horse Long Run, who had disappointed at Cheltenham before, finally put everything together at the right time and charged up the hill under his amateur jockey Sam Waley-Cohen, the man who had reportedly got Prince William and Kate Middleton together. That was a story in itself, with Simon Barnes in *The Times* reflecting that: 'once professional used to be a dirty word in sport, now it's amateur.' Despite that, Waley-Cohen's victory reminded many that the original meaning of the word, rooted in the Latin that many have to parrot at a certain kind of school, *amo, amas, amat*, amateurism is about love.

And it was the love that made that Friday so special, and reminded me that Cheltenham is a lot more than just a betting medium. There was a fondness for Long Run, and a sense that he could win the next three Gold Cups. But the real stars of that day were the two older horses, Denman and Kauto Star, who were 11 years old and seemingly past their best. Not many were giving them a chance this year. And yet Kauto Star had moved into the lead a few furlongs out, and his stablemate Denman had cruised into contention alongside him, with the whole field in behind them, apart from Long Run. For one time-freezing moment it had looked like Denman and Kauto Star would fight out the finish of the Gold Cup for one final time, but then the younger horse, as he should, had too much for them up the hill. The two old men had gone out on their shields, though, and the receptions that they both received when they came back into the winner's enclosure were like nothing that I've ever heard at Cheltenham, rarely heard in sport. Denman had finished second, and yet it felt as if he'd won. And if you ever wonder why we, those of us who are lucky enough to know how great the place is, come back to Cheltenham year after year, then that was the moment to understand. A place of bravery, of emotion, where it doesn't matter what you wear or how much money you have but simply that you love racing. A place of possibility, and one that makes you, as you drag yourself away from the course on Friday night, start thinking, straightaway, about next year. About punting plans, about anticipating the noise, and about how a new approach, one that combines research and instinct, and one which takes more care, might just work again. For all that I revelled in the success, I couldn't decide whether I'd been good or just lucky, and I wouldn't know that for sure until we all came back next time, tantalised by hope, lifted by possibility.

CHAPTER SIX

So to the venue which had captivated me more than any other as a child, which fills me with more early sporting memories than any other. I love sport because of my grandfather, a man who was good enough to win one rugby cap for Wales and who delighted in sitting of an afternoon and filling his grandson's heart with his love for sport. I'd sit in my favourite spot at my grandad's feet and together we watched everything, and his opinions became my own. That's why, as an Englishman born in Liverpool, I have a passionate hatred of the English rugby team that lasts to this day, and why I preferred Steve Ovett (good, solid lad) to Sebastian Coe (bloody mummy's boy). I could name a hundred sporting prejudices that linger somewhere on the fringes of my mind and they're all down to him. What grandad Charlie said I believed, and even now I wouldn't have it any other way.

And he loved his snooker. Every year we'd sit in that position, me at his feet, and watch the World Championships from the Crucible Theatre in Sheffield. He was a tough man who'd worked all his life, and so his players were Cliff Thorburn and Eddie Charlton, the grinders from the pool halls of Canada and Australia, rather than the more flamboyant younger men, like Tony Knowles and Kirk Stevens. The only allowances that he'd make for flair were to a left-handed South African called Perrie Mans, who had a razor sharp parting and a smooth style, and Alex Higgins. When you've grown up as a battler, you'd forgive Higgins the bright shirts and the long hair, and recognise instead the constant fight against authority and against himself. The brilliance of Higgins was that he was always 'one of us,' whoever 'us' might be.

And so I watched Mans lose the 1978 final to Ray Reardon, a Welshman, but not one that Charlie liked, and then the unknown Terry Griffiths win a year later. Thorburn's triumph in 1980 was a joyous moment, but the defining one, as is the case for every snooker fan of my age, was 1982. That was the year that Higgins won, and famously cried and called for his baby, and I'm pretty sure they were the first tears that I ever shed over a sporting event. Even as a ten-year-old, I got what it meant, saw something in Higgins. But the truly hypnotic moment of those championships, and still the most astonishing piece of sport that I've ever seen on television, came in the semi-final, on the last weekend of that year's event. My mum and dad were out, and so it was just me and my grandad in front of the telly, praying that Higgins could beat the young Londoner Jimmy White, who seemed like a good bloke, but who would surely have many more chances to win. If I'd known then what I know now, that White would fall short time and again, then I might not have greeted what happened with such open arms. But then again, I was hooked on Higgins.

The story of that semi-final has been told many times, and so it won't delay us long here. That match was the best of 31 frames, and White led 15-14. Higgins had felt that it was his destiny to win the world title that year, and yet at 59-0 down, and with the balls spread unhelpfully, it looked as if White was certain to cause an upset and win 16-14. And then Higgins, dressed in an electric blue shirt that I can still remember, cleared the table in the most perfect example of genius that I've ever seen. This was nothing to do with snooker sense or the positioning of the balls; it was force of will and natural ability. The long black, the red cut along the cushion into the middle pocket, the strangely angled blue. The twitch of his head, the smile to a friend in the crowd, and the grinding of the jaw as he forced ball after ball in. That break lasted 353 seconds, from the moment that he hit the first red to the one when the final black hit the pocket. Jim Meadowcroft came up with one of the most memorable, well-placed lines of commentary as Higgins reached the colours and neared the end. 'I'm feeling nervous for him, Jack,' he said to his colleague Jack Karnhem. We all were, glued to the gaudy colours on our television screens. Higgins, won, of course, and after that was unstoppable. And he'd never be world champion again. So I went to Sheffield, with thoughts of my grandad Charlie and of Higgins too. I'd never been to the Crucible, and I was expecting a lot.

Sheffield has had a facelift, but my first thought was that it could probably do with another. A friend of mine had told me about the fantastic fountain that was waiting for you outside the station and the way that the clouds reflected on it and seemed to open up the sky. That particular friend has a habit of being fanciful, and when I got there it was pouring down and there was an old man sitting on the fountain, coughing up phlegm and yelling the word 'Marie' over and over again. Through the rain, the fountain reflected parts of him and little else. I wondered where this thriving city that had been described to me was hiding. You couldn't see Jarvis Cocker and the Arctic Monkeys, but you could see where they got their ideas from. In Sheffield's defence, I didn't see enough of it to make too many value judgements. I missed the Devonshire quarter and Eccleshall Road and plenty more. I was fixated on the building that was in the square near the Town Hall and the Lyceum Theatre. And I wasn't far away.

But when you walk up the hill opposite the train station the place brightens. On the right, there's an Andrew Motion poem called 'What If?' written large on the side of a university building, and then when you've turned another corner you see a small square at the foot of which lies a squat and grey regional theatre. Given the part that the Crucible played in my early life, I don't know what I'd expected. It always seemed like a palace to me, but could this really be the place where all of those things happened? Where Taylor beat Davis and Higgins wore his fedora, and Hendry broke Jimmy's heart, not once, but twice? Deep down you know that the Crucible is nothing more than a successful local theatre that gives itself up to snooker once a year, but somehow you expect it to be more. To have an aura and light up the city. But it doesn't. It just sits there as buildings do. It's what's inside that counts.

With the World Championships a day away, I knew that I didn't have much time to find the winner. So I slalomed around the goofy kids playing something called Street Snooker and watched a local TV personality do one of those soul-sapping links which ended with the words: 'Yes, Street Snooker does look great, and I'm going to hand back to the studio and have a go myself!' No you're not, I thought. You're going to take your fixed smile back to your car and spend the journey home hating yourself. Street Snooker, if you're interested, seems to be an exercise in kicking multi coloured balls into holes, a bit like *Soccer AM*. And so it's not really snooker at all.

Outside a nearby hotel in a kind of glass covered shopping centre with no shops that they call the Winter Gardens, I found the BBC pundits doing their thing and playing to a crowd by recreating significant shots from the Crucible's past. No sport repackages the same memories better than snooker. There's only one tournament that the general public care about and it's only been televised for just over 30 years. And each year we greet those same pictures like old friends. No television coverage of a World Snooker Championship is complete without Ray Reardon shrugging his shoulders and doing his Dracula grin, or Cliff Thorburn picking up his fags and double punching the air after his 147. And we all love it.

So in the Winter Gardens Ken Doherty hams up Steve Davis' famous missed black from 1985 quite brilliantly and doesn't really get the applause that he deserves. And then Davis himself gets up to mock what is probably the most famous missed ball in snooker history. As he cuts it and misses, he stands with his shoulders a little hunched and his head tilted towards the sky and just for a moment you're transported back to that night in 1985 and remember how much you hated him then and how much you like him now, and you watch Dennis Taylor chuckle away and mug to the crowd and you ask yourself how on earth you could have wanted *him* to win. And yet you did. And, as Davis stares into the distance on a warm afternoon 26 years on, you see the glint in his eye that tells you, just for a moment, that it still hurts him, and that he still cares. And that he cared deeply about not being at the Crucible this year, much more deeply than many watching would guess. At the age of 52, the great winner of old still believes that he can win. Otherwise, a man like him wouldn't be playing.

They don't have much of a presence, these snooker players. A lot of modern sports people have a glow that makes you feel the need to touch the hem of their garments. A highly familiar face or the flex of a muscle and you want more of it. But as former world champion Doherty walks through the hotel reception you see that he's tiny, like a mini version of the man you see on the television. These are not men of physical stature and they don't carry any particular aura, seeming unremarkable. By common consent Ray Reardon was the only player who ever lit up a room when he walked into it, and, apparently, if you came close to beating him then you felt like you were annoying your headmaster.

There's a likeability, lovability even, about the old players who stroll around the hotel, though – a camaraderie and a sense of how their sport has stayed the same as the world has changed. They're unfailingly polite, and there's something reassuring about watching John Virgo pose for a photo over there, Terry Griffiths sign an autograph here. The person that I wanted to talk to, though, was Davis, as he more than anyone knows what it takes to win here. But first I needed to take the walk that he has taken a hundred times. Wanted to get as close as I could to feeling what it was like to actually be part of the World Championship. And it goes something like this.

You arrive at the Crucible entrance at the bottom of the gently sloping Norfolk Street and you won't find many fans. The gathering outside the players' entrance resembles one that you might see for a minor TV star in panto, rather than anything more spectacular. A Joe Swash crowd rather than a Graham Norton crowd. You'll still sign a few autographs though and then you wander through reception past the slightly over-familiar security guard and tap a code into the pad to the left of the double doors. You walk past posters for upcoming productions (The Crucible is a theatre, after all, and *Journey's End* is coming up in April) and then into the dressing rooms. There are only a couple of them, the names on the doors are frequently changed, and the rooms themselves are tiny. There's no sense of permanence, and you're constantly reminded of how quickly it can all come crashing down.

You'll more than likely hit a ball or two on the practice tables next door and then gather yourself in the dressing room until a few minutes before you play when there's a knock on the door from the security guard. He'll escort you out, through a double door which says 'To Stage Left' in red lettering, then you'll turn right and go through another double door that says 'Upstage left' in black writing. You'll walk on past the commentary box on the left in which sometimes you'll see an open door and possibly even overhear the next few hours of your life being discussed. Then you'll make a final left turn before standing behind the black curtain that all of us have only seen the stage side of. It's not as heavy as I expected, it has that diaphanous IKEA feel rather than anything more worthy and weighty, and when the lights are up you can make out shapes in the crowd. And then Rob Walker, all chin and mouth and gangly sincerity, whips up the crowd while you listen and hear your name. Only then will you emerge from behind the curtain and down a small flight of stairs that are narrower than they look on television into an arena which is impossibly tiny.

And that's the bit I don't understand: how your heart doesn't stop and how you don't forget how to play and how all of the hard work that you've done doesn't stay frozen in your brain and become impossible to access. Because the inside of the Crucible Theatre is chilling. Even standing there when its empty starts you shaking. And snooker players don't simply have to stand there. They have a job to do.

Steve Davis didn't just conquer those Crucible nerves. By the end of his run of success in the 1980s, the arena was scared of him. He made the leap from being a prodigy to a champion, something that many others have since have failed to do, and won the World Snooker Championship six times. Had he not been beaten by Dennis Taylor in 1985 and Joe Johnson a year later, both matches that he was supposed to win, Davis would have eight titles to his name, one more than the only other player who can challenge him as the greatest ever, Stephen Hendry. For all Hendry's later dominance though, it's still Davis that you think of when you consider snooker. And the first thing that you notice when you meet him is how familiar he still looks and how much love he still has for the Crucible, the place that both made him, and that briefly broke him.

The Friday before the start of the 17 days of the World Championships is a busy time for a pundit, and I'd already heard Davis do a few interviews: he's a kind man who doesn't mind turning up at a venue the day before and answering the same questions again and again. Yes, he thinks that Ronnie O'Sullivan can be a force here this year, yes he thinks it's as hard to win as ever, and no, he doesn't think the tournament will throw up too many surprises. But, as always at the Crucible, you never know. Not all great sportsmen are as generous with their time, or as thoughtful with their answers.

Another ex-player, and a very good one, Neal Foulds, had told me just how obsessed Davis was when the two of them became famous. It was the early days of Matchroom, the Barry Hearn management stable that so perfectly publicised the sport in its 1980s red top zenith. Foulds told me that all Davis ever loved was snooker. Not money, or fame, but the game that was to bring him both. At one of the early Matchroom meetings, when all of the players turned up in brand new cars to celebrate their fame and freshly inked contracts, all that Davis wanted to know was where he could get an MOT done. He'd had his car for three years and it simply hadn't occurred to him that he might buy a new one. The other players all laughed at their friend who wasn't wearing a new watch and hadn't been out the night before. But perhaps that was also the moment when they knew, deep down, that he would be the truly special one. Daley Thompson used to train on Christmas Day, because he knew that his rivals wouldn't. The story of Davis's MOT was his Christmas Day training.

Davis smiled when we finally sat down together and I told him the car story, a recollection from a different time and place. He seemed politely embarrassed when I told him that Foulds still called him his 'hero'. 'That's a nice thing to say, very nice,' said Davis. 'Good player Neal, you know, very good.' I was still full of the feeling that I'd had standing behind that curtain, and rather over eagerly asked Davis how he had managed to cope with the experience. He looked into the distance and took a few stabs at answering, as if it was a question that he hadn't been asked for a long time, or more likely something that he's become so good at that he didn't need to think about.

The first point he made was that you had to enjoy yourself: 'You have to be in the moment, and the best way of doing that is to enjoy the experience of playing and then you can't help but stay in the moment.' As it's widely acknowledged that Davis simply loves snooker, it was probably never too hard for him to do: 'You play your best golf when you're having a laugh and not over thinking it, and the same thing applies to snooker... but you have to try to become immersed in the match and enjoy it. You either do or you don't, and I guess I'm lucky that I have always been able to do that.'

Enjoying the game itself is one thing, and enjoying the competition is another, but that's what a lot of sportsmen talk about. It's a step away from being 'in the zone', that place that the real greats – Woods, Nadal, Bolt and Taylor – talk about, but to which none of us normal people can truly relate. And yet the most striking thing about Davis is his normality. Even at the height of his fame, when *Spitting Image* christened Davis 'interesting', they weren't really lampooning him for being dull, they were pointing out how like us he is. He wasn't Alex Higgins, who seemed like a creature from another planet wearing a green shirt and a purple fedora; Davis was the bloke you might meet down at your local. The one who'd quietly ask if you'd had a good day and then go and put 10p in the jukebox. Ordinary, yet extraordinary.

As a normal man, who's able to have run of the mill conversations about run of the mill subjects with run of the mill people, I wondered if there was anything else in his life that mirrors that walk from the tiny dressing room and into the main theatre? I suggested a job interview as a suitable comparison, but he thought for a little, gently flat-batted that, and then his eyes lit up and he said: 'I've got it. It's like going on a first date. When you're standing outside the pub or the restaurant or wherever, you're excited as well as nervous. You feel the need to sell yourself and give it your best shot. It's butterflies, but butterflies in the knowledge that something really special could happen. A first date, yeah, I like that. Playing at the Crucible is going on a date.'

That's an image to treasure. The greatest snooker player who ever lived standing outside a pub as a nervous teenager, wearing a pair of suit trousers and smart shoes, and waiting to go in and impress a girl in stonewashed jeans and high heels. And one day using all of that to calm his Crucible nerves. Maybe extraordinary people are the ones who can best use the everyday to their advantage.

While I was enjoying that thought, Davis dragged me back to reality and pulled out the copy of *Uncut* magazine that was sitting under his notes. He'd found an example of his competitive edge in a story about two of his 1970s idols: 'I've just been reading about Frank Zappa and Captain Beefheart and when they were both at the height of their powers they used to have pissing competitions to work out who was better. They'd stand in a urinal and see who could piss the highest and then they'd stand in a forest and see who could piss the furthest. Winning a match at the Crucible is like trying to win a pissing competition, if you'll forgive the analogy.' He was warming to his theme. 'You're trying to be yourself, but the competitive part of yourself, a version of yourself. Like an actor going on stage who gets into the role. He's still himself, but he's not standing there thinking about his shopping list is he? He needs to play the role of the snooker champion and become a gladiator that breathes fire.'

So, I was looking for a player who'd be good on a first date, was handy in a urinal, and could breathe fire. So far, so confusing. Part of my briefly scribbled Perfect Punter mission statement had been to avoid simply interviewing experts and asking them who they thought would win, but when you're sitting there with Steve Davis what can you do? So I asked, and he liked the idea of how badly John Higgins would want to win, and how much it would mean.

I'd lazily thought, as many had, that Higgins might have too much pressure on him and could want it too much, but Davis laughed at that and said that it was impossible in sport to want something too much. That was just something that people like me said. And Higgins wanted it. As everybody watching knew, he'd been implicated in a match fixing scandal during the last World Championships from which the sport's governing body had exonerated him, but from which he had never really recovered. Many people around the sport were clearly still suspicious of him, although the opinion among the players that I spoke to echoed the official verdict that he'd been terribly naive but nothing else. That may have been men involved in the sport toeing the party line, but I sensed that it was genuine sympathy, and that there was a feeling of just how easy it could be for any of them to be drawn into a sting as Higgins was. Maybe those of us who believe Higgins is innocent are as naive as he claims to be, but my gut feeling is that he's OK.

The Scotsman was there to be shot at, though. He'd already won the world title three times, but last year had fallen to one of the craziest defeats in the history of the Crucible, losing to, of all people, the veteran Davis, and seemingly out psyched to boot. Higgins would start the tournament this year as the 11-2 favourite, and the main challenger was seen to be the man they call the Jester from Leicester, Mark Selby. His nickname has always seemed like a desperate attempt to glam up the sport. Selby is a perfectly pleasant man, but not one who's prone to practical jokes. An occasionally wry smile, a penchant

DAVE FARRAR

for dying his hair, and a schoolboy rhyme would seem to be the only reasons for him to be in any way a jester. But that's snooker for you: a sport in which television dominates, and the tiny picture becomes very, very large. If telly wanted Selby to be a jester, then a jester he would be. He was 6-1, and then there followed a host of players seemingly in with a chance. Ding Junhui, still young, but already touted for years as the first Chinese world champion and always playing as if he carried that burden. Mark Williams, twice a champion here and back to his best form, Shaun Murphy, another former champion, Neal Robertson, the louche Australian who'd won last year, and the likes of Ali Carter, a onetime finalist, and Graeme Dott, a brave and troubled man who'd won the title as an outsider and reached the final last year. Dott and Robertson had served up one of the worst World Snooker finals ever, littered with mistakes and played at a somnolent pace. I'd had my wisdom teeth out just before their final session, and that match as well as an armful of painkillers sent me blissfully to sleep, but apparently viewers who had tuned in with a different motivation turned off in their tens of thousands. With the flamboyant and business savvy Barry Hearn back in charge, snooker needed a big World Championship, and yet the fact that the sport would get its biggest lift in years had nothing to do with any of players that I've mentioned, nothing to do even with Ronnie O'Sullivan.

As Steve Davis wrapped up the interview on that dreary Friday afternoon, he said one thing to me, almost as an afterthought: 'You might want to look at what price Judd is to beat Robertson tomorrow. It's very hard to come here and defend when you've won your first title. And Judd's good. Very good.' As he walked away he said: 'You are going to come and see a match aren't you?' I nodded.

123

'Because you'll never really understand it unless you come and see a match.' With that he tucked his *Uncut* Frank Zappa special under his arm and wandered back to the hotel. I wasn't too far behind him, but hung back so as not to seem over-familiar and was amazed that this person I regarded as an absolute sporting icon, a real hero of my childhood could make it through the streets of Sheffield without being noticed. It seemed unfair. But that's Davis: normal, unobtrusive, one of us.

Having pledged to listen, I ignored his advice about that Saturday match. Judd Trump, with his peacock hair and his attitude, had long been considered to be the future of snooker, but that tag had started to look a bit shop soiled. Granted, he'd managed to win the China Open a couple of weeks before, but he seemed flaky to me, not one who had handled the Crucible well before. And yet, as Davis had suggested he might, he went out and beat the world champion. As a punter, the greatest player of all time in a particular sport had told me one thing, given me one wink, and I'd ignored it because I suppose, deep down, I thought that I knew better. Sometimes you just deserve to be a loser.

It was clear that I needed as much help as I could get, and spent half an afternoon with a man who'd had a different experience of the Crucible in the shape of Neal Foulds. Foulds is a fellow gambler, and one who works at Ladbrokes, and he too proved to be engaging company for half an afternoon. He tried to help me narrow the field by telling me that 'only seven or eight of the players here really want to win. Trust me. It's a lot to handle, being world champion, and you've got to look into your soul and ask yourself. Do I want to walk out of that door in 17 days time with the eyes of the world on me?

A lot of these players are happy to earn their money, and they don't want it.'

Foulds is in a good position to judge what it's like to be a brilliant snooker player but ultimately an also-ran. He was a consistent member of the world's top ten, and was good enough, remember, to be part of that original Matchroom gang, but his best performance at the Crucible had been when he reached the semi-final in 1987. And that was a match that he ended up not wanting to win. Seriously. I can remember watching that semi-final and being desparate for Foulds to get to the final, but seeing him fade badly and being upset for him. And here he was, telling me that he was so mentally shot in that match that he knew if he'd reached the final he would have been humiliated. That's what this place does to you, and I wondered if, as he talked about those players this year that didn't want it enough, he was talking about himself. Davis disagreed with Foulds about the theory of only certain players wanting to win, pretty vehemently, but I think that's to do with the kind of players they were and the kind of career trajectories they had. Foulds knows what it's like to see the top of the mountain and feel your legs give way. Davis can't understand why anybody wouldn't want to come out on top. It's what makes Davis the legend and Foulds the more interesting analyst of the game.

Because of what had happened to him in that semi-final, Foulds wanted to emphasise how important it was to stay the course at the Crucible. The reason that Sheffield rookies very rarely win is because this tournament is longer than any of the others in which the players are involved, 17 days rather than a week. There can be serious downtime between matches, and you have to be able to handle it. When Shaun Murphy won as a qualifier in 2005 he made good use of the fact that he was local, and would spend his days off at home and unbothered, and that made him fresher as he approached the latter stages of the tournament. Murphy was involved this year, and had a chance, but his image as slightly aloof and unpopular meant that he'd never really fitted in since his win five years ago. And that brings its own pressure. The draw had thrown him a second round match against Ronnie O'Sullivan. Which could turn into anything. No matter how much chance he realistically has of winning, O'Sullivan will dominate the snooker headlines for years to come. He is the character that sets the sport on fire, the natural successor to Alex Higgins and Jimmy White, and is widely regarded as the greatest natural talent ever to play the sport.

O'Sullivan had to be included on any shortlist, but had been struggling so much with his form and his mind that he was pretty easy to ignore. He'd reportedly been seeing a psychologist that week, and Foulds made the valid point that the fact he had taken to the couch meant that he was confronting his demons, and may be a force to be reckoned with again. If you have a bet on Ronnie, you know that you have the best player in the tournament on your side, but the risk that you're taking is whether he'll turn up and play like it. It was possible that he would this time, but I was prepared to swerve him. I hope that he wins the World Championship a few more times before he gives up the game, and I'll happily let him carry my sporting heart into any tournament, but not my money. Not this time.

As I was talking to Foulds in the hotel reception a strange thing happened. I'd just wondered out loud how on earth someone could come to the Crucible for the first time and leave it as world champion when I felt a hand on my shoulder. Foulds smiled and said: 'Here's someone who knows.' I turned round, and standing there was Terry Griffiths, the hero of 1979 who'd arrived as an unknown and walked away with the title. I'd always felt that I somehow knew Griffiths, probably due to the resemblance that he has to a friend of my mum's. I think it was something to do with his hairstyle, which became more coiffed and styled the more famous he'd become. So, whenever I saw Griffiths on television, I'd nodded, as if to a family friend. Maybe I was looking for it, but as he smiled and spoke with self-deprecation about how he'd been fortunate to win in 1979 I'm sure that he did a double take, as if we'd met before. He had no idea who was going to win this year, he seemed happy to be there, working, and enjoying every second. As he walked off to 'have a nap' in his room, Foulds was paying the bill and also had something to say about sleep, almost as an afterthought: 'You know one thing that you shouldn't underestimate. They were great sleepers, Davis and Hendry. I'd get a long-haul flight with Steve and he'd sit down, pull the facemask over his eyes, and that was him. He wouldn't wake up until the cabin lights had come on at the other end. Didn't matter where we were going, whether it was Singapore, Australia or wherever, but he was away. I'd be there, drinking coffee, trying to watch a film, worrying about what we were doing when we got there, and get off the place like a nervous wreck. And Steve would be fresh as a daisy alongside me.'

Davis had laughed when I told him that and had a similar recollection of Hendry: 'I used to watch Stephen and in-between sessions you'd see him casually reading the paper and not thinking about the snooker. He never used to clutter his mind, just kept it absolutely clear for the snooker and that's such a big key.' It emphasised the point that dealing with breathing space between matches is a much-underestimated part of winning here, as much of an issue as the matches themselves.

The other person that I wanted to talk to before I made up my mind about a bet was John Parrott. As well as being a former world champion, Parrott is one of the faces of the BBC's racing coverage, and is a keen gambler. Somehow it felt wrong not to talk to him. He spared me some time on the Saturday morning, just before the tournament got underway, and what he said finally made up my mind. I was already veering towards a bet on John Higgins after what Davis had told me, and as the two of us wedged into hotel banquettes, I secretly wanted Parrott to confirm what I was already thinking.

This is the man who was humiliated in a final by 18-3, still the record winning margin in any Crucible final, and who showed the strength and courage to come back and win what would be his only world title in 1991. I always got the feeling that Parrott should have won more it than once, but then this is a world in which Jimmy White never triumphed, and so I supposed he should be grateful he got what he did.

The first thing that Parrott spoke about was how claustrophobic the atmosphere is. 'There are two games going on, there's a dividing wall, and even when you're playing, you can't help but have one eye on the score on the opposing table. You have to sit next to your opponent, and when you swing your cue back you're very aware of just how close the people sitting on the front row are.' It's not necessarily something which comes across on TV, but the players can't stand by the side of the table while their opponent is playing; they always either sit down or stand at the end, where there's a bit more room. As the World Snooker Championship goes on, there'll be people playing in snooker clubs, even in rooms at home, who have more room to manoeuvre than the best players in the world. And you can hear the audience breathe. Every sweet paper, every sigh, can be an exquisite torture. And you have to do all of this, as Parrott puts it, with 'a camera up your backside.' Two cameras in fact, as well as one above the table and two long thin microphones which pick up the clickclickclick of the balls.

Parrott was also keen to stress the two different personas of the arena. For the first few matches, you're playing in this tiny claustrophobic world, and then for the semi-finals, they take the screen away, they move the table to the middle, and then suddenly there's space all around, every single one of the spectators is focused on you, and there is absolutely no place to hide. To win at the Crucible, you have to win two separate tournaments.

Parrott fell in love with the place when he came to see Cliff Thorburn play Doug Mountjoy as a 14-year-old. From that moment on, he knew what he wanted to be. He's also a big fan of the idea that, in horse racing terminology, you have the stay the trip, that mental strength is as important as snooker ability. When he watched Graeme Dott play Peter Ebdon in the final that Dott won, no one marvelled at the standard, but Parrott was incredulous at the extraordinary staying power that both players exhibited. He's been in the situation where 'you can't see straight, and that each ball looks like two or three balls,' when the game that you have embraced on practice tables and enjoyed throughout the upward curve of your career that has got you to the Crucible, suddenly turns on you and tears you to shreds. Parrott was also keen to stress that the best player pretty much always wins at the Crucible. Of course, there have been surprises over the years, but this is a place where the strong pretty much always survive.

Unlike Davis, he was a little bit down on the chances of Judd Trump, who had just won the China Open, because sometimes it's harder to be playing well coming into this than to have no form at all, and winning that tournament would bring its own pressures. Rather than being an outsider coming into the tournament against the world champion, Trump was perhaps expected to do well, and that can be very hard to cope with. And Parrott liked Higgins: 'I think that he's a worthy favourite because he's the best matchplayer of all time.' I'd heard this phrase a million times about Higgins and had always seen it as a rather pat, throwaway line, used by TV commentators like, erm, John Parrott. But when I asked him just what that meant I realised that there was plenty of depth behind the comment, behind the idea of a matchplayer.

Parrott looked into the distance, as if he was trying to remember and block out bad memories all at the same time, and then after a serious moment's thought, he turned and said with particular emphasis: 'Because he's made from girders.' This sounds like another pat TV line, a weak Irn Bru reference, and I suppose that if pop culture references are what you reach for, then this is how you express yourself. I was about to mentally patronise Parrott as much as I just did in that last sentence, but then he repeated the word, and his Scouse accent made it somehow more evocative: 'Ger-ders'.

Parrott said that when two snooker players start a session then you always get an idea of how well you're playing and how well the other fellow is playing. If your opponent starts to pot everything cleanly and control the cue ball well then you have a little think to yourself and realise that you're in trouble, and that your job is just to try and hang onto his coat-tails. But there are other times when you're cueing really well and the other player is playing badly. The thing that sets John Higgins apart from any other player is that if he's playing badly, he seems to find a way to keep going, to stop his opponent winning. 'You'll absolutely pulverise him in a session and then at the end of it you'll realise that he's managed to stay level with you, or only lose it by two frames, or even beat you. And that creates a massive psychological burden on you because you know that at some point in the match [it's the law of averages after all] he'll be playing well and you'll be playing badly, and he'll draw away from you then. That's what matchplay means, and that's when he'll really hurt you.' And there's something about the way that Parrott looked when he talked about Higgins that's convincing, something awestruck and reminiscent of fear. Higgins would be my man.

Parrott also liked Selby because he had staying power too, and had recently started running. I'd also noticed that Selby had a 'means business' haircut this season. In the past he'd walked around with coloured hair, but always wore it slightly uncomfortably. Now, with a short back and sides, he looked every inch the serious young man who wanted to be world champion. Parrott said that he'd be very surprised if we got a winner above 20-1 as that happens here so rarely; in fact he had told everyone who had asked him (and he was just back from Aintree, so you have to believe that *everyone* had asked him) that backing Higgins and Selby to win was the right thing to do. As he put it, if they don't win, then you can at least tear up your betting ticket and know that you got a run for your money, and as a gambler that's all that you can ask for. I was convinced. I'd ignore his advice on Selby, and go for the matchplayer, the favourite, the man made from girders. Higgins to win the tournament at 11-2 was the bet.

As I left Parrott to patiently sign autographs, I asked him if he fancied anything for that afternoon's Scottish Grand National, and told him that the horse that I liked had been put up by Pricewise in the *Racing Post*. Amidst all of the noise of the first day at the Crucible, I think he must have forgotten that the race was actually on, and so when I mentioned it his eyes lit up and he said: 'Blazing Bailey's running in that, isn't he? He looks well handicapped. I think I'll have a bet on him.' When I checked the result later, I saw that neither my horse nor Blazing Bailey had made the frame, and I felt guilty that Parrott probably wouldn't have had a bet if I hadn't mentioned it. And it turned out that he'd helped me find a winner.

Davis had told me to make sure that I went to a session, that I'd never really understand the essence of the Crucible until I'd done just that, and so, on the Friday that London filled up with Union Jack waving invaders keen to catch a bit of William and Kate, I headed back to Sheffield on a near deserted train, travelling, it seemed, in the opposite direction to the rest of the population. My selection, Higgins, had reached the semi-final where he was playing the casually brilliant Welshman Mark Williams. And there was every chance that I was going to see my bet go down. Higgins was losing 5-3, and had been outplayed up until now. His matchplaying instinct had to kick in, and fast, because so far there hadn't been any sign of a girder.

It was strange to be back in the same arena, but this time full of people. There's something of the holiday camp about the atmosphere, as soft rock floats out of the speakers while the crowd files into the theatre, and if you look up, you seen tiny pins of light in the ceiling, stars picked out against the black background. Plenty of the crowd come in early, as they want to soak it all up, even before the players have made their entrance.

I'd already seen Mark Williams arriving through that Norfolk Street entrance with two friends. He seemed delightfully haphazard for a top sportsman as he shambled into reception and asked if there was a chance of him having a quick knock on the practice table before he plays. He looked a little scruffy, with his shirt out of his trousers and his beaten-up shoes. He carried a red waistcoat under his arm and I presumed that he was going to change, but half an hour later he emerged into the arena dressed exactly the same, but with the shirt tucked in and the waistcoat on.

As Williams came out into the arena, looking relaxed in that lopsided way of his, I thought of something else that Davis had said to me: 'It doesn't matter what you're outwardly showing, it's what you're feeling inwardly that matters. Although it definitely helps to look confident. Mark Williams may spend a match laughing and joking but I know that he's gone to the toilet and been physically sick before matches in the past.'

I wondered if he had been this time. Between that relaxed arrival and the sheepish entrance, before or after he'd slammed home a practice ball or two, had Williams got nervous and let the negative thoughts creep in? As I watched him take his seat on one side of the table, the human being in me hoped that he hadn't, but the punter prayed that he had. I needed Higgins to come roaring back, and Williams to lose belief. It's a sad symptom of being a gambler. Sometimes, you just can't afford to behave like a human being.

There were a few celebrities in the Crucible for much of that week, and now I found myself sitting just to one side of one of them. The next few lines will mean nothing to you if you don't watch the BBC2 quiz show *Eggheads* in which a team of amateur pub quiz players take on five hardened quiz professionals, or full-time smart alecs, depending on your perspective. One member of the resident quiz team is a man called CJ De Mooi, a former male model who seems to change his hairstyle on a weekly basis and changed his name to include the word 'Mooi' as it means 'beautiful' in Dutch. His job on *Eggheads* seems to be to mug to the camera whenever another contestant gets an answer wrong, and affect an air of casual superiority at every turn. I don't know anybody who watches *Eggheads* who doesn't hate CJ. Possibly the most interesting thing about the man is that he's a snooker fan, and spends many of the 17 days of the World Championships sitting in a press seat and watching the matches intently. And he was there to study Williams and Higgins. There's a lull between the theatre filling up and the players being introduced, and in that time CJ eagerly engaged Rob Walker in a conversation about running half marathons. It must be strange for Walker: about to whip up the Crucible crowd, go on national television and introduce the players, and yet there he is, faced by an intense man in sensible shoes and an armful of charity bracelets, being spoken to about training regimes. CJ wanted to be part of things, and his eager presence added something to the feel of the place.

When Walker finally does his introductions, the players make that walk and come blinking into the arena. Higgins bounces down the steps, and his smart shoes make a hard noise as moves to his left and takes his seat. Williams shoulders are more shrugged, and his soft slip-ons barely make a sound. Both players know that this is a key session, and that any advantage they can take forward from here could end up being a match-winning one.

And once Walker has retreated, you're left with the starkness of the arena, and that feeling that every player needs to conquer every time that they come here. Twenty-two balls shining under the two angled lights which hang over the table, beautifully symmetrical and simultaneously daunting. Both players know that they have the skill to make mincemeat of this game when they're practicing or playing with friends, but the intensity and the sense of what today means changes everything.

One of the odd things about the Crucible is that it hosts the World Championships, and yet is a long way from being the biggest venue in the sport. It only seats 984 people, is claustrophobic and noisy, and makes it very difficult to concentrate. Foulds and Parrott had both said that you can hear people breathing when you're trying to play a shot, which I found hard to believe, and yet now I realised that it was true. Every noise seems amplified, the buzz of the commentary headsets that many of the audience wear, the smallest whispers, and the breathing from next to me. Heck of a breather, CJ.

There'll be eight frames today, and Williams knows that if he can take five of them, then he'll go into the final day of the match with a four-frame lead and will be thrillingly close to a place in the final. He knows that he has to play at his best to do that, and here he is quite brilliant. The softness of his walk belies the ruthlessness of his play, as he noiselessly prowls around the table, and starts to take Higgins apart. He goes 6-3 up, and then 7-4, missing out on a 140 break in that 11th frame. The 11-2 that I have about Higgins to win the tournament looks an awful price, and my man is in trouble. And he looks it. The chubby face and the sad, watery eyes give the impression of someone who is perpetually on the brink of cracking. Higgins wipes his forehead with his sleeve and continually fills up his glass of water as he watches Williams pot everything in sight. Parrott's comment about Higgins being a great matchplayer seem redundant. How can it matter if he never gets to the table?

I curse my decision to back the tournament favourite, and, just like in 2009, am starting to see my chances evaporate in the semi-final. Williams is about to go 8-4 ahead, and is playing like a man who will extend that lead. The fact that his apparent frame-winning break has broken down seems irrelevant, as at 64-0 Higgins moves to the table, nervously pointing his cue in front of him. And then, for the next ten minutes, I finally get what Parrott meant. Because, in that space of time, Higgins finds a way to win the frame, and in that moment, the match. He induces a couple of bad shots from Williams, and then manoeuvres the white ball around the table and clears up to win the frame. And there's nothing beautiful about it. Whereas Williams had played with smoothness and style, and every ball had thudded into the middle of the pocket, Higgins is staccato and sweaty, and on two or three occasions he looks to have missed, but somehow the ball creeps in. This is what being a matchplayer means. As he gets closer to winning and moves to the colours, the pressure increases, as any miss now will gift the frame to Williams. But he doesn't miss. He pulls a 64-0 deficit around and the score at the mid-session interval of 15 minutes is not 8-4, but 7-5. The session started at 5-3 and Williams has comprehensively outplayed Higgins. And yet still the deficit is the same. As the players walk off,

Williams looks shell-shocked. Like David Haye in Hamburg later on in the summer, he had caught his opponent with his best shot and still he was standing in front of him. And when it's man-to-man, with cues or with gloves, it's moments like that which break one man and make the other stronger. Higgins was winning the pissing competition hands down.

As if that clearance wasn't enough, Higgins did it again in the final frame of the session. Williams had come back from that mid-session interval and stood up to the psychological battering. With two frames to go, Williams led 9-5, and was in position to take a commanding lead. And once again Higgins, nowhere near his best, ragged and awkward, came back. He won the last two frames, and even though the scoreboard said 9-7 and the bookmakers still had Williams as favourite, anyone who had been watching knew that Higgins would go on and win the match. He had proved before that he had the psychological edge over Williams, coming from 9-5 down in a UK Championship final to beat the Welshman 10-9. And he would do it again here. One of my biggest regrets of this whole six-month experience was that I didn't go out and back Higgins to win the match after watching that session. The fact that I already had the Scotsman to win the tournament stopped me from doing so, but that's the kind of flawed logic that plagues you every day as a punter. One bet should never stop you from placing another. You do the right thing at any given time regardless of your wider gambling picture. Another rule that I know, and even recite to others, and yet rarely put into practice myself.

That session was the only one that I saw, but Davis had been right. All of the theorising that I'd done in the build-up to the tournament would have been irrelevant if I hadn't gone and seen it for myself, and spoken to the men who know just how hard it is to play there. That tiny arena, perfect because of its imperfections, hadn't disappointed, didn't let me down. Seeing it for myself had made me realise just how mentally strong these current players were, and how much it took to win this tournament. It made me respect those heroes that I'd grown up with a little bit more, and for all his faults, made me see that John Higgins is up there with the finest sportsman of his generation. Able to play, but more importantly able to cope, to sleep, to play every session as if it was his last. He beat Williams, as I'd known he would, and then, under enormous pressure once again, he outlasted the younger Trump in the final. Trump had been the star of the fortnight, with his thrilling style and casual charm, but Higgins wasn't ready to give up just yet. As he took the trophy late on Monday night, I expected Higgins to break down in tears. But he spoke haltingly, talked of the year that he'd had and the father that he'd lost, and he refused to crack in public as he would surely do later when it all sunk in. Made of girders, and on his way to redemption.

CHAPTER SEVEN

Football is supposed to be the sport that I know most about, but I'm never entirely convinced that this is a good thing. For all that this book is about trying to understand sport and find a bet, I think that you can sometimes get too close, and when you're surrounded by too many fellow devotees, you run the risk of Groupthink. They may not call it by the same name, but Groupthink is something that tortures every gambler. In the first chapter of this book, I spoke about how differently someone will answer the question: 'What do you think the score will be?' to how they'll approach the near statement: 'It looks like there'll be goals in this, don't you think?' Now that is an obvious example, but Groupthink is there in any sport that you watch frequently, with friends who know as much about it as you. And even though I was aware of the danger, the G-word was about to hit me hard in Paris.

I first heard the term used by the American boxing presenter Max Kellerman. Kellerman is a man who gives the impression of loving his sport, but knowing at the same time just how ridiculous the hullabaloo can be. Boxing seems to produce a lot of frontmen like this, with Harry Carpenter and Reg Gutteridge in the old days and the more current Adam Smith of Sky having a similar perspective. It makes them more realistic, more measured ringmasters than most. Maybe it's because frequent exposure to the desperation of the ring makes you see through the gloss of an event rather more quickly than others. In no sport can hype turn more quickly to dust than in boxing.

A while ago, Kellerman was anchoring the American channel HBO's coverage of a tricky looking fight between a Mexican-American from Houston called Juan Diaz and the all-action Australian Michael Katsidis. Diaz is what's known in the boxing world as a stylist, and beforehand, he wasn't only the pick of the HBO team, but you sensed as a viewer that he was the fighter that they wanted to win. Not because of any grudge against Katsidis, more because Diaz was seen as one for the future, and Katsidis as approaching his sell-by date. As the fight progressed, Diaz seemed to be in control, and the HBO commentators made that point forcibly. Diaz was using his skills and reach advantage to blunt the power of the shorter man, and was strolling to victory. Sitting in my hotel room, I agreed that Diaz was ahead, but the ringside expert Harold Lederman was giving him round after round on his scorecard, and I thought that I saw Katsidis having a bit more success than I was being told. By the end of the fight, the HBO crew had Diaz by a landslide, and then there was genuine shock in the commentary box when the ring announcer said: 'We have a split decision.' For those of you who don't understand the significance of that (and why would you? You're out having lives while I'm in a hotel room watching HBO), it meant that at least one of the three judges hadn't given the verdict to Diaz, and the result wasn't quite as clear cut as it had appeared to the HBO team.

In the end Diaz got the win, but only just, and Lederman started to splutter about how wrong the judges were, but after that had died down Kellerman did something that I've rarely heard from any American broadcaster: in a solemn piece to camera, he admitted that the whole team had perhaps been wrong, and he said that perhaps they'd been guilty of Groupthink, the phenomenon which leads a roomful of people to eventually come to the same opinion, no matter what their starting points. Kellerman clearly felt that the strident views of one or two members of the team had influenced the calling of the fight far too much, swaying others with different opinions into having the same opinion.

I was shocked and impressed by this admission of weakness and naively thought that Kellerman had invented the term 'Groupthink'. When I looked a little closer, I realised that it's a phenomenon that has been discussed by psychologists for many years. I found an explanation of it in Irving Janis's study on the subject, *Victims of Groupthink*, which was published in 1972. He said that the structural faults which would lead to the phenomenon occurring were: 'insulation of the group, a lack of impartial leadership, a lack of norms regarding methodological procedures, and the homogeneity of members' social backgrounds and ideology.' So, if we hang around with people like ourselves too often, and don't actively seek other opinions, then we're in trouble. It's the kind of thing that gamblers should instinctively know, but often fall foul of. Think of the times that you've discussed a football match with your mates, and no matter how different your points of view may have been at the start of the conversation, after a few beers you'll end up at least seeing each others' points of view, and even finish the argument with the same opinion. And then think of the number of times that you've said after the game that 'I knew I was right.' That's Groupthink in action, leading to the second-guessing of yourself, and that's why it's to be avoided.

Later on I'll be extolling the virtues of a book called *The Wisdom of Crowds*. But, while the crowd can be an exceptionally good thing, it can also be a disaster if it's used in the wrong way. A Scottish journalist called Charles Mackay published a book back in the middle of the nineteenth century that went by the splendidly caustic title of *Extraordinary Popular Delusions and the Madness of Crowds*. His theory was that a crowd always reaches the level only of its lowest common denominator, and a herd mentality gets in the way of any intelligent thought. That day in Paris, the lowest common denominator in my crowd was me.

Before having a bet on any football match, any sporting event in fact, you need to have a picture of just how things are going to develop, and work out the course of events in your own mind. It's not enough to simply say: 'I think there'll be goals in this,' or 'I fancy Manchester United to win.' More often than not those sorts of suppositions can be based on a lazy logic, rather than something more specific. The rest of sports betting, a relatively new pursuit, can take a lesson from a far older betting medium in the shape of horse racing. A proper punter would never think about placing a bet on a horse race without knowing the going, or having a look at the horses in the parade ring. They would know which horse would lead, how significant that was, and which would be finishing fast. All of those factors give them an idea of the shape of the race, and allow them to build up a picture from which they can draw a conclusion.

One of my best gambling lessons came before the Cheltenham Gold Cup of 2007. I was interviewing Graham Cunningham of Racing UK, and I wanted his thoughts on that afternoon's big race. Graham didn't simply say that he thought that Denman would win, he described in passionate detail *how* he would win, how the race would unfold. He described Denman taking an early lead, winding up the pace and breaking his stablemate Kauto Star's heart on the second circuit. And he was right, almost disturbingly so. What Graham does, like many excellent tipsters, is read the way that the race will unfold and *then* decide the right bet to have. There's a big difference between the clarity of that and the muddiness of the way that I can often approach things. As I sat on the Eurostar surrounded by violent children, it was something to ponder. Could I ever call a football match the way that Cunningham had called that race?

I was heading to Paris for the French Cup Final. Of all the bets that I'd lost during my period of chaos, that defeat for Rennes against Guingamp was the one which had hurt the most. The Coupe de France has always been special for me, mainly because of the exploits of a group of amateurs from Calais back in 2000. They were a truly remarkable bunch, who somehow got to the big game at the Stade de France while they were all doing other jobs. One, Mikael Gerard, was a cheese salesman in a big hypermarket, another was a student, and the captain Reginald Becque was a social worker. In that final Calais played one of the best teams in France at the time, Nantes, and the amateurs led 1-0 at half-time. It would have been one of the great upsets if they'd managed to hang on, but they lost 2-1 thanks to a dodgy last minute penalty and the football world had righted itself just in time, as it so often tediously does.

I lived in Paris back then, bought into the Calais story big time, and was absolutely shattered by their defeat. After the match, I went to a bar to meet friends for a consoling drink, and found that I wasn't able to drink anything without feeling sick. It must have been nervous energy, some weird release of emotion. I jumped into a cab, and halfway home I felt sick again and had to ask the taxi driver to stop. I jumped out and was violently ill for five minutes and when I turned round he was still there waiting for me. That was a surprise in itself, as most Parisian cabbies are particularly harsh on people they think are drunk foreigners with funny accents. I climbed back in and rather pleadingly said: 'I'm not drunk,' and I realised that he was looking at my bag, over which I'd tied the Calais scarf that I'd bought at the final. He looked at me and said: 'I know you're not drunk. It was pretty hard to take wasn't it?' The French Cup Final and it's unifying quality has been in my bones ever since. The intervening 11 years had produced a healthy number of surprising finalists and some strange winners. This year, though, it would be a high-class affair, romance maybe of a different kind.

Paris St Germain, one of the strangest football clubs in Europe, would play Lille, one of the grand old teams of France who were enjoying their best season in years. Lille were on the brink of winning the French title for the first time since 1954, and they hadn't picked up the French Cup since 1955. Lille had been rejuvenated by their coach Rudi Garcia, who had produced a fantastically entertaining team during his time as coach at Le Mans and had sorted out the bigger club in much the same way. They'd got to the brink of a double by playing entertaining football, and Garcia had got the best out of a group of talented young players. The main man was the Belgian Eden Hazard, the best of the bunch, who was already being linked with Arsenal and Bayern Munich, and around him were the Ivorian pair of Moussa Sow and Gervinho, with 40 league goals between them, and a talented cast of less appreciated players, led by Yoann Cabaye and Rio Mavuba. PSG would start the final as favourites, but that was more because of a feeling that they were playing at home, not in their own ground the Parc des Princes but in their own city, and because they had won the trophy in two of the previous three years. In reality, though, it seemed like a 50/50 game.

Paris was an interesting place to be during that strange and sunny week. The previous Saturday, Dominique Strauss-Kahn had been arrested in New York and the waves from that moment were still crashing. In many other cities the tone of the newspapers would have been of shock and betrayal, of outrage and dismissal. But they live in a curious moral world, the Parisians. The same people who routinely use the word 'Arab' as a pejorative term made clear their opinions of what Strauss-Kahn had or hadn't done wrong. There was far more shock at the image of this potential future President in handcuffs than there ever was at the allegations of what he had done to a hotel chambermaid. The insouciance and the arrogance is why Paris can be a great place to visit, but a very hard one to become a part of. It's why many of the ex-pats who pass through, like me, end up being centred around English and Irish bars. It's not entirely a lack of imagination, more a sense of belonging. I lost count of the amount of times that friends would come to visit and wonder why I didn't have a regular seat in the corner of some smoky bar full of strangely glamorous women and artists in berets. I think that you have to live there for a long time, a lot longer than I did, to truly belong.

My local in Paris, and I'm not ashamed to say it, was, and still is, a pub called The Bowler on Rue d'Artois just north of the Champs Elysees. The place is run by an old mate of mine called Eddie. Eddie is pure gold, the nicest guy in any room he's in, and when I go to The Bowler, we talk about a lot and not very much all at the same time. There's a cast of characters there that you'll find versions of the world over. A big friendly Swede called Richard, an alluring Danish girl whose name I never catch, a Bostonian Walter Mitty and a fantastically bright American barman who wears an Aquaman T-shirt but hates *Entourage*. The last I heard, he'd quit bar work to become a glassblower. It's that kind of place.

At the start of every football season Eddie and I place a bet. For six years now we've tried to predict the winners of the five major European football leagues and for six years our accumulator has come up one short. Bayern Munich let us down one year, Chelsea another, and four out of five has become an annoying habit, but still we both chase the dream and look for the rainbow. And it's the looking that's the fun part. The choosing of it in the first place and then the hope that sometimes lasts a season, and then the denouement, which has so far left us short. I'm not sure that someone who regards himself or herself as an intelligent gambler should even be placing bets like these, but then there's a large part of me that doesn't care. It's about the fun that the bet brings us, rather than the knowledge that one day it will pay out. And every year, when Eddie and I sit down to work it out, I wish that was the only bet that I had all year. But it isn't, and it's never going to be.

So The Bowler was the place to sit and get my own back on the French Cup Final, and for a couple of days I agonised over it. The logical starting point was that I saw it as a tight game and the book-makers made PSG the favourites, and therefore Lille were value, end of discussion. But I never make things that simple. A look at the two squads told me that PSG had a lot more big game experience, and a glance at recent results suggested that Lille were starting to feel the pressure of contending for both the League and the Cup. They'd been fine under the radar, but were struggling in the spotlight. They would have a chance to wrap up the League title back in Paris, away at PSG, the following week, and surely that meant that the focus, which should have been on the Cup Final, would be elsewhere. Maybe the prices were right, and PSG were worthy favourites.

One of the problems about trying to work things out was my personal history of gambling on football: many of my football bets over the years have been made in blind faith rather than through any more scientific method. No idea of the conditions, the state of the pitch, whether or not it's blowing a gale, or indeed if the Marseille midfield are all hungover. And yet there I go: bet placed, sometimes successfully, but in the dark and unscientific. That's why the Palermo experience opened my eyes so much. And it wasn't the only one which had taught me how there was another way, a better way.

Back in February, I'd been back in Rome, managed to avoid going anywhere near that internet cafe on Largo Argentina, and I'd had an uncharacteristic bet on the Serie A match between Lazio and Bari. Lazio share the Stadio Olimpico with Roma, and even though much of the way that a football match will be played out depends on the atti-tude and ability of both teams, I firmly believe that the circumstances and the atmosphere really can't be ignored. It's a vague distinction to make, but that afternoon in Rome felt like the opposite of the night in Palermo that convinced me to go on this journey in the first place. You could walk within a mile of a Lazio home game on a Sunday afternoon and not have much idea that there's even a match taking place. Lazio had been going well in Serie A, and this was the best position they'd been in at this point in the season for nearly ten years. You'd think, then, that the area would be buzzing and the stadium would be packed. But that's rarely the case at the Olimpico. They come in their hordes for the Rome derby, but stay away for the more bloodless games. My image of the stadium in Palermo is of noise and blood and passion, of the Olimpico it's a paper cup blowing down the street.

Bari had won just one of their last 20 matches in Serie A, they were on the fast track to relegation and they'd gone for 346 minutes without even scoring a goal. Lazio were by far and away the more obvious winners, and it didn't seem likely that Bari would score. It was at this point that I thought of a mate of mine who approaches every weekend by saying: 'I love a correct score.' He's far happier to have a bet on a team winning a match 1-0, at say, 7-1, than he is to simply back the same team at even money to win the match. You'll be wrong more often, but when you're right, the price will be worth the wait. Like a large section of their fan base, Lazio's style wasn't particularly attractive, and I couldn't see any result other than a win to nil. So rather than lump on them to beat Bari at a prohibitively short price, shorter than 1-2, I tried instead to picture the game. The home team would try and score early, try and break Bari's hearts, and then be happy to hold on, and would probably do so comfortably. A score of 1-0 was priced at 11-2, and that seemed fair.

I remembered something that Gianluca Vialli once said about the Stadio Olimpico. Vialli used to feel that, because of the running track around the pitch, the goals always seemed smaller there than they did at, say, Highbury, where they felt pretty big. As a result of that perception, he found the Olimpico harder to score at than many other grounds, and ridiculous as that might sound, the shape and the feeling of a ground is important when you consider what might happen in a football match. It won't always work out, but the feeling at the Olimpico that day was of boredom and inevitability, a half-full, half-paced walk in the park. Lazio scored early, very early, after six minutes, and even though they went close a few times, the score did end up 1-0 in their favour, the second or third time in 25 years of gambling that I've won a Correct Score bet. The stats and the match conditions had come together perfectly.

So, rather than come to some vague conclusion in Paris, those Italian lessons had taught me to think it through, take advice and work out the best bet, I had time, and I should use it. I also had a useful friend. The French football expert James Eastham lives in Lille, having decamped there to try and make his dream of being a talent scout and agent come true. James fell in love with Ligue 1 while going on family holidays to France as a kid, and he's the genuine article. You'll find a lot of charlatans in the football world, who see 20 minutes of a Spanish game on a Sunday and then talk to you on a Monday reciting a bundle of received wisdom. James could actually tell you, without recourse to notes, who was playing left back for Dijon five years ago. And, remarkably, despite so much of his brain being filled up with this kind of stuff, he's engaging company, able to talk about things other than football. James wouldn't be coming to the French Cup Final, muttering about a pressing family engagement, but I wanted to get his advice on the game, and we sat in The Bowler a couple of days before and tried to picture it.

I was keen on the idea that this would be an open attacking game and that the possibility of that was being underestimated by the bookmakers. Rudi Garcia's natural desire was for his team to attack and I didn't think that Lille could curb those instincts. PSG were that way inclined as well and defending had certainly been the Parisians' major weakness all season. Over 2.5 goals was available at around 2.38, and I thought that looked like value. The problem was that I took that opinion into the conversation with James. Rather than ask him what he thought and allow the bet to flow organically from that, I went into our chat with an agenda. And that's where the problems began.

James is normally crystal clear in his opinions on football, but even he was struggling to get the big picture of the Cup Final, despite having a number of beguiling small ones of which he was much more sure. His first thought echoed mine, that it was a 50/50 game, and he felt that trying to pick a winner was a route to madness and that was a market to be ignored. I pressed him on the possibility of goals and he said that he thought that both teams might well score, but that we should remember that this was a Cup Final, and that there would be nerves, which often stops teams from expressing themselves. That was a perfectly measured opinion, but the only part of it that I heard was that 'both teams might well score.' And as we talked, and I enthused about the probability of there being goals, of Garcia being a fantastic attacking coach, and of PSG being good at one end of the field and vulnerable at the other, I sensed that James was coming round to my opinion. He could see the logic in what I said, and was allowing that to drown out his own more measured conclusions.

Before I had swamped him with my dog with a bone approach, James was keen to talk about substitutes. He said that he was interested in the strength of the Lille bench. In fact, he uttered the following sentence within a couple of minutes of us sitting down to discuss the match: 'Pierre-Alain Frau, Ludovic Obraniak and Tulio De Melo were the best attacking substitutes in Ligue 1, and the stats back that up. Lille to win the match in extra time at about 16-1 is tempting, and I think that one of those could get the winner.' He was wrong about extra time, but right about much else, and even though it's hard to have a bet on something as vague as a substitute affecting a match, I ruefully reflected afterwards how right he had been. He was also keen to point out that the pressure wasn't just affecting Lille: 'PSG could still finish third in Ligue 1 and that is a *huge* deal for them, as it would mean Champions League football next season.'

The more that I thought about it, the more it looked appealing. I sensed, though, that James had been initially uncertain and that my enthusiasm was starting to influence him. All that he had said was that it could be a lively game, and 'could be a lively game' shouldn't automatically translate into 'there'll be a lot of goals.' The more that you convince yourself of something, though, the more likely it is that you will end up holding the opinion that you want to have, rather than the one that you should have.

There are many reasons why a football match will or won't contain goals. You might think that it's to do with having high-class forward players, and, of course, that helps, but they tend to play against teams with high-class defenders and so can cancel each other out. And the same holds true if your basis for the bet is that poor defenders tend to concede goals. They'll often be playing against strikers at a lower level who won't take many of the chances that come their way. The perfect storm for this kind of bet is the rare occasion that a top-class attacking team comes up against an awful defence, or at least a defence which is significantly worse than onlookers had expected it to be. If Barcelona played a team from League One in England, for example, they'd rack up a hatful of goals, but the pre-match prices would reflect that. When Manchester United beat Arsenal 8-2, for example, Arsenal were significantly worse at the back than anyone had predicted, and over 2.5 goals in that game were available at the decidedly backable price of 10-11.

So, as is always the case with gambling, you're looking for something that other people might not spot. I asked a few of the experts who I know why they think that football matches have goals and the former Arsenal player Stewart Robson, one of my favourite television pundits, told me straightaway that 'the game must have a tempo. Both teams must be looking to play at pace, and looking to get in behind defences. If you can see a way that an attacking team can over-load a defensive side, can get into a position where two players are up against one, then those are the games which are likely to have goals.'

The former Tottenham man, Gary O'Reilly, who in his time at Crystal Palace was part of a team that lost 9-0 to Liverpool, said that it was all about special players, at whatever level, being able to create angles. As a centre back, he says that your nightmare is the player who can make you turn and be unsure about where the next bit of attacking play will come from. O'Reilly used the example of Picasso's painting 'Dove'. The four lines on the page look like nothing until the fifth is added and that's O'Reilly's point about attacking play. You always need the man who'll paint the fifth line. Michael Cox of *Zonal Marking* website, who along with Jonathan Wilson is the country's leading expert on football tactics, told me that he always looks for space in the midfield, for unprotected defenders, and attacking players therefore having the ability to roam free. And, for all that I was guilty of forcing myself into a bet, rather than letting it come to me, all of those factors looked like they'd be at play in the Cup Final.

The basis of my theory was a player called Clement Chantome. He would play in the centre of PSG's midfield, alongside the 38-year-old Claude Makalele. Makalele has always been described, lazily in my opinion, as the thinking-man's footballer, the kind of player who attracts those who like to feel that they see beyond the obvious. Three years ago, in the season that Cristiano Ronaldo scored over 40 goals for Manchester United, a Fleet Street journalist wrote in his column that he felt Anderson, rather than Ronaldo, should be the player of the season. That particular journalist has a habit of trying to prove that he sees something that the rest of us don't, but this was pushing it, even for him. I bet that he loves Makalele. The man who, in his days in West London, made Chelsea tick, the one who none of the rest of us see. We're too busy naively praising the goal-scorers, the shot stoppers, the obvious. So I was never that much of a Makalele fan, and certainly didn't rate the 38-year-old version. PSG had played with three midfielders for much of the season, and Makalele was able to hide his decline, his crumbling body, in amongst two men who would do his running. But the PSG coach Antoine Kombouare had decided to play 4-4-2 in recent weeks, with creative players out wide, and only Chantome and Makalele in the middle to protect the back four. I knew that Makalele wouldn't be able to cope with Lille's fit and strong running youngsters, and so the onus was on Chantome to try and stop Lille getting space. If I tell you that the player to whom Chantome is most compared is Arsenal's Andrei Arshavin, then you'll understand why my eyes lit up. His natural instinct is to get forward, and as I tried to picture how the game would develop, I could see Chantome trying to do his best for the team, but constantly being drawn out of position, leaving space and only Makalele to fill it. And the Lille forward players, Hazard and Gervinho and Sow, would love space.

The Lille players were fully aware of what a big week this would be for them. If Marseille failed to win in the league the following night, then Lille could be crowned champions on Wednesday night with a victory against Sochaux. That would render next week's game back in Paris largely irrelevant. Those four days were the biggest in the lives of those players – they could end up a Double-winning squad, or could throw it all away. They had to know that this was their time, and one or two of them knew a thing about having nothing. The captain, Rio Mavuba, had been born on a boat in the middle of the Atlantic Ocean, to a mother who was a refugee, trying to get to Europe to get the best for her unborn child. And alongside him in that midfield would be Idrissa Gueye, a kid from Senegal who had grown up with nothing and then got his chance at a football academy on the outskirts of Dakar. In his first few days at the academy, Gueye had cried for his mother, and yet here he was playing in the Cup Final. Lille might have been top of the league, but their very natures meant that the players saw themselves as underdogs. When another Lille player, Aurelien

Chedjou, was asked in the build-up what he most envied about the PSG players, he said, quite simply, 'Their salaries.' With PSG on the brink of being taken over by a consortium from Qatar, this could be a benchmark game.

So, as Cup Final day dawned, I was excited. Too excited. Over 2.5 goals at 2.38 would be the bet, and I was certain that I was right. Before I got to the stadium, though, there was an experiment that I was keen to try. I didn't think that the people of Paris cared, or even knew, that the Cup Final was being played that day. Think of the great London sporting events, the FA Cup Final or Rugby League's Challenge Cup. You picture those events and you have in your mind the image of a sporting presence. There are tens of thousands of fans cramming into mainline stations and heading off to Wembley and you see them all over town, families and bellies crammed into shirts and groups of lads who look like they could be trouble. And it's the same up and down the country at clubs at every level. The game feeds into the town.

At midday, I walked from the south of Paris, right through the centre, veered off towards the Champs Elysees to the west and then swung back along the river, covering just about every busy thorough-fare and all of the tourist magnets. I went down the Boulevard St Michel and saw two fat tourists, one in a sweaty blue shirt with a white collar, the other crammed into Armani, and they headed off like Tweedledum and Tweedledee, but there was no sign of a football fan. Just over the river, next to the Hotel de Ville, a man in a white hat and spats was being sung to by a pretty girl. But there was still no sign of a football fan. The eccentrics outnumbered the football fans. Because there weren't any football fans. I started to ask people if they knew about the sporting event that was going on that evening in Paris, and most didn't, and some, when they were told, said: 'Oh. *We're* in it? Allez PSG.' They knew what to say but they didn't know what was going on. I'd walked for two hours now, and there was still no sign of a football fan.

I went north, moved nearer the stadium, and thought that there would be more chance of seeing supporters take their chances in the roads near Les Halles, where the dreamy Paris ends and things get a little nasty. There are shops called things like Ruffneck and Kiss Me and Paris Sexy and Videodrome and the trainers get bigger and the T-shirts get longer and you feel like you're in someone else's town. But they hadn't come here. I saw a yellow old man shuffling round a corner and giving money to a woman with wrinkles and a painted face. And there was still no sign of a football fan. I moved west and found some petanque courts under a shabby canopy of trees. There was a woman with red shoes surrounded by a group of men and there was a noise, a clickclickclick, but there was still no sign of a football fan. And even on the Champs Elysees, where it was busier and louder, and stiflingly hot, there was a pompous Englishman deconstructing the ingredients of a sorbet and trying to impress his family, but there were still no colours, no shirts, no sign at all of a football match.

I got the impression that the Cup Final would make absolutely no dent on the daily life of the city. One man summed it up perfectly, and unintentionally, by railing against 'the kind of people who support PSG, the Arabs and the blacks from the suburbs, the ones who hate the state and try to destabilise things, and yet are more than happy to take our money. You cannot complain about things like this, because immediately you're a racist, and so why should we [the bourgeoisie, in effect] give a shit about this match? And trust me, if we win, there will be trouble in Paris tonight, big trouble.' Once again, it was the 'we' that I loved.

That man is not alone in his opinion. I make the point again that I love Paris for many reasons, but when you go over on the Eurostar for a weekend of food, wine, and being ignored by waiters, don't think that everything there is as good as it looks. You don't see it in the centre, but in the suburbs that the man was talking about, the *banlieues*, there is discontent and desperation. The picture that was painted after the 1998 World Cup, the *black, blanc, beur* idea that France is a multi-cultural melting pot, is simply not true. The weeks before that Cup Final was played, there was controversy in France over a meeting at the Football Federation. The senior people in French football had discussed the idea that more white players should be brought into the academy, at the expense of those with African heritage, as they might care a little more about playing for their country. It was disgusting, but plenty of the Parisian bourgeoisie agreed. That's why a Cup Final, with PSG supported by kids from the suburbs, had little interest for the rest of Paris.

Once I'd reached the Stade de France, everything felt alive again. The Lille fans had made the short journey from the north in coaches, or grabbed the train, and the PSG supporters had simply bypassed the city centre. Most of them aren't welcome there anyway. It was a proper clash of cultures, of cities, with most of the PSG fans super-cool, with scarves tightly tied, or sticking out of their back pockets, and the Lille fans looking far more like dads and uncles, smiling and enjoying the day out. The rest of France looks down on the north, the saying goes that they talk in funny accents and aren't as bright as they might be, and this meant that there was little chance of crowd trouble. The PSG groups have a fearsome reputation, but they need someone to fight against, and weren't going to get it here.

I went to get the pass that had been organised for me by an old colleague and then found out that he'd forgotten. Or not cared enough. After an hour of begging and bullshitting I realised that I wasn't going to get in, and so did my best to try and analyse what the conditions would be like from behind the railings and through gaps in the stand. Outside the Tribune Basse at Gate Y, I could get as near as anywhere to pitch level, and so I craned my neck and did my best to see through the gaps in the stand. I was worried about the wind, with a nod to Philadelphia, but it didn't seem that bad, and the pitch looked, from what I could see, in good condition. All of this, though, felt desperately unscientific, and I thought about pulling out of the bet. But faith in my flawed logic kept me going, even though, unlike that one in Palermo at the start of the book, this day felt wrong.

Thanks to the old colleague who had let me down, I had to leave the PSG and Lille fans to it, go against the crowd, and scurry back through Paris to find a suitable bar. From there I would see if I was right. The first thing that I noticed from the television pictures was the state of the pitch. Football isn't the only sport they play at the Stade de France, and it looked like it had seen a little too much rugby this season. I felt a bit of a mug for not considering that more and actually wondered whether if I'd got a bit closer to it then I might have cancelled the bet. Lille were coping with it much better, but I noticed that in the early stages that Cedric Chantome was turning in an uncharacteristically disciplined performance, tracking back and helping Makalele. The young referee, a new star in the officiating firmament by all accounts, wasn't booking anybody but wasn't letting the game flow either. He seemed happy to blow for fouls, but not to issue yellow cards to stop them happening again. It was more than a little galling to watch this 29-year-old Robert Downey Junior looka-like miss an elbow by Gueye, and then allow a hack by Chedjou on Giuly to go unpunished. It was stop start, and unpromising

But then, halfway through that first half, Chantome started to wander, leaving space in the midfield into which Gervinho and Hazard merrily ran. Gervinho was electric, but could never seem to find a telling final ball. PSG were stretched, and a goal for Lille now would make the game even more open. But it never came.

PSG pushed forward, nearly scored, and then looked vulnerable on the counter attack. Moussa Sow shot over, Gueye shot wide, and the watching Nicolas Sarkozy looked bored. It was 0-0 at half time, and to my mind the over 2.5 goals bet was almost certainly finished. It was a question now of who would win the game.

The match was being played in bursts, with no discernible tempo. Chantome continued to wander, and just after half-time Makalele was withdrawn, presumably injured after having to do just a bit *too* much running. He looked every bit like the boxer who grows old during a fight, and I wondered if he'd ever play again.

PSG's star striker Guillaume Hoaurau missed with a Robbie Keane style miskick after the permanently angry Mevlut Erding had teed him up and with the PSG fans going a little quiet you genuinely sensed that it might just be there for Lille, who had spent the season, after all, as the best team in France. And then Lille made a substitu-tion, and I remembered what James Eastham had said to me back in

The Bowler. Lille had the best substitutes in France, and he fancied one of them to make the difference. And so it came to pass.

With a minute remaining, a man who had only been on the pitch for ten minutes, Ludovic Obraniak, curled a free kick into the top corner with the PSG goalkeeper Gregory Coupet rooted to the spot and that was the end of that. It looked like being a sad end to a brilliant career for Coupet, and ultimately was, but at least he had the satisfaction of saving a penalty in stoppage time. He'd lost his team the game, but still gone out on a sort of high.

Lille had won the match, I'd lost the bet, and I kicked myself for not seeing the signs. Despite the nature of the two teams, it was a Cup Final after all, and Manchester City's 1-0 over Stoke earlier that day should have given me a hint. In his wonderful history of football tactics, *Inverting the Pyramid*, Jonathan Wilson quotes the former Arsenal manager Herbert Chapman: 'The average standard of play would go up remarkably if the result were not the all important end of matches. Fear of defeat and the loss of points eat into the confidence of players... what it comes to is when circumstances are favourable, the professionals are far more capable than may be believed, and it seems that, if we would have better football, we must find some way of minimising the importance of winning and the value of points.' The very act of caring too much can destroy a game of football, and it wasn't as if I hadn't been warned.

One of the many mistakes you can make as a gambler is to impress individual emotions and states of mind onto a team game. 'They'll want to win it inside 90 minutes'; 'They'll be worried about closing out the league title the following week.' We talk of a football club, of a team, as if it is an entity with its own thought processes, rather than as a set of individuals, each with a different job to do. So all that the 11 players of Lille wanted to do that evening was to win the Cup for their team, and PSG's team wanted the same, possibly a little less given their recent success. And they would do that regardless of the atmosphere and the desire for an attractive match. In French Cup Final history, in any Cup Final history, it's the teams who genuinely have nothing to lose which are most dangerous. A bet lost, and I hoped, a lesson learned.

CHAPTER EIGHT

That PSG against Lille game hit me hard, and left me with a dilemma. The two clubs were playing again the week after the Cup Final, and surely with the stays loosened they would produce a game worthy of the description. Having had some time to reflect, I felt it had been the pressure of the occasion which had got to both teams, particularly later on in the game, and even though Lille could win the League at the Parc Des Princes in the south west of Paris, they didn't *have* to, as they would have several more chances in the coming weeks. I was tempted to treat the new game as a fresh gambling opportunity, and have exactly the same bet, over 2.5 goals, which had cost me in the Cup Final.

The problem was that I'd walked away from that Cup Final resolving never to have another bet on French football, echoing the views of two friends of mine, one Irish and the other Scottish, who are oddly obsessed with Ligue 1. They'd both been prescient enough to back Lille at 11-1 to win the title before the season began, but had probably pissed away any potential profit by betting *every* Saturday night, and getting things wrong more often than not. Each Monday they'd tell me: 'That's it, it's a ridiculous league, it's so unpredictable, I'm never going to bet on it again,' and yet the following Saturday there they were, asking each other questions like: 'Do you think the Lorient game will have goals in it?' or 'Marseille should beat Montpellier shouldn't they?' They start those Saturday evenings with hope of what might be, and more often than not end them wanting to kick in their computer screens. After the Stade de France, I knew how they felt, and would never again think that there must be a joke to be invented about the Irishman, the Scotsman and the bloody Frenchman.

I needed some time to clear my head and regroup, but my problem was that I was headed straightaway to Roland Garros for another event which had cost me dearly during those six months which had cost me so much. Back then, I'd lumped a sizeable amount of Rafael Nadal winning the men's tournament, on the reasonable basis that this was his venue, and that he had won here for the previous three years, I was on reasonably safe ground. And his knees chose that year to start hurting him, and he lost, famously to Robin Soderling, in one of the biggest French Open shocks for many years. That was the curious thing about my meltdown, it had neither rhyme nor reason. One moment I would back a golfer at a big price only to see one of the favourites oblige, and then I risked all on a favourite as big as Nadal, only to see him lose.

I could only smile when I read one of the pre-tournament statistic packs ahead of this year's event. Simply looking down the list of winners made me realise how badly the stars must have been aligned against me two years earlier. Since the Argentine Gaston Gaudio ground his way to a win in 2004, the roll of honour went like this: 2005 – Rafael Nadal, 2006 – Rafael Nadal, 2007 – Rafael Nadal, 2008 – Rafael Nadal, 2010 – Rafel Nadal. All that was missing was the year that I had backed him. Why *that* afternoon? Why *that* year?

Nadal wasn't as hot a favourite for this French Open as he had been previously. And there appeared to be solid reasons for that. The Serb Novak Djokovic had gone on a blistering run of form, during which he'd beaten the Spaniard in two of the big clay court events, Madrid and Rome, and even though Djokovic had never performed particularly well on the clay of the French Open, he was favoured by many to continue his run of 39 wins in a row, and cruise to the title here. The draw dictated that Djokovic would avoid Nadal until the final, and would play a fading Roger Federer in the semi-final, if they both got that far.

Djokovic had shocked many in the tennis world by suddenly displaying a maturity that had never before been apparent. He would turn 24 the day before the French Open started, and yet up until the end of the previous year, had still appeared to be little more than a teenager. A nice guy; but immature and petulant. And yet now he had changed. He was incredibly fit, the result of a punishing routine, and had decided to go on a gluten free diet, which he said gave him more energy than he'd ever dreamed of. But it was more than that. Djokovic had seemed to embrace how much of an icon that he'd become back home in Serbia. His country needed its heroes, and rather than see it as something which cranked up the pressure, Djokovic was able to handle it.

The three time French Open winner Mats Wilander told me that if I wanted to get to the root of Djokovic and why he had changed, then I should watch the video of the Serbian Davis Cup players celebrating their win in the competition at the back end of last year. Nenad Zimonjic, Victor Troicki and Janko Tipsarevic all did impressions of Djokovic that made him look sulky and moody, the man who thinks he's it. And Djokovic had smiled and gone along with the joke in a moment of such glory for his country. Yet privately he had been badly hurt by the way that the players spoke about him, and that their impressions had been so easily recognised by those watching. Was he really that much of a spoilt brat? Wilander says that Djokovic resolved to change the way that he approached the game that night in December, and that he had never turned back. He couldn't come from a country like Serbia, one which struggled so much with the weight of recent history, and let down people who needed a hero, a role model. And that had been the genesis of his new found form. He had trained harder, he had eaten more sensibly, and his attitude had been right. He was super fit and playing better than ever, and had beaten Nadal four times out of four this year.

That passing on of the mantle hadn't gone unnoticed in Paris. There was a lot of coverage of Djokovic in the French sporting papers in the week building up to the tournament, and it was interesting to see how the journalists were anointing him as the most obvious winner. It doesn't take much for a French sports journalist to change horses just before a race, as they hate nothing more than being seen to be old hat, and so the story of Djokovic, and how good he was feeling now that he had adopted a new diet, had their attention, and the only picture that was receiving wider coverage than his was that of the still ubiquitous Dominique Strauss Kahn.

Roland Garros is just down the road from Paris St Germain's home ground the Parc Des Princes, and I've always had this rather dreamy image of the place, the redness of the clay such a striking TV memory, and the sun always apparently shining. Despite living five miles from the stadium for a few years, I'd never managed to get there, and so I was excited by this first visit, imagining something whimsical yet edgy, a midsummer Parisian garden party with a little attitude thrown in. And the approach to the stadium and surroundings was exactly what I expected. The atmosphere around the Metro stop at Porte D'Auteuil is pretty rarified, a beautiful garden lights up your journey to the stadium, an oasis of peace as the crowds gather.

Inside, though, the place caught me by surprise. There were plenty of predictable things, like the outfits worn by the young and beautiful people who greet you at the gate. They're clay coloured on the bottom and white on the top, and made the women look amazing, the men like Dale Winton prototypes. What I wasn't ready for was the concrete ugliness of the show courts, far closer to Flushing Meadows in New York than to SW19. Roland Garros is much nearer reality than the fantasy that I'd built up. In his diverting memoir of a year on the tennis circuit in the 1950s, *A Handful of Summers*, the South African player Gordon Forbes said: 'The Roland Garros Stadium in Paris was disappointing after the splendour of the city; a gaunt, concrete amphitheatre which held 13,000 people, inflicting each with a raw behind and softening only when it filled up.'

It certainly needs people, and the mix is fascinating, in that it's not really a mix at all. This doesn't feel like Paris, it feels like a version of it, one in which the bad stuff has been edited out. Roland Garros is just like a suburban tennis club, one in which you can book a court and play when it's your turn. In fact, on the qualifying days, the Thursday and Friday before the tournament proper starts, you could mistake the place for a posh Parisian park, a place where a grumpy janitor might tell you to clear off once you'd exceeded your time.

Just standing in the alleyway between the back of Suzanne Lenglen and the outer perimeter of the club, and listening to the noise of the balls tells you a lot about the rhythm of the tournament itself. At Wimbledon, where the serve dominates and where points are short, you can close your eyes and hear. THWACK – applause. Or possibly, THWACK–THWACK–THWACK – applause. Here it's far more hypnotic. THWACK–THWACK–THWACK–THWACK–GRUNT–THWACK–SILENCE–SCAMPER–SQUEAK–THWACK–THWACK. The back of the court booms only interrupted by drop shots and lobs. This is a place where subtlety still matters, where artfulness and guile can still get you somewhere. Not as much as it used to, maybe, but more than anywhere else.

The qualifying days are interesting; in fact the build-up to any major sporting event will tell you a lot about the event itself. It's good to see the players walking back through the fans on their way to the concrete walkway that takes them down under street level and into the changing rooms. It's not so good to be occasionally greeted by some of the rudest security men I've ever encountered. I lost count of the number of supporters who were trying to do something as subversive as 'go through the wrong gate' who walked away from a man in a blazer saying: 'charming' or 'thanks for your help'. They were the ironic British visitors, of course, the more literal Americans and French simply said 'putain' or 'asshole'.

Sitting in the East Stand of the Suzanne Lenglen, effectively the number two court, you're very aware of the concrete nature of it, the grey seats which only fade into green when they reach the area where coaches and friends sit. One side of the court, the west, is curved concrete, and both ends go straight up. I'd expected it to be more beautiful, somehow more Parisian than this, and despite all the attempts at style from the visitors, including a man wearing a pair of lime green brogues, I was disappointed.

By the surroundings perhaps, but not by the playing surface. The clay itself is stunning. The colour is deeper than you imagine, and stands out the higher that you go up. You can see deposits at either end of the court where the clay has been brushed, and so the area in which the players will come out, will slip and slide and try to bluff and counter bluff, is clearly defined. The brushing of the clay is done by bored-looking men with an arrogant demeanour who drag the weighted end of a net which skims the top of the court, and who then get to work with brushes. Everyone who works near the court is covered in clay, including the players. This place may look clean and pristine, but the play here is down and dirty.

In terms of trying to find a bet, something to lay to bed that Nadal memory once and for all, I was drawn to the idea of Djokovic. Nadal started the tournament as favourite, but given the dominance of the Serb I felt that the man from Mallorca was being rated so highly because of previous glories here, rather than anything that he'd done this season, and I love it when players and teams are priced up on reputation rather than reality. It means that those taking them on are bound to be too big a price. And that was certainly the case with Djokovic. He was available at 5-2, and that would do for me, given that Federer is past his best and the only other realistic winner, Andy Murray, is a player that I'm always keen to oppose as I'm not sure that he has the steel when it matters to win a Grand Slam tournament. Effectively, in my mind, I was backing Djokovic to beat Nadal in the final, and no one that I spoke to beforehand felt that the Serb wasn't capable of that.

No one, that is, except someone whose opinion I respect and who had won me money betting on tennis in the past. In a previous lifetime, I had worked for Eurosport, and their excellent tennis commentary team had always provided me with fun and friendship. The former Wimbledon doubles champion Frew McMillan was there to talk cricket and American politics, Sam Smith to bemoan the fate of her beloved West Ham, and Chris Bradnam to make you smile with his self-deprecating sense of humour and ability to take a joke. My favourite was always: 'I'm a former British Number One, not that that narrows it down much.' Bradnam had pointed me in the direction of one of my best ever bets, at the 2002 US Open. I believe that sporting knowledge should be separated from betting knowledge, and before that tournament I was interested in who Bradnam thought could win, rather than who he thought was a good price. He knows plenty about one subject, next to nothing about the other. He reeled off a list of names, seven in total, and included in them Pete Sampras, by that point 33 years old and with fading powers. 'Sampras?' I said. 'Really? Has he still got the game?' Bradnam replied: 'He's Pete Sampras. He wouldn't be playing if he didn't still have the game.'

Sampras was 33-1 to win that year and so I backed him on the basis of Bradnam's advice, without really holding out too much hope. I was wrong to doubt. Sampras won, pretty comfortably in the end, and as he celebrated what would be his last Grand Slam title, McMillan uttered one of my favourite commentary lines, surreal and spontaneous, yet utterly appropriate: 'There's nothing finer than a trip to Carolina,' he whispered. I still don't really know what it means, but love it all the same. With Djokovic on the brain, I emailed Bradnam and asked him who he thought would win this year at Roland Garros. I got a one-word reply. And it featured five letters, rather than the eight that I'd expected. 'Nadal.' It said. I felt the need for more. 'Not Djokovic?' I tentatively said. Bradnam was adamant: 'It's the French Open,' he said: 'Nadal.'

Having determined that I would do whatever Bradnam had advised, and having noted that Nadal was available at a far bigger price than he had been in recent years, even money or thereabouts rather than heavy odds on, I went out and backed Djokovic. Nadal had cost me here before, and after the French Cup Final, I could see the fates ganging up on me once more. After the Judd Trump incident at the Crucible, I'd sworn never again to ignore the advice of someone that I rated. And yet, here I was, once again, presuming that I knew better.

Bradnam was nowhere near as certain about the women's tournament. That looked wide open, and the best that he could offer was that if Kim Clijsters was fit, then she had the best chance, but that was a case of waiting to see how she moved about the court. Clijsters had won in Australia, and was the obvious favourite in a weak looking field, but if her injury played up, then she too was opposable. I felt that the fact that she was injured was already built into her price, and so I added Clijsters to my portfolio along with Djokovic, taking Bradnam's hesitant advice in the women's but ignoring it in the men's draw. The kind of selective listening that I really should have grown out of, both as a person and a punter.

The other person that I wanted to speak to was my old boss at Eurosport, Simon Reed. Unlike the other three members of the tennis team with whom I got on easily, my relationship with Simon was always more complicated. I wouldn't have the career that I have now without him, and I'll always be grateful for that, but there's definitely a spikiness in our friendship, probably because I'm a younger version of him: opinionated and ready for an argument. We've had a few over the years, but always come back from them, although when I emailed him for French Open advice, I wasn't certain that I'd hear back. I underestimated him hugely, though, because not only did he get back to me but explained that he thought that Djokovic *did* have a big chance in the men's, and that Clijsters should be a stronger favourite for the women's than she was. If she was fully fit then she had an unbelievable chance.

Unoriginal though it seemed, I was happy with backing Djokovic at 5-2 and Clijsters at 6-1, but still thought that it might be fun to have a flyer in the women's draw, back a player at a bigger price in a competition that was extremely hard to predict. After all, there were only five players in that women's draw who had ever won a Grand Slam, and this was the first Slam since the 2003 US Open in which neither of the Williams sisters was taking part. Their influence in Paris had never been that strong, but their absence made the tournament feel even more wide open. There was no point in just picking a name out of a hat, though, and so I decided to stick with what I had. And then I woke up, and realised that I'd received a second email from Simon. 'Just one other thing,' it said: 'don't forget Li Na. She reached the final of the Australian Open and has been terrible since, but she's just got a new coach, a guy that I really rate, and I think that she might have a big couple of weeks. Don't blame me if she goes out in the first round, but I just have a feeling about her.'

This was exactly what I was after: a player with a pedigree. Li Na was being quoted at 28-1 to win, and so she was the final part of the portfolio. I'd gone from the sport that I know most about, football, to one that I have next to no idea about. And yet, with the wisdom of a couple of old friends, I felt that I had a chance. One statistic that I liked was that this was the 104th women's singles at Roland Garros – and only twice in that time has it been won by someone seeded outside the top ten: in 1933, and last year, by the Italian Francesca Schiavone. Li Na was the 6th seed, and that made it feel that I had the stats on my side.

At around the same time as those email conversations, another friend of mine who has an occasional big bet on the horses got in touch. I'd told him about the project, and the fact that I would be concentrating on the specific events that had cost me money in the first place, but that if he had any strong feelings about particular races along the way, then I was all ears. In my mind, he's the kind of punter who will come up with something running in the 8.30 at Wolverhampton on a Friday night, but this time he surprised me by telling me about a fancy that he had for a big race. In most people's eyes, *the* big race. There was a horse running in the Derby in a couple of weeks, he said, that he felt had a massive chance. The French horse, Pour Moi, had been working well by all accounts, and with my mate keen to oppose the likely favourite, the Queen's horse Carlton House, he felt that Pour

Moi was a serious bet. He hadn't given me anything at Cheltenham, and this was the first time that I'd spoken to him in about a year, so I blindly followed him in. And unwittingly set up Saturday 4 June, and what would turn out to be the most remarkable ten minutes of my gambling life.

During that first week of Roland Garros, I watched intently from back in England as first Nadal struggled desperately with the new Babolat balls and was taken to five sets by the giant American John Isner. He looked anything but the winner, and his price to win the tournament went out from that pre-tournament even money to 13-8; with his inability to control the balls as he usually did, he was looking vulnerable. In contrast, Djokovic was cruising through, far too good for a series of opponents and all set for a semi-final against Federer. Li Na had started a little shakily but made her way through, but the big disappointment was Clijsters. She hadn't been anywhere near fit, and had gone crashing out in the second round.

One thing that surprised me about the French Open was how similar it seemed to the other big tennis tournaments. I'd always grown up with the idea that the Grand Slam season started with one kind of test in Australia, on a synthetic surface which favoured hard court specialists, then moved to Paris where the clay slowed the ball down and brought a certain kind of rugged yet soft-handed baseliner into the picture. These players were often South American, and often not heard of throughout the rest of the year. The season then continued with the lightning fast courts of Wimbledon, which played into the hands of the serve volleyers, and then ended in the passionate and noisy surroundings of Flushing Meadows in New York, where once again the hard court players who'd done well in Melbourne would come into their own. And for many years, this was the case. Certain players, like Bjorn Borg and Mats Wilander, bridged the gap and were able to win on all four surfaces, but more often than not even the most famous names struggled in at least one of the Grand Slams. John McEnroe, for example, reached one French Open final and played in only five Australian Opens, while Pete Sampras never got beyond the semi-finals at Roland Garros. But now, all of that seemed to have changed, at the other Grand Slam events first, but now even here. There's a homogeneity about what should be four different events, and, as the men's tennis world stands at the moment, before each Grand Slam the probable semi-finalists are the same for each event. Nadal, Djokovic, Federer, Murray. That was never the case in the 1980s and 1990s.

I spoke to Wilander on the balcony of the Philippe Chatrier court and, as we looked down at the gaiety of the walkways beneath us, I asked him what he thought had changed. He's a nice guy, a ball of energy who rushes from event to event, but he was considered and a little melancholy in the time he spent with me, telling me: 'I think it's a really bad thing that the Slams have changed and that the differences between them are now not so great. You used to get players who were excellent on one surface and then others who were a little bit more all courters, and as an all courter myself, it was always a big challenge to play a clay court specialist here. But now it's different, and, yeah, it makes me really sad.'

The main issue seems to be the one that was troubling Nadal, that the new balls being used are quicker and take less spin. There were those who felt that the courts at Roland Garros were also quicker this year, but Wilander felt strongly that this was down to nature, rather than anything deliberate on the part of the organisers: 'Yeah sure, the courts might be quicker in certain years because of specific differences in the weather, but that doesn't mean that it's deliberate, it means that it has been sunny and that they've dried out, and that's really not rocket science.'

I was interested to hear from Wilander about the mechanics of playing on clay, just how you coped with a surface that was completely alien to many of the players when they were growing up. It's all to do with the bounce, as Wilander explained with his arms waving, his eyes suddenly bright: 'When you play for the first time at the French Open and you see the way that the ball bounces and you think "holy shit," I never saw a ball bounce like this before, now I have a whole set of new problems to deal with. You see balls here that you just won't see anywhere else and that takes some getting used to.'

Now that the balls were a little quicker, though, and absorbed less spin, the power players could still dominate, and so the days of the manipulating Italians of the 1950s, the likes of Giuseppe Merlo and the American Art Larsen, seemed further away than ever. It seemed a shame that a style and an era that had been so rich in so much could so easily have been forgotten, and I found myself thinking of all that I'd read about the old days on clay. The craziness of Larsen, who in the words of former South African tennis stars of the time Gordon Forbes '…seldom missed the opportunity of ending points with extraordinary strokes – like making sliced drop shots come back over the net, or turning what appeared to be enormous smashes into the softest of pats,' and Merlo, whose racket was 'so loosely strung that you can't hear him hit the ball.' Merlo used to hold the racket half way up the handle when he played his fore-hand and in Forbes's words, 'his shots sneak past the net-rushers like bullets out of a gun.'

The day I spoke to Wilander, I would get to watch Li Na. With the women's tournament played at a slower pace, there is still room for some of the old clay virtues, and she had embraced them. She had grown in confidence as Roland Garros had moved into a second week, and now she would play in a quarter-final against the Belorus-sian Victoria Azarenka. Li Na was the outsider, available to back at 5-2 for the match, with Azarenka seemingly able to play at a higher level and attack Li with her power. The ticket that I had wasn't supposed to get me anywhere near that match, which was played on the main Philippe Chatrier court, but I smiled and flashed my wallet, and found myself with the perfect vantage point, as the sun started to beat down. This would be one of the key days of the Championships, with Li and Azarenka followed onto Chatrier by Nadal and Soder-ling's quarter-final, and Maria Sharapova and Andrea Petkovic on the other court, preceding Andy Murray and the Argentine danger man Juan Ignacio Chela.

I left Roland Garros that evening feeling confident, if not overly so. Li Na had outperformed her price and that in itself was cause for celebration, but now she would face Maria Sharapova in the semi-final, a match that she seemed certain to lose. Of my three bets, she and Djokovic were still alive, and Djokovic was looking fantastic. He seemed certain to beat Federer and then face a rejuvenated Nadal in the final.

And then the semi-finals produced a double shock. Li Na moved Sharapova around the court, made the Russian look one dimensional, and beat her. I now had a 28-1 shot going for me in the women's final. The gloss was taken off that when the old man Federer produced a performance for the ages to beat Djokovic on a dramatic Friday evening. The Serb had done little wrong, had just been undone by a talent that was raging against the dying of the light. Without a Grand Slam victory since the 2010 Aussie Open, his performance against Djokovic was one of his greatest ever. Nadal beat Murray, of course he did, and Bradnam's five letter pre-tournament email was looking pretty accurate now. The Nadal team had been happy to see Federer beat Djokovic, as the Serb had looked to have the beating of their man, even on clay, and now the way seemed clear for Nadal. The match between Murray and Nadal showed us just how high class an era this is. Murray knew that he needed to play better than he ever had on clay and he did. And yet he was beaten in straight sets. It was a windy day and Murray even accounted for that, keeping the ball flat and cutting down the number of lobs that he hit. Great tennis players have the habit of seizing the moment, having sensed it just before they seize it, and this is the instinct that Nadal has, that possibly Murray never will.

So onto that Saturday, 4 June, forever etched into my memory, and what should have been the key moment on this road to redemption. On my friend's advice, I'd already backed Pour Moi for the Derby at 6-1, and now I noticed that Pricewise in the *Racing Post* was tipping the horse to win. It's relatively rare for Tom Segal to support horses at shorter prices, and his art is to find something at a double figure price, and this somehow filled me with confidence, as did the fact that the *Racing Post* was supporting Li Na for the women's final against the previous year's winner Francesca Schiavone. I'm not sure how I made it through the morning, but was relieved that I finally had some sport to sit down and watch. Li immediately took control of the match, cruised through the first set, and looked as if she would win easily. I was counting my money, and then her old uncertain self came to the surface.

Li was a set up and 4-2 up and she looked for all money like the winner – and then she started to freeze, and Schiavone got to within two points of forcing a third set which she surely would have won with momentum on her side. I thought that she was going to throw it away, but somehow Li coped. She stretched her lead in the second set tie break to 6-0 and she had the luxury of enjoying a large handful of match points, giving her time to realise what she was about to achieve.

I was flicking between TV channels, as the build-up to the Derby was in full swing, and the race wasn't far from getting underway. Pour Moi's confident young French jockey Mikael Barzelona was looking a little too confident for my liking, so I switched back to Roland Garros and saw Li Na's reserved and refined celebration. Not for her a climb into the stands, just a quiet punch of the air and the knowledge of who was watching – 65 million Chinese fans. The pressure of who she was representing had nearly got to her, but she kept her head when it really mattered.

Schiavone had said before the final that to be successful on clay 'you have to use your head… you can't just use power. You have to be good physically, mentally and tactically… it's a good mix to keep going, to use the mind, the heart, the body, everything that you are.' Li Na had quite simply been the best at that, and her move to a new coach was the main contributing factor. That second email that I'd received from Simon Reed had been the key, and I had a 28-1 winner.

I left Li Na to her celebrations and turned back to the Derby. The BBC appeared to have rewound to the 1950s, as we were being told that the whole country wanted to Queen's horse Carlton House to win, and that the nation would be on the edge of its seat. I'm not sure that, outside the older members of my family, I know any royalists, and so I was unconvinced by this argument. Carlton House winning would be a great story, and would be carrying a few casual bets, but those who had taken Tom Segal's advice that morning and backed Pour Moi would have no problem cheering on the French horse.

The stalls opened to signal the start of the Derby at almost exactly the same moment that Li Na won, and so one bet segued perfectly into the next. Gamblers often relate bets to each other and talk about fate, and I found myself doing that now. Because Li Na had won, my fuzzy reasoning went, there was no way that the horse could follow up. It's all about applying your own specific story to the ones that you're following, and is, of course, nonsense, as if what a Chinese tennis player has just achieved has any bearing on a French racehorse. Pour Moi and Barzalona clearly hadn't been listening to anyone, because, with the two furlong pole approaching, the horse seemed to have far too much to do, let down by the tactical naivety of his young jockey. And then Pour Moi produced an unbelievable burst of acceleration, and before you knew it Barzalona was standing up in his irons and celebrating. No one seemed quite sure what had just happened. And I was in a state of disbelief. A 28-1 winner had been followed in by a 6-1 shot, both improbable in different ways.

Both winners had been achieved by a willingness to follow the advice of people in whom I believed. Simon Reed had suggested Li Na as an afterthought, but the fact that he even saw her as a potential winner made her hard to ignore at 28-1. If you took the leap of faith that she could get past the first few tricky rounds then she would always grow in confidence and have a massive chance, far better than the 28-1 that had been available. Plenty of bets like this will fall early, but I was gradually starting to realise that they're worth chancing because of the margin for error that they give you. If you continually back odds on and even money shots then a large percentage of them need to win for you to be profitable. If you're prepared to take more of a chance, then you give yourself plenty of chances to get things wrong. This, of course, is one of the most important fundamental principles of gambling, and it had taken 20 years of watching short-priced favourites lose and two weeks of seeing Li Na win to make me understand it.

The Derby, too, was about opinion. That of a very good judge who rarely rings me, and of Tom Segal, Pricewise at the *Racing Post*, who is rightly the hero of any Saturday punter. In previous years, I would have been determined and proud enough to sit down and work the race out for myself, and more often than not, I would get it wrong. Accepting the fact that someone knows more than you about a sport isn't a sign of weakness in a gambler, it should be viewed as one of real strength. I felt as if I'd found a way to escape from a few punting traps into which I'd always previously fallen, and emerged from that day with real hope. In Hamburg a month later though,

I'd realise that getting a lesson and learning from it are very different things.

The final footnote to that stellar Saturday came the following week, when I remembered that Paris St Germain and Lille would be playing their League match on the Saturday night. I wondered if I should have exactly the same bet as last week, knowing that there were likely to be goals, but I decided not to risk ruining everything, and went to a friend's 40th birthday instead. I forgot all about the match, but then remembered it the following morning. And there was a fateful feeling when I checked the score, and realised that PSG had won 3-1, and so the game had indeed produced goals. Despite having one of the best betting days of my life, somehow I finished the following weekend still feeling that something was out of reach.

CHAPTER NINE

It was the day after the fight that was supposed to be the greatest show on earth, and my flight was delayed. I bumped into a friend at Hamburg Airport, who told me that he had been talking to a sportswriter of repute, a late night debate in a hotel bar, and that things had got heated at just after 3 a.m. The writer had told him that he was going to describe David Haye's performance against Wladimir Klitschko as 'pitiful'. My friend had argued with him, saying that no man who is brave enough to get into a ring with the World Heavyweight Champion should ever be called pitiful, and that Haye was deserving of some respect in defeat. That was my opinion too, and I bridled at the thought of the newspapers going for Haye now that he had lost. The writer, though, had twisted his face into a smile and said that Haye had it coming, that after his behaviour of the previous few months he was finally getting what he deserved, and that he had brought all of this on himself. I was surprised to find myself feeling sorry for Haye, a man who I had come to loathe the idea of, and I thought of how quickly opinion can turn in the face of overwhelming defeat.

A while ago, after yet another one-sided battering, another show that wasn't really a show in a far corner of Germany, the American channel HBO decided that they would stop covering the Klitschko brothers' fights. They might be interested if the two men fought each other, or took on somebody who could actually beat them, but the Sports President of the network, Ross Greenburg, said that most Americans couldn't tell the difference between them. It might have sounded scathing and arrogant, but above all, it was true. And lack of recognition means loss of ratings. And in American television in particular, loss of ratings means end of story. In the country which had produced Jack Johnson, Muhammed Ali and Mike Tyson, the identity of the World Heavyweight Champion no longer mattered.

I've watched a lot of Klitschko fights, an awful lot. They've never been much of a punting vehicle, as, ever since Vitali took Lennox Lewis to a desperately dark place, and Wladimir lost, shockingly, to both Corrie Sanders and Lamon Brewster, both men have rarely fought an opponent worthy of the name. The only man who has since troubled either brother was the Nigerian Samuel Peter back in 2005, when he had Wladimir on the floor three times, but still couldn't finish him. That was arguably the fight that made the younger Klitschko, the one that proved he had a heart and not just the ability to train hard and develop an impressive physique. The one that earned him respect from his peers, and from those observers who care enough to know.

Since that first Peter fight, though, the Klitschkos had fought 17 times between them, and at no point had either looked in any danger, at no stage had there been that element of doubt, that sign of a proper contest that is so crucial for boxing to gain a big TV audience. I've been lucky enough to commentate on pretty much every Klitschko fight since I saw Wladimir destroy an overmatched Cuban called Eliseo Castillo in Dortmund back in 2005, and trying to generate excitement for a worldwide viewing public has got harder and harder. I'll admit that I have bigged up fighters who I didn't really feel had a chance of winning, and I'm not particularly proud of that, I just felt that a guy sitting on his sofa in Malaysia or Australia or wherever had the right to feel that it was worth watching once he'd made the effort to tune in.

Two years ago, during a snowstorm, I sat in the jauntily named Post Finanz Arena in Berne in Switzerland, wondering whether an American journeyman called Kevin Johnson had a chance against Vitali, the older of the two brothers. Johnson was, is, a decent stylist, and knew how to look after himself in the ring. But he had admitted before the fight that he had no punch, and that the only way that he was going to win was to outpoint the bigger man. And given the fact that Klitschko was almost certain to overpower him and had the judges on his side anyway, Johnson did not have an earthly.

A colleague of mine from Las Vegas told me beforehand that he had placed a hundred dollars on Johnson to win, and my ears pricked up. Perhaps this guy knew something, maybe he had worked out a way that Johnson could climb into Vitali's head and stay there. And so I asked him, and he told me, bluntly, that he had placed the bet because he knew that he'd be bored, and he wanted to make the fight interesting. Like me, the Las Vegan had been at so many Klitschko fights that flights of fancy were starting to take over from reality. Johnson performed well, and lasted for 12 deadening rounds, at the end of which Klitschko was declared the comfortable winner. My mate had chucked away his hundred bucks, which struck me as an entirely Las Vegan thing to do, and not for the first time I wondered whether it would be worth backing the brothers at prohibitive prices every single time they fought. I've never been drawn to gamble at heavy odds on, as your margin for error is so tiny, but sometimes you wonder if, in the right circumstances, it can make sense.

There's a quote which is always credited to the gambler and race-horse owner Harry Findlay that goes: 'What do you mean there's no such thing as value at 1-10? If a racehorse was running against a donkey and I offered you 1-10 about the racehorse, then you'd take it, wouldn't you?' He's right, and the Klitschkos were thoroughbreds who'd come up against an awful lot of lesser men, albeit incredibly brave ones. I thought back through every single fight of theirs that I'd covered, and considered with how little trouble they'd won. Whether it was Castillo that first time, with the build of a middleweight, who had fallen in the fourth, or Chris Byrd and Ray Austin, who'd both been destroyed in Mannheim, or Lamon Brewster in Cologne, or Tony 'the Tiger' Thompson in Hamburg, or Hasim Rahman back in Mannheim, or Fast Eddie Chambers in Dusseldorf, or Ruslan Chagaev in Gelsenkirchen, or Samuel Peter, for a second time, in Frankfurt. All comfortable wins for Wladimir, all delivered behind his frightening left jab, all relatively risk free. It was hard to see how he would ever lose again, especially given the lack of opposition. It's often been written sneeringly of the Klitschkos that they have never fought anyone, that they only take fights they know that they can win. I've always felt that it's not their fault, and that it's the weakness of the division that allows them to dominate. There are always those shouting from the sidelines that they're being avoided. Alexander Povetkin, Robert

Helenius, and, of course, an Englishman that you may have heard of called David Haye.

As if it ever needed questioning, the Klitschko dominance was confirmed when Vitali came out of retirement in 2008. He was always the superior boxer, and the braver of the two, and he too started to demolish every fighter who stood in his way. Samuel Peter (him again) was taken apart in Berlin, then Juan Carlos Gomez in Stuttgart, and Johnson in that Swiss non-event. Albert Sosnowski's excuse for a challenge in Gelsenkirchen summed up for me what the heavyweight world had become. Sosnowski is a Pole who now lives in London, and a man who had built up a decent record, but one which was very much at domestic level. He was lucky to get a shot at the title, but there was no need to behave in the build-up to the fight as if he knew it.

He was almost thankful, and the big pre-fight show that always accompanies the Klitschkos exaggerated the nonsense of it all. A giant fire-breathing mechanical dragon had been brought into the arena to accompany Sosnowski's ring walk. As the ring announcer Michael Buffer went through his routine, Sosnowski waited back-stage, until finally Buffer filled the arena with the words: 'The Challengerrrrrrrrrrr... Albert, 'the Dragon', Sosnowskiiiiiiiiiiiiiiiiiiii'. Buffer has the trick of taking the microphone away from his mouth so that he leaves nothing more than an echo. As his words tailed away, the dragon started to move, and the fire from this diabolical construct's mouth lit up the dark of the football stadium along with tens of thousands of camera flashes. Sosnoswki appeared in a spot-light and the atmosphere built up into something that was genuinely terrifying, until the Pole's choice of ring walk music began. Surely it had to be some barely identifiable rap, something with a thudding beat and an attitude. Anything would have done. But then the strains of 'I Feel Good' by James Brown filled the arena, and any tension, and indeed any doubt, was gone in an instant. Sosnowski didn't want us to know that he meant business, or that he was going to hit Klitschko hard, or that he was going to take him to a dark place. He wanted him to know that he felt good. He put up a brave, brave display and was one of the rare fighters who tried to stand and trade punches with a Klitschko, but any chance that he had was gone long before he got in the ring.

I thought back to the stories that I'd heard about the likes of Roberto Duran, and what he would do to opponents before fights to unsettle them. This is a man who faced Sugar Ray Leonard back in 1980 in Montreal, and who started his mind games at the pre-fight press conference. Duran ate a grapefruit as if it was an apple, and then ripped a steak apart with his teeth. As the boxing writer George Kimball recalls in his classic book *Four Lions*, 'Leonard blinked a couple of times and looked away. He must have been thinking: "this guy is a friggin' animal."'

Leonard went on to announce to the world's media that he wasn't just going to beat Duran, 'he was going to kill him' and the nice guy admitted that he'd been drawn into making such an uncharacteristic statement because 'Duran had been pushing all the buttons.' Duran continued his tactics in the build-up to the fight. Leonard's trainer, Angelo Dundee, is quoted in Kimball's book as saying that Duran's tactics beforehand had proved most effective. Dundee says: 'Leonard got out-psyched. Duran abused Ray, and Ray couldn't handle it. Duran would see Ray walking with his wife in the streets of Montreal and he'd yell: "I keel your husband, I keel your husband!" The night of the fight, Ray wanted to keel him. Ray wanted to fight the guy, not box him.' The stylist Leonard was drawn into a street fight by the ultimate brawler Duran and lost. It's still widely thought that if Leonard had fought his fight then he'd have won, and he proved that theory by knocking Duran out in the eighth round when the two fought later that year. But in Montreal in March, Duran had set the perfect example of how mind games, as well as skill and bravery, could win you a fight.

If Sosnowski, the fire breathing dragon, and James Brown was the most obvious example of allowing your more fancied opponent to further seize the initiative, doing the opposite of Duran, then in the Pole's defence nobody ever seemed to get inside the head of either Klitshcko. They do inscrutable well, and Vitali in particular strikes you as a man who would be prepared to fight anyone, anywhere, at a moment's notice. I once stood next to him in a lift and slightly too cheerily I asked which floor he'd like, 'probably the penthouse?' The look that he gave me made me wary of ever being cheery again. If you took both men at their peak, then Vitali was certainly the better fighter, but I had seen what I thought were signs of weakness in him, and was hoping that he would fight someone soon who had the style that could beat him. There's a famous saying that boxers can get old overnight, and I felt that Vitali, with his reflexes starting to slow, and his feet moving a little less fluently, may be there for the taking by the right kind of opponent. Wladimir, who had never reached the heights of his brother at their peaks, was definitely the better man now.

There's a danger as a gambler when you come to an opinion about a sportsman. You read stories over the years about certain punters earning the majority of their capital by identifying a talent, and following it through. If you'd latched onto just how good both Roger Federer and Tiger Woods were round about the turn of the millennium, for example, managed to tap into their success before they became prohibitive favourites for every big tournament they played, then you'd have done pretty well. It's all about identifying a talent or a weakness before most other people do and placing your faith in that person. The danger with this philosophy is that you out-think yourself. You decide something is set in stone, and then you ignore all evidence to the contrary in the hope, rather than expectation, that you'll be right. My big weakness on that score is with major golf championships. I watch a good performance and I say to myself: 'He's good enough to win a major.' I then back said player in every major, somehow scared that I'll miss the one that he wins. It's about liking to think that you're a better judge than you actually are, and it's proved a route to the poorhouse for me over the years with the likes of Brad Faxon, Mike Harwood, Mark McCumber, Jesper Parnevik, and in more recent years Sergio Garcia, Ian Poulter and Brandt Snedeker. Everyone on that list, apart from Faxon and Snedeker, have finished second in a major, and Poulter and Garcia still have chances but no longer carry my money. I like to think that I wasn't completely wrong about any of them. But I was still wrong.

I was starting to get that dangerous feeling about Vitali Klitshcko. That a shock defeat may be on the cards for him which would send him into retirement, and that those of us who could see it coming would be in a perfect position to profit. My reasons were pretty solid, far more than those that had led me to believe that Brad Faxon may one day win a major. Klitschko is a proper fighter, a powerful man, and has an iron will that has never been broken. His two defeats have both come about, not because he was being outfought, but once, against Lennox Lewis, because cuts caused the fight to be stopped, and secondly, against Chris Byrd, because he had dislocated his shoulder. He would certainly have beaten Byrd without the injury, and many feel that he was on top against Lewis when the fight was stopped.

We'll get to David Haye in good time, but earlier in the year, Vitali was due to fight a Cuban called Odlanier Solis in Cologne. Solis is an exiled Cuban who lives in Miami and had been good enough to win an Olympic gold medal in 2004. Like many Cubans who find the good life elsewhere, he had lost his discipline, and had looked horribly blown up and bloated before fights. He'd still been good enough to win them, and the feeling around boxing was that if he could ever get himself in shape then he could have a chance of a world title. I was looking to oppose the older Klitshcko, and if Solis was fit enough, then I felt that his speed could lead to an upset. It was an outside chance, but Solis was 8-1 to win, which I felt was too big. The Cuban was confident as well: he looked in good shape and announced at the pre-fight press conference that 'we will see the best fight of all time.' You should never take pre-fight comments seriously, but Solis wasn't going to be walking to the ring accompanied by James Brown. And confidence could take him a long way. With fast hands and feet, Solis had the skills; he just needed to believe that he could use them.

Just before that fight, I was sitting ringside and looked up at Solis. He had sat down on his stool to receive some final words from his trainer, and I looked at the roll of fat that was sitting just above his garish shorts. I started to lose confidence as he seemed a little sluggish, but the bet was on and I had to wait and see what happened. Klitschko won in the first round, as the backside fell out of Solis's career. He wasn't beaten by a punch, although a glancing blow had caught him high on his head, but as he had fallen backwards he had twisted his knee. He got to his feet from the knockdown, but wasn't able to continue. Klitshcko stood over him and roared his disapproval, thinking that his opponent didn't have the stomach for a fight, and many of those in the arena felt the same. I felt sorry for Solis, though. I thought that he was genuinely hurt and admired him for refusing the offer of a stretcher to take him away from the ring. He had dignity in defeat, at least.

I also wondered if David Haye had been watching. Haye was rumoured to be fighting the younger Klitshcko brother, Wladimir, later on in the year, and he would have been intrigued to see the fact that Solis had managed some success against Vitali before his knee gave way. It was nothing earth shattering, but the skills of the Cuban had allowed him to feint and move and get inside the reach of the bigger man. And that's exactly what Haye would have to do if he was to have any chance against Wladimir. That Solis v Klitschko fight will end up as a footnote, I thought at the time, but may just have wider ranging significance.

Eventually, the Haye v Wladimir Klitshcko fight was made, and it would take place in Hamburg, not in the purpose built arena in the city, but in the football stadium. This would be what so many fighters dream of: an outdoor summer fight for the world title. A spectacular on 2 June, finally a Klitschko taking on someone who could beat him.

Haye had shown real ability in his career to that point. He had won a world title at cruiserweight, had produced a stupendously brave performance to stop the Frenchman Jean-Marc Mormeck in Paris, and so far as a heavyweight he had barely been troubled. He had beaten an American called Monte Barrett, and then had won a world title with a smash and grab performance against the enormous Russian Nikolai Valuev. That had been about a tactical plan perfectly executed, as the smaller man used his speed to confuse the colossus. Haye had then beaten a former world champion in John Ruiz, and then humiliated Audley Harrison in Manchester. Haye deserved his shot at Klitschko's title, but even if he hadn't, he would have talked his way into the fight. He'd used every tactic that he could think of to rile the brothers: insulted their family, called them cowards, and then notoriously turned up wearing a T-shirt which showed a picture of him holding the severed heads of the brothers. He must have been reading about Roberto Duran, but not even Duran had suggested that a fight would be 'as one-sided as a gang rape' as Haye had before he fought Harrison. Haye made himself easy to hate, and I took full advantage.

Because I despised him for months before the fight. I think that it was the gang rape comment that finally did it for me, and I'd found myself wanting Harrison to cause an upset, knowing deep down that he couldn't. There were those who defended Haye, who said that all he was doing was selling the fight and that deep down he's a nice guy, but if he never shows us that then what are we expected to think? The 'you don't know the real him' defence reminded me of that feeling you have when you meet a partner's friends for the first time. You generally get on and then there's always one of them who's a bit of a dick. Maybe too loud, maybe too quiet, but seemingly intent on making you, the newbie, feel uncomfortable. And on the walk home from the bar you say something inoffensive like: 'Your friends seem nice, but I'm not sure that Andrew liked me.' And the response comes instantly: 'Oh, you don't really know him, that's just his way.'

I'll admit that I don't know Haye at all, but if insulting people's families and talking of ambulances and disrespecting old fighters as a result is his way then I don't want to know him. The Brits travelled over to Hamburg in force in the hope that their man would win, but I wanted him to lose. And lose badly. Not get injured, because that would be stooping to his level, and besides, I have a deep respect for anyone who's prepared to get in a ring and fight. But a humiliation from which his body could fully recover was all that I craved.

And, of course, it's hard to gamble sensibly when you want something so much. Klitschko was, in my eyes, an absolute certainty. Firstly, I always knew that he was far better than those who had an opinion but had never seen him fight told us that he was. His fights are dull, certainly, but that's because his style is so efficient and his mind so strong that no one ever gets near him. And he'd beaten everybody that he'd been asked to, every challenger, every wannabe. And I'd watched them come with their boasts, some more convincing than others, and all been sent packing.

Haye and Wladimir had been supposed to fight back in 2009, but Haye was injured in the build-up, and so the massive stadium in Gelsenkirchen had watched Klitschko beat up the Belorussian contender Ruslan Chagaev. I'd backed Chagaev to cause an upset that night, at the height of my madness, an illogical bet that couldn't possibly win. So I was in Hamburg looking to put that right. I was going to have a massive bet on Klitschko to beat Haye, and the more that people suggested that Haye might win, the happier I was.

And plenty of good judges were giving Haye a chance. The argument went that the Englishman could punch, and if he could use his speed to get inside the Ukrainian's jab and land his right hand, then we already knew that Klitschko could be vulnerable. I was so sure in my own opinion, so cocky about a Klitschko win, that I loved every minute of exposure that the pro-Haye lobby was given. Anything that would drive Haye's price down, and Klitschko's up, would do for me, because their man was in for a beating.

Both fighters had advantages. Haye has always said that he was born to fight, whereas Klitschko is a considered individual who admits to not really liking the sport. That's why his first win over Samuel Peter had been so surprising. He had had his fighting heart tested and come through, looking stronger ever since. The big advantage, though, was Klitschko's, and that was simply his size. He stands at 6 feet 6½ inches, and has a reach of 81 inches. That means that when Klitschko walks to the middle of the ring with his left arm outstretched, trying to jab his way to victory, an opponent has to find a way to get inside his reach and get to his body and his chin. Haye is 3½ inches shorter with a reach that is inferior by 13 inches. And regardless of the rest of the hullabaloo, that was where the key to the fight lay. Every time that Haye would try to get near the big man, he would be repelled by a punch. If he wanted to dish out punishment, then he would have to take plenty himself, and I wasn't sure that he could.

And I wasn't alone. Haye may have been talked up in England, but *The Ring* magazine in the United States polled 20 experts about the outcome of the fight, and only three said that Haye would win. I was convinced by Klitschko at 4-7, having said to friends for years that I thought he's beat Haye, and now was the time to take advantage. And I wish that I'd stuck to that: a straightforward opinion about the winner, but then I thought back to the lessons of the football in Paris and how important it was to see exactly how an event would unfold, rather than simply predict it. The thoughtlessness that had cost me there would have saved me here, and I wasn't laughing too much at the irony.

Because an alternative bet came into focus. I was so sure that Wladimir would win, and would do so by connecting with a big right hand onto the fragile jaw of Haye, that I looked at the prices for Klitschko to win by a stoppage. He had stopped 49 of his previous 58 opponents, and Haye would be giving him the chance to get a 50th. Klitschko's trainer Emmanuel Steward says that pretty much all of Klitschko's opponents have gone into the ring just thinking about survival and haven't wanted to take the risk that would leave them open to a right hand, but I thought that Haye would do that, risking a knockdown to give himself a chance of winning. Haye said that 'the public will be guaranteed a violent early knockout.' And he's fond of qualifying his statements to try and add to their power. 'That's not a prediction, that's a promise,' he said. For once, I agreed with Haye about something. There would be a violent early knockout, but Haye would be the one looking at the stars.

Now that I can sit back and consider the build-up to that night in Hamburg, I realise that I allowed myself for the first time on this journey to get complacent. I was so convinced that I was right about the result of the fight that I blocked myself off to the possibility of anything else happening. The ethos of this book was to talk to those in the know and pull that expertise together to arrive at a considered conclusion. And maybe because I was tired, more probably because I was arrogant, I passed up the chance. At various times in the days before the fight, I stood in a lift with one of my favourite ever fighters, Roy Jones, I had the opportunity to talk to the brilliant Mike Costello and Steve Bunce of the BBC, and likewise ignore the chance to get the opinions of the incredibly knowledgeable Sky Sports team of John Rawling, Jim Watt, Glenn McCrory and Spencer Oliver. It wasn't that I didn't value their opinions, it was that I didn't want anyone to dissuade me from my view. Klitshcko would win by a stoppage, and that was the end of it. It was the first time that my old punting persona had resurfaced, and I should have known better, but didn't allow myself to.

Nature weighed heavy that day and night in Hamburg. From early in the morning, the rain hammered down, and there were doubts from late morning as to whether the fight would take place. The ring itself was protected by an overhead canopy, but the rain seemed to be driving sideways, and there seemed to be a risk of the fighters being unable to plant their feet firmly enough. Emmanuel Steward was having breakfast with Ola Afolabi, one of his undercard fighters, and I wondered if they would sneak a small pot of honey out of the dining room. When conditions are like this, Steward likes his fighters to put honey on the soles of their boots, sticking them to the canvas just enough. Afolabi would later throw an amazing right hand to knock out the British fighter Terry Dunstan, on an undercard that was the usual mix of hope and desperation.

There were those like Afolabi, and the British fighters Ashley Sexton, Mike Robinson and Ryan Aston, who seemed to be going places, and there was Tony Harrison, a laid back kid from Detroit who'd stalked around the hotel all week, and effortlessly took care of an overmatched German called Uwe Tritschler. But there's nothing glamorous about being on an undercard. The early finish to the Afolabi fight meant that the swing bout got an airing. On nights like this, two fighters sit backstage and never know if they're going to get on. They're there to fill in the gaps at a moment's notice, and so they stay loose and ready, just in case they're needed. The two swing fighters in Hamburg were a young Hungarian called Gabor Veto and a Kenyan James Kimori, who had travelled to Germany without a trainer, and had sat alone at the previous day's weigh in, a million miles from home, a fighter going wherever he could to earn.

Kimori was brave, but suffered a predictable beating from Veto, and when the fight was finally stopped, the Kenyan wandered around the ring, dazed and bruised. The young German trainer who'd been brought in to look after Kimori for a couple of hours simply stood and watched until Steve Bunce stood up behind me and yelled: 'You.' The trainer turned to look at him. 'Go and get your fighter. Go and get your fighter. Get him a stool and take care of him.' I liked Bunce a lot in that moment. And Kimori at least had an arm to support him as he staggered back to the dressing room.

As Kimori sat alone and wondered where he would go next, the preparations for the big fight began. The rain was still ferocious, the pockets of British fans around the stadium started to make some noise, and those who had bought expensive ringside seats were given ponchos, and sat bedraggled, looking up at the covered cheap seats. The rain created an atmosphere of near bedlam at ringside, with the security guards failing to keep track, and fans were wandering around the ring, in between journalists and commentators, taking photos and taking their chance. The Klitschko fights are usually well organised and glamorous – this was anything but. Both fighters were given the option of a postponement, and had one of them said yes, then the show would have delayed for 24 hours, but the word came out from both camps, that, rain or no rain, we were on.

The sense of mayhem continued when the cue was given for Haye to begin his walk to the ring. Backstage, the TV executives were delighted with the mini mock up of London that they'd created, with phone box and black taxi, and in the afternoon's rehearsal they'd clapped their hands in glee. But then, when the cue came for Lennox Lewis to get out of the cab and knock on Haye's dressing room door, he didn't come out. Lewis waited, the big intro was ruined, and some at ringside wondered if self-doubt had finally taken over the Englishman. But then he emerged, smiling and confident, wearing England's new football shirt and a look of determination.

What happened next made the evening seem odder. The afternoon rehearsal for these Klitschko fights is always worth watching. Michael Buffer stands in the centre of the ring in casual clothes and technicians stand in for the fighters. The ring walks are precisely choreographed, and producers and cameramen know exactly where each fighter will go, and when. I'd watched in the rain as they practised their show, and seen the routes both men would take to the ring. But Haye was taken off course. He wasn't guided to the ring via the preordained route, and instead was forced to come through the crowd, giant security guards pushing fans out of the way. When Haye said afterwards that he'd had his feet trodden on as he walked to the ring, he was laughed at, but that part of the story was true.

And I'm sure that it was done deliberately, that someone was trying to mess with Haye's head.

Wladimir had cut a more sympathetic figure in the build-up to the fight, and so journalists seemed happy to give him the benefit of every doubt, but his trainer Adam Booth's post-fight claim that there had been 'dirty tricks' wasn't as mealy mouthed as it sounded. I don't know if the Haye camp was spied on throughout the week or given a bottle of ephedrine by a supervisor, but I do know that the home fighter's advantage was pushed to the limit that night. Haye had said, with a nod to the spirit of Roberto Duran, that: 'We're doing everything we can to get under Klitshcko's skin, to rattle him, to wind him up. If we succeed and I win that's all that anyone will care about.' What Haye was trying to do so overtly was being skilfully done to him.

There is a tradition of these big fights being a disappointment. You get carried away by what *might* happen and then are presented with what normally happens – that both men need time to assess their opponent, that things necessarily remain risk free and that fireworks are often absent. The French Cup Final had been a turn-off because both teams were scared of making a mistake, and the same was true here. Klitschko pawed at Haye, and twitched, and tried to avoid danger, remembering his pre-fight comment that 'it takes one step for a champion to become nothing.' Haye seemed a little sluggish and couldn't get within range. It's remarkably difficult to win rounds against either Klitshcko brother, and Haye was discovering that. As the fight moved forward, neither man had sparkled, but as the bigger man, doing marginally more work, and at home, Klitschko would be taking every round on the scorecards of the three judges. Even in the early stages, Haye looked as if he needed a knockout, but then again he always knew that.

After seeing the cagey attitude of both men, particularly Haye, at the start of the fight, I started to worry about the bet. Klitschko looked too strong for Haye, but didn't look like stopping him, and on a fairly predictable evening the biggest surprise was how strong the chins of both men looked. I'm convinced that one of the key moments in the fight was in the third round, when Haye caught Klitschko on the chin with his right hand, having used footwork to get within range, and Klitschko stayed on his feet. Haye had believed all along that if he caught the bigger man with a clean shot, he would go down, and when he didn't Haye's driving ambition must have died a little.

Klitschko was definitely stung, though, and it was in those early rounds that Haye proved that he belonged at this level. The fight was competitive, and I've never seen Emmanuel Steward look as animated and worried as he did in that period. Steward said that they'd watched Haye and noticed that 'every time he throws his right hand he loses his balance,' – and that's what he reminded Klitschko of throughout the fight, sometimes more hysterically than others. There was no question that this was a very different Steward from the one that we had seen in the corner in previous Wladimir fights – he was jumpy, and edgy, and not giving the impression that he thought his man was winning the fight as easily as ringside observers said that he was afterwards. He knew that his man was up against a live opponent, and when Klitschko had a point deducted for pulling Haye down by the neck, Steward charged to the centre of the ring and remonstrated with the referee. That was one psychological area which Booth and Haye had played to perfection, insinuating that the referee Genaro Rodriguez was a friend of the Klitshckos, and that he would somehow show a favour or two. Rodriguez wanted to prove his honesty, and deducted a point from Klitschko the first chance that he had.

That was about the only battle that Haye and his corner won. After that early success, Haye faded badly and the champion dominated. There was still the latent danger that Haye could rock Klitschko with a big shot, and in the final round in particular, he threw huge punches over the top and came close to connecting, but Steward summed up the general disappointment by saying afterwards that he: 'expected David to be more aggressive.' He wasn't the only one, and Haye's reluctance to risk everything to try and achieve his goal was what cost me the bet. I'd been absolutely right about Klitschko having too much for Haye, and yet I'd lost my bet because I'd been greedy; 4-7 hadn't been good enough for me, and I'd been tempted by the odds against and paid the price.

I felt a little hoodwinked by Haye but also felt the need to defend him. He was by far the best opponent that I've seen either Klitschko face in six years, and, for a man who had been written off as a charlatan in some places he had proved that he belonged. He judged his pre-fight publicity campaign perfectly, and it was taste-less and crude, maybe he's only giving the people what they want. I wish, as he probably does, that he'd thrown a few more punches against Klitschko, but ultimately, for all his ability, he too was more concerned by self-preservation. At Roland Garros, I'd wondered about Andy Murray's ability to seize the moment, and the same seemed true to his good friend Haye.

Murray's issue the previous day at Wimbledon had been that fail-ure to open up when it matters and feel that he has to play safety first, albeit high-quality tennis. It takes that leap of faith to become a Grand Slam champion, that moment when you have to take a risk. Murray struggles to go from being a baseliner who can put away poor opponents to a risk taker who can beat the best. And that's what Haye did. Stayed in there for a couple of rounds, landed in the third, and then backed off. Klitschko recovered and dominated. Booth said afterwards that Haye was meant to throw punches and then move in with a second wave, but that his legs wouldn't work as they had done in the gym. Possibly it was a flawed plan, or maybe, as he later claimed, Haye really was carrying an injury.

The judges gave Klitschko the fight by six, eight and ten rounds, and that meant open season on Haye. I had the fight a little closer, and wasn't alone at ringside. Klitschko had certainly won, but my margin was four rounds, and while I was frustrated by getting the name of the winner right, but the method of victory wrong, I felt that I'd been wrong about Haye. He was a lot better than I'd realised, and with more belief and awareness of his moment he could have had Klitschko in all kinds of trouble in that third round.

Klitschko had seduced many of the travelling journalists, and Jeff Powell in the *Daily Mail* typified the slightly hysterical reaction from some quarters by saying that he only gave Haye a share of two rounds, one of which because of a point deduction. That's a one-eyed reading of the fight, and the punch stats show that Klitshcko only threw one more punch than Haye, but landed 45 per cent of the time to Haye's 26 per cent, 99 to 57 – proving that he deserved to win but that it was a long way from a landslide.

I hope that Haye gets a fight against the older Klitschko brother, as I think that he could beat him, although this time he'll be a much bigger price to win. Having been overrated against Wladimir, he may be seriously underrated when he fights Vitali.

Back at the airport, I continued to fume about the treatment that Haye was likely to receive from the journalists, the avalanche of *Schadenfreude* that would be coming his way. Sporting ignominy would be piled on him because of his character and the way he behaved, and that somehow seemed unfair. He had given Klitschko a better fight that any opponent in six years, and yet his efforts were being dismissed as amateurish, as pathetic, as pitiful. And then I saw Haye. He'd admitted afterwards that 'there would have been a lot of people hoping that I lost. They can have a little smile and feel glad about it.'

And there he was: limping through the airport with his face still bruised and his eyes covered by sunglasses, but smiling and relaxed. He was talking to Adam Booth, protected by his security guards, and heading home no longer a champion. And at that point I stopped feeling sorry for Haye. He would take a beating in the papers the following day, and he had lost his title and his dream of being unified champion. And yet he had played the game to perfection; £15 million richer, Haye didn't care what anyone thought of him. He may fight again, but if not then the great braggart and self-promoter is still clear eyed enough to make a success of an alternative career. Maybe he really will be the next James Bond, as he's frequently claimed. As Haye swaggered off, beaten but still full of attitude, I thought of two things that Klitschko had said directly after the fight, in that strange press conference when Haye had revealed his injured toe and been laughed at by a room full of reporters. Klitschko said: 'I hate you but I love you too.' An acknowledgement that the pre-fight talk had been distasteful, but that it had made the Ukrainian an even wealthier man.

And the second thing, astute and yet smelling a little of amateur psychology, was that: 'I think everyone in life deserves to be in the place that he is'. And this was Haye's place. Beaten, and destined never to be a great heavyweight, but with enough money for the rest of his life, and still somehow a winner, ready for the next challenge.

CHAPTER TEN

A young fellow with a long fringe bumps past me as I clamber up the steps into the carriage. 'This is the race train, the race train to Belmont Park,' says a small neat grey man with a uniform that looks like it was pressed an hour ago. He busily clips tickets while the fellow with the fringe joins a group of different young men, all with fringes, and starts to noisily joke about who might win the big race that evening. 'I like the Irish horse,' brays one. 'What's it called?' says another. 'I dunno. Something to do with dogs I think.' The group of them find this hilarious and the race train continues on its way.

Another group of young men, a little scruffier and less expensively dressed, have their copy of *Daily Racing Form* open and are engaged in an animated debate. One of them likes the Irish horse too, and is winning the argument until a small woman carrying a child turns to them and says: 'I can see why you like Master of Hounds, but he's certain to be overbet. I'd need at least 10-1 before I bet him, and he'll be somewhere nearer 5, so I'm not interested. He's no value, no value whatsoever.' Even the fringes are impressed, and, warming to her audience, the woman's face brightens and she tells the young men that the Irish horse Master of Hounds is definitely one to include in exactas and trifectas and superfectas, but she'd stop short of backing him to win. She launches into a description of all of the different combination bets available that afternoon and she concludes that she'll stick to those kind of bets, as there's no value around this afternoon. 'You know,' she says. 'Everyone wants to come and enjoy this day, and I won't enjoy it if I have a whole load of stupid bets and lose. So I'll keep trying to use a dollar or two to win thousands, and then I'll enjoy my day.'

The race train is taking all of us to Belmont Park on Long Island for the final leg of the series of races known as the Triple Crown. They start with the Kentucky Derby at Churchill Downs, move on to the Preakness Stakes at Pimlico, and finish here with the Belmont Stakes, New York's biggest racing day of the year. The woman's name is Veronica, and this is her 20th Belmont day out. She's from Yonkers, and she was here as a 14-year-old back in 1991 to see Hansel win. She's with her little girl Maisie, and this is Maisie's first Belmont Stakes. Veronica wants to start her off young in what she thinks is the finest New York tradition. They're both totally charming, and the brightness in Veronica's eyes drowns out the rest of the noise on the train: 'This day at Belmont Park is just the best day of the year. Everyone dresses up, all of the New Yorkers, and we *own* this race. And we get to see some of the best horses close up. Maisie can't wait, can you Maisie?'

Maisie is sweet and shy and so I leave them to it, although kick myself for not asking Veronica who she thought *was* going to win. She's a friendly face, and for all the jollity, there aren't too many of those on the race train, the Belmont Special. There are lots of checked shirts and blue blazers, there's a whole heap of loud bonhomie and guffawing, and every wallet contains store cards from Brooks Brothers and Banana Republic. This is serious WASP territory, and on New York's big racing day, they've all come out to play.

On its way to Belmont Park, the Long Island Rail Road takes in a stop called Jamaica. A nothing place which seems full of red warehouses and little life; a part of the city that has died. As the train pulls away in the mist, I spot a couple of US flags on top of one of the factories, and wonder if they've been put there simply because it's race day. A kind of 'hey folks, enjoy your day out', a gesture which is lost in the fog as soon as it's noticed.

After Jamaica, the train gets slower and the mist thicker, and no one seems sure where we are. A man uses the phrase 'horses for courses' and then struggles to respond to his wife's snappy request to explain exactly what that means. 'Well it means that certain horses like certain courses,' he says. And when that doesn't work he falls back on Federer at Wimbledon and Nadal in Paris. She understands now, and I'm silently amazed that someone can know enough about sport to know the difference between grass and clay, and yet so little as never to have heard the phrase 'horses for courses.'

We stop, and we see a line of buses, and I'm briefly wary at the thought that I might have to get off this train full of ruddy cheeked and brutish posh boys and climb onto a bus with yet more of them. If we're switching transport, then I'm sticking with Veronica and Maisie. At least I'll have someone to talk to. But then, a miracle. To the left of the train a large expanse of grass appears and a cheer goes up. It's a racecourse. It's the racecourse. And it's not the grass course in the middle that concerns us, but the muddy brown one that snakes around the outside. At Belmont, chinos and checked shirts or not, we'll be getting deep down and dirty.

The Belmont Classic is widely regarded in America as the race like no other. Part of that description is down to the fact that it brings the pizzazz of New York to the sport, but the main reason is its length. Most US races are run over any distance up to a mile and a quarter, with the emphasis on speed and not stamina, but to win this third leg of the Triple Crown the horses have to go a mile and a half, something that nearly all of them will never have done, and for that reason, it can be a dream for a certain kind of gambler. If you forget about what the noisy crowd tells you, and if you're brave enough to ignore the favourites, then you can get lucky here. Four winners of this race in the last 15 years had been returned at odds of bigger than 60-1, and as the rain continued to belt down, you could smell another upset here.

It hadn't been a vintage year for three-year-old horses in America. Achieving the Triple Crown is one of the holy grails of US sport, and yet not since Affirmed in 1978 had a horse managed to win in Kentucky, in the Preakness and then in New York. Legends such as that surrounding Secretariat had been made here. But there'll be more of Secretariat later. Much more. The favourite this time was a horse called Animal Kingdom, which had won the Kentucky Derby, and then finished second in the Preakness to another of today's runners, Shackleford. Animal Kingdom was clearly brave, having produced a storming finish in the Preakness despite the dirt which was kicked up from the track and into his face and which then caked in between his blinkers, rendering him severely discomfited at best and blind at worst.

Not many horses come into the Belmont with a chance of the Triple Crown, and so to win the first leg and then finish a brave and close runner-up marked out Animal Kingdom as a seriously good horse, what a friend of mine who is prone to horse racing hyperbole would describe as a 'quality individual'. And Animal Kingdom had been in Long Island the week before, taking a training spin around Belmont Park, and he had looked sensational, with his jockey John Velazquez complaining afterwards of sore arms, so much had he been compelled to pull the horse back.

Animal Kingdom would more than likely go off at a pretty short price, round about 2-1, and so he wasn't for me. Sometimes when you go racing you have to learn to let a horse win, allow a chain of events to unfold as you thought they would and not profit from them, like Hurricane Fly at Cheltenham. And that comes down to the price, always the price. I was happy to let Animal Kingdom become only the third favourite to win the Belmont Stakes. If he did, then at least I could mutter the words 'I was there' as I tore up my losing ticket.

Given the make-up of the racegoers on the train, I was expecting Belmont Park to be something rather different to Aqueduct. If that is a place where the disenfranchised and desperate while away their Saturday afternoons, then surely this was a place for people who belonged. People like this, the preppy types and their giggling companions, don't go to places where they feel anything less than comfortable. And, from the outside, the racetrack is beautiful: it has that red brick and ivy look that I'd always associated with a dreamy New England educational establishment, the place where the men spend days debating their forehand and the women are all fiercely intelligent and sexually charged. When I saw the facade of Belmont and the view from the parade ring, I half expected to see Jay Gatsby stroll out onto the lawn. Then I woke up.

Because once you walk away from the parade ring and out towards the racetrack, you are in a venue *exactly* like Aqueduct. It's a three-storey stone floored aircraft hangar, which operates at a low capacity on just about every single week of the year except this one. And the regulars were here to curse at the June intruders and bemoan the fact that the queue for a doughnut was that much longer, and the wait for a betting terminal more frustrating. More than once I heard an elderly fellow with a blue sailor's cap grumble: 'These motherfuckers don't even know *how* to bet, let alone pick a winner.' Jay Gatsby, if he was ever there, had hurriedly left the building.

If the rain hadn't been lashing down, then the day may have felt a little less like an excursion to a shopping mall for the upwardly mobile and the mentally ill. Belmont had made an effort, with a park to one side of the aircraft hangar turned into what looked like a frat party for the day, all beers, bands, and haircuts, and there were a few stabs at eclectic catering, from Philly Cheese Steaks to Lobster Rolls. The problem was that the rain kept much of the crowd huddled in the central part of the racecourse, the aircraft hangar, and so finding room to breathe was hard.

My punting plan for the day was to avoid anything with the words 'Moon' or 'Raven' in its name and to only bet on the big race, which was coming up at 6.35. That gave me ample time to go out and have a look at the track, make a few judgement calls about conditions, and see if I could find anyone who knew what they were talking about.

At 2 p.m., down by the finishing post, out in front of the soulless grandstand, conditions were gruesome. The rain was beating down and I was one of 20 or 30 people who were anywhere near where the race would take place. Water was already standing on the course and the tractor which ploughs along the track between every race, trying to flatten the dirt down and make it more even, seemed to be making things worse, all churned up and inhospitable. Unless the weather turned dramatically, the horses in the Belmont would be walking through Long Island treacle as they turned for home and went that extra quarter mile. I looked to the large scoreboard in the centre of the course, the brightness of the display accentuating just how dark and murky it was, and, amidst all of the facts and figures, I saw the going described as 'muddy'. Never miss a trick, these Americans.

There were ten races before the big one, and as the afternoon went on and the scoreboard looked ever brighter, the course was getting worse. You got the sense that anything could win, and so logic dictated that it was time to find a long shot. Time to put a line through a few names and see what was left. I went through the card in numerical order and what I was looking for were two logical selections, albeit two that veered towards being bigger prices. As I sat shivering inside, I knew that these conditions levelled things out so much that there was no point in backing any of the favourites unless there was an overwhelming reason to do so. Aiden O'Brien had sent over Master of Hounds from Ireland, the horse that they'd all been talking about on the train. He had stamina, which I was looking for, and class. My worry was that he had travelled back and forth over the Atlantic on three separate occasions in the last few months and that, at the end of such a tough season, a muddy straight at Belmont might prove too much for him. And he was sure to be third favourite at least. So he was gone. Stay Thirsty was a horse that loved Belmont

Park, a real horse for the course in the words of my friend on the train, but he didn't look to have the requisite class to win a race as good as this. He'd run well on the wet dirt before but his rating was well below many of the others in the field and he didn't look like he had the scope to improve. I thought that he could run better than his likely price suggested, but probably into a gallant fifth, so he was gone too.

When they go racing for the day most people try to look at a long list of horses and pick the winner. What I was doing was trying to work out what wasn't going to win and then see what was left standing. Number three on the list was Ruler on Ice, who had finished in the top three in his last five races, winning two of them. His rating was also low, but he'd been running over shorter distances than this, always finishing strongly. He could run badly, but if you took the leap of faith that Jose Valdivia, the Peruvian jockey, could manoeuvre him into contention as they hit the famous final turn, then he definitely had a chance, and because of his perceived lack of class, he'd be a big price. I left him on the list for now.

Next was the horse that had finished sixth in the first leg of the Triple Crown, Santiva. In that Kentucky Derby he had been stuck against the rail for much of the race and had actually done amazingly well to get out and get into as high a place as he did. He was another one who looked as if he might run better over the slightly longer distance, and his sire was Giant's Causeway, one of the bravest horses that I can remember, and a real favourite of mine. Giant's Causeway won five Group One races in a row in Europe, each of them by less than a length, and I hoped that some of those guts had been passed down to Santiva. I imagined the final furlong of the Belmont playing out with Santiva cast in the role of a mini Giant's Causeway, and there was no way that he was being left off the list.

If you're finding this a little hard to read, then I apologise. But I really wanted to explain to those of you who *don't* gamble the kind of thought process that goes on when you *do*. Belmont Stakes day would turn out to be the craziest, maddest punting day of my life, and the ending of this chapter involves a parrot, a pretty girl and a bruise on the side of my head. So you may want to read on.

At this point in my race analysis, I was still sitting in one of the corners of the aircraft hangar, water forming into a puddle alongside me and the music of a tragically bad grunge band thumping through the floor. Royal Ascot this most certainly wasn't. Brilliant Speed was the outsider that most of the experts felt had the best chance of causing an upset. He had gone off at 27-1 for the Kentucky Derby, and finished seventh despite finding little running room. He had to have a chance, but I just wondered that, with so many people looking for an outsider, that he might go off at a shorter price than he should. I could see Brilliant Speed winning, however, and so he stayed on the list too. I loudly heard a man in a pink shirt and tie, which he'd decided to wear with shorts and flip flops, tell his soon to be girlfriend that Animal Kingdom could not lose and was going to 'payyy for our holidayyy.'

You've probably guessed that I was feeling bitter and bullish, and with numbers 3, 4, and 5 already on the shortlist I hoped that I'd be able to rule a few more out quickly. Nehro was next, and was instantly crossed out. The horse had finished second in the derbies of Kentucky, Arkansas and Louisiana and had only ever won once. He was clearly classy, and had every chance of being in the top four, but I never touch horses that show no guts at the end of races. Particularly in races like this. That long run home through ploughed up dirt would find Nehro out, and he was 7-2. Gone. As was Monzon, number 7 in the race, who had attracted me initially because he made me think of Carlos Monzon, an Argentine footballer for whom I always had a soft spot. He was also the son of the 1995 winner Thunder Gulch (the horse, not the footballer), and another long shot with a chance. Every time he'd run against better horses, though, he'd failed, so I couldn't have him. Line through Monzon.

The next in line, Prime Cut, looked consistent but little else and wasn't going to win a race like this, and the next was the favourite Animal Kingdom who I'd already decided to ignore. The ridiculously named Mucho Macho Man (I hate people who spend fortunes on a racehorse and then give it a name that sounds like a burger chain advertising campaign) was a horse that a friend of mine back home had texted me about and suggested that he fancied. He'd finished stongly in third place in the Kentucky Derby and then been disappointing in the Preakness with little or no excuse. Animal Kingdom had already brushed him aside twice and he was another that looked solid rather than particularly gifted. He would be the choice of many who wanted to back a horse that would 'give them a run for their money', and as a result would definitely be too short a price. Because, strange though it is to relate, that's how it works on these big betting days, when a heap of people with money to burn descend on a race-track with people to impress.

I'd heard one of the fringes ask one of the regulars at Belmont who he fancied for the race, and with a wink he had said Mucho Macho Man. I then heard the fringe relaying this information to a group of increasingly drunk friends as if it were his own opinion, and then I followed splinter groups from this main group pass on the feeling that Mucho Macho Man was the one to be backed, an ill-conceived ripple effect that was spreading around the racecourse and, for all I knew, beyond. The reasons behind people recommending horses like Mucho Macho Man are worth closer inspection, and get right to the heart of why certain bets are such bad bets.

When most people go to a racecourse, what they want is to have a fun day. There are various elements which will come together to provide that fun: having a drink, sitting in the sunshine, being excited by the spectacle. And then there's the joy that can be gained from backing a winner, and more pointedly, the joy that can be gained from simply having a horse in contention. People want something to cheer on, with a hard luck story being preferable to nothing at all. A horse like Mucho Macho Man, that seems likely to finish in the top five but on closer inspection, unlikely to win, then becomes what New Yorkers call a 'wiseguy horse', a word of mouth fancy whose chances of winning are exaggerated in every telling. The hum of the racecourse was muchomachoman, muchomachoman, and all because people wanted something to cheer in the big race, but didn't mind about winning.

After that patronising dismissal of the average racegoer, I know that most of you will now want this chapter to end with Mucho Macho Man winning, and me being forced to eat my vicious words. We'll see.

The last two horses on the list for the Belmont were at either end of the betting. Isn't He Perfect seemed to be anything but, and despite my search for a long shot just required too much of a leap of faith, then Shackleford, the second favourite would wear number 12.

Shackleford had won the Preakness Stakes, and beaten Animal King-dom in doing so. Shackleford would be the horse that would make the race. He would sweep to the front from a wide draw, and then dictate the pace and try to stay there. Of all of the favoured horses, he was the one that I found hardest to discount, and so he stayed on my list.

So I'd whittled the field of twelve down to just four fancies. Shackleford, the game, front-running Preakness winner, who loved the rain and wouldn't go down without a fight. Brilliant Speed, the expert's outsider fancy, who may not like the rain and yet could take to the race like a horse to, um, water. Ruler on Ice, the horse who had been described by his trainer as 'insane', and who had been moved from his main stable to a smaller one, because he was 'causing too much trouble and disrupting the daily goings on.' And, while you all brush aside the image of a horse leaning against a bus stop and smoking a cigarette and chugging a bottle of brandy, a reminder that the fourth on my shortlist was Santiva, the son of Giant's Causeway and as courageous as they come. One of the four was second in the betting, the other three considerably lower down in a race that fancied horses rarely won. And, for those of you who aren't racing fans and who don't know the eventual outcome of the chapter, I'll give you a clue. One of the shortlisted four runs into a valiant fifth place, one of them finishes third, one of them never really gets into the race. And one of them wins.

The next few hours were spent awkwardly. I do have friends in New York, but none of them wanted to come racing, and so I stood on my own at what is very much a big group event. There's fun to be had people watching, but only so much, and so I went outside, got wet, tried a lobster roll, regretted it, and kept walking. I had the names of the four shortlisted horses running through my head and I decided to get rid of the fancied outsider, Brilliant Speed. The reason was as simple as the one that had bothered me in the first place, and one of which Veronica had warned me on the train. So many experts seemed to fancy the horse that it was bound to be overbet, and therefore too short a price. It was being given an unrealistic chance of winning simply because a few guys in a TV studio felt the need to tip something at a big price. It could win, but wasn't for me. And then there were three.

I wanted to leave the second favourite Shackleford out, again because the price was short and the day seemed made for an outsider. But the knowledge that the horse would almost certainly be leading going around the final turn was enticing. When conditions are this bad, a lead like that can be more decisive than it normally is, as the horses coming from behind are struggling to quicken and dealing with more dirt than usual being kicked in their faces. Front-runners were going well in the races throughout the afternoon, and it seemed crazy to kick Shackleford off the list just because he was one of the favourites. I didn't think that he was too short in the betting, I thought that he was about the right price, and so he stayed, along with Santiva and Ruler on Ice.

As my shortlist was trimmed to three, I realised that the rain had stopped for just a moment and that I was in the small tented village that stood between the parade ring and the frat party. In one of the tents, a small man was sitting behind a table and signing things. There didn't seem to be much of a fanfare about who he was, and so I went and took a closer look. The pictures he was signing were of Secretariat, arguably the greatest horse in American racing history, and the man was his jockey, Ron Turcotte. He was smiling and flirting and looking good on his 69 years, and I couldn't believe that there wasn't more of a crowd for a photo with him, for his signature. He had been on board Secretariat in 1973 when the horse had spreadeagled the field in the Belmont, and he deserved more exposure and respect than he was getting here. It's the nature of the event though, that he should be ignored. People were here either to party or have a bet on every race, not to catch a slice of history.

And so Ron sat there, and periodically did his stuff. I wanted to do something out of the ordinary, buy him a coffee and sit down and talk about Secretariat, but he seemed a little tired and distracted and so I asked him to sign a photo and spoke to him across a table. I told him about my dilemma, and said that I had the horses in the field for the Belmont down to three, Santiva, Ruler on Ice, and Shackleford, and what did he think. He looked at me with his eyes bright and asked why I'd got rid of the rest of the field. I told him that I figured that a long shot might win and that I was going to leave Animal Kingdom alone because of his price, but that I couldn't discount Shackleford. Ron said softly: 'Shackleford is the front-runner, right? What does the course look like now, pretty wet?' When I told him that it worse than wet, he whispered with his hand theatrically to one side of his mouth: 'Just remember that when it's that wet, front-runners are hard to pass here. Very hard.' I thanked him for his advice and shook his hand. And as I walked away I realised that there was still no one in the queue for autographs and he might soon feel devalued again, and so I turned round and saw him waiting patiently. 'Can I ask you one more question?' I said. And he nodded and I pointed to the famous picture of

Secretariat winning the Belmont by miles, and knelt down next to him and said: 'What did that feel like?' 'Easy,' he said, 'just easy.'

I shook his hand for a final time and wondered what it must have been like to be here in 1973 and to have seen Secretariat. The picture that Ron had signed shows the horse crossing the line with the rest of the field just a blur in the distance. That wouldn't be happening today, but it's the stories of moments like that, and the potential to witness them that make every day you go racing filled with wonder. And now I was walking around Belmont Park clutching one of those photos, signed by Ron. A sucker, as always, for a memory.

When I left Ron there was still an hour to go until the race, and so it was time for a final decision. I could just have backed all three of the horses on my painstakingly logical shortlist, but I'd gone to the race-course saying that there'd be only two, and I stubbornly stuck to that. I had two text messages to send, one to a friend who wanted some course-side advice, and another to Dan Roebuck, the conscience of this whole project to whom I had texted every single bet that I placed. I walked out once again to the front of the grandstand, and looked at the state that the course was in. The rain had come again, and cigars were being chewed rather than smoked, summer dresses protected and not displayed, and rather than there being expectation ahead of the big race, there was a feeling of wanting it to come so that we could all go home.

I decided that the heavens had decreed that the day would be like this, and that something surprising was more than likely to happen, and so I texted the friend in England that my two against the field were Santiva and Ruler On Ice. I got a text back saying that one was 60-1 and the other was 80-1 on Betfair, and was I sure? I replied confidently, and waited to see what happened. After a disappointing sandwich, I remembered that I'd forgotten to text Dan Roebuck, and before I did, I had another look at my notes, glanced out of the window one final time, and changed my mind. I thought about what Ron Turcotte had said about front-runners and remembered how dominant horses going from the front had seemed to be throughout the afternoon, and so my text to Dan read: 'Santiva and Shackleford to win the Belmont Stakes.'

I couldn't tell you, short of that scrambled reasoning about front-runners, why I did it. I placed my bets on those two and felt confident that I had come close to getting things right, and that the crowds of punters and Long Island smart guys who were shouting for Animal Kingdom and Mucho Macho Man were onto a loser, were chucking their money away.

The final build-up to the race was like nothing I had ever seen. As the horses came from the parade ring and down through the tunnel underneath the main grandstand and emerged into the rain of the racecourse, the tinny speakers around the place, which up until then had only been used to make announcements about prices and non-runners, suddenly struck up with the sound of 'New York, New York.' A grubby racetrack, a thunderstorm, and Sinatra. I didn't see anybody at the course, whether trackside with me or high up in the grandstands, who wasn't singing along, and there was a soaking wet conga starting all around me, pretty girls and old guys, cigars and lollipops.

I realised then what Veronica had talked about on the train. This was a day for New York to be proud of, and they had all come together. The preppy guys that I'd seen on the train might still have been a little aloof, but even they were joining in. It was sport and gambling as a leveller, not about how much you had, but how much you might be about to win.

Like Cheltenham, Belmont has a roar as well, and I heard it when the gates opened, and when, after an entire afternoon of anticipation, the race that I'd thought about so much was finally underway.

The first thing to notice was the extent to which the light had faded. I'd never before been to a race meeting at which the feature takes place at the end of the day, rather than at its heart. It was a marketing man's nightmare, but as the rain drove down and the colours of the jockeys shone through the twilight, it added to the drama. What drew a gasp from the crowd was that the favourite Animal Kingdom, carrying a lot of money, had slipped coming out of the starting stalls. John Velazquez had nearly fallen off, and used every ounce of experience to balance himself and try to ease the horse back into the race. But, in that moment, his chance had gone, and Animal Kingdom would not be adding the Belmont Stakes to his Kentucky Derby.

As I'd expected, Shackleford led them out, and Ruler on Ice was settled just in behind him, with all the other names that had been going through my head all afternoon tucked in behind. I quickly realised that the noise of the crowd was going to completely drown out the racecourse commentary, and I would have to rely on the colours to tell me how Santiva and Shackleford were doing. Shackleford was easy to spot, as he was still out in front, and Santiva was in a good position too. As the mud splashed up from the course, the colours became harder to distinguish, and so now I focused on the numbers, mercifully big in American racing.

Shackleford was number 12, and Santiva number 4. As the crowd got louder and louder, the horses came around the final turn with Shackleford still leading but starting to struggle. After the race, Shackleford's jockey Jesus Castanon said that his horse had done everything right but had got a little tired, and that looked a fair analysis: no excuses, just a long season getting to his legs as he tried to plough through the mud. As Shackleford dropped away, I was looking for the number 4 of Santiva, but he was struggling in the conditions and too far back and so I watched a thrilling finish develop between horses that I couldn't recognise.

I heard the crowd go up, and realised that Animal Kingdom had rallied from the back and was charging down the centre of the course, but too late, and as they flashed past the winning post the colours of the horse that had finished first shone through the darkness. Pink and orange with the number 3 standing out beneath them. It was Ruler on Ice, the horse that I had recommended to a friend and then discounted at the last minute. The rank outsider that returned 24-1 on course but had been 80-1 on Betfair before the race. I had had him in my grasp and had somehow let him go. My head started spinning as I tried to work out what had happened.

Later on that evening, once the madness had subsided, I went into a bookstore near Penn Station and picked up a book called *The Art of Choosing*. Having made such a series of bad choices, it seemed like something that I needed to read about, as I tried to get to the bottom of what had gone on. Why had I spent all afternoon whittling down a list and then changed my mind late on? What had led to that choice? I could have blamed Ron Turcotte, but that wouldn't really be fair:

it had to come down to me. Maybe, having wanted to take a leap of faith and back an outsider, I'd played safe and gone for what seemed like the safer option in Shackleford. It was agony to know how close I'd come.

There's a marketing concept called Vuja De, which encourages you to approach things with fresh eyes, rather than tired ones which have seen it all before, Deja Vu. And I had tried so hard to do that. Having been able to apply freshness of thought to Cheltenham it was frustrating to fall back into the old habits here, to come so close to nailing an outsider and then give it up at the last minute. I wasn't helped by a text from my mate back in England thanking me for the tip and asking: 'How the hell did you pick Ruler on Ice?' 'I didn't', I thought, 'I didn't.'

The Art of Choosing, written by a professor at Columbia Business School called Sheena Iyengar, will teach you a lot about yourself and the choices you make. There's one section of the book that fascinated me, and which taught me a lot about what went on that afternoon at Belmont Park. Iyengar claims, under the heading 'I am Unique, just like everyone else' that she can give the reader a personality assessment without ever having met them. And it reads as follows:

'You are a hardworking person. Others don't always appreciate that about you because you're not able to meet everyone's expectations. But when something really matters to you, you put forth your best effort. No, you're not always successful by conventional measures, but that's OK because you're not someone who sets too much store by what the average person thinks. You believe certain rules and standards exist for good reason, so you don't go out of your way to defy them, but what you really rely on to guide you is your strong inner compass. This strength isn't necessarily visible to others, and they may underestimate your resourcefulness, but sometimes you surprise even yourself with your abilities. You enjoy learning new things, but you don't think all education has to take place in a formal environment or have a specific purpose. You would like to be able to do more for the less fortunate, but even when you can't, you are caring and considerate in your own way. Life has dealt you a few harsh blows, but you've pulled through and you intend to keep up your spirits. You know that if you stay focused and confident, your efforts will bear fruit. In fact, a special opportunity is about to present itself in either your personal or professional life. If you watch out for it and pursue it fully, you will achieve your goal!'

Her profile is scarily accurate. The same tricks used by psychics and fakers, by women in underground rooms in New York and by those who tell us that they can see into the future, and she says that they all come down to three basic facts:

People are more alike than they think.
What people believe about themselves, or what they would like to believe, doesn't vary much from person to person.
Each person is convinced that he or she is unique.

It might be a crushing blow to finally realise that you're not unique but Iyengar proves it at every turn. And I think that was at the root of my problem at Belmont Park. I wanted to believe that I was different enough from the crowd to make my own decision, but in the end I had the choice between an outsider and a fancied horse, and I went for the fancied horse because it was the right thing to do. Normality is what changed my mind for me. People are more alike than they think.

I sat down on a step after the race, with my head in my hands, not out of despair, but more out of disbelief. I had been within touching distance of a really big one, and yet had somehow let it slip away. I could hear the chatter of the crowd as they filed back to the race train, and they were talking in astonishment and resignation. The outsider had won, but there was always next year. I felt a tap on my shoulder and looked up. There was a man standing there. He looked a little odd and so I moved backwards to take in the sight a little more fully. And he was grinning, while using his index finger to stroke the parrot that was sitting on his right shoulder. He asked if I'd had a bad day, and I said not really, just an interesting one. And he put his hand on my shoulder and said: 'Don't worry buddy, tomorrow's another day and your luck will turn.' I thanked him and walked away, and as I walked towards the train all that I could hear, over and over, was a parrot: 'Don't worry buddy your luck will turn. Don't worry buddy your luck will turn.'

As I waited for the train, cutting a dejected figure and soaked through, a girl in a blue dress, short black hair and sassy looking, came and asked me for the time. She heard my accent, looked me up and down, and said: 'All this way to lose money, huh, that's some trip. You should have a drink or two tonight.' I asked if she knew anywhere good, and she recommended one or two places. 'Fancy coming?' I said. And as she walked off I'm sure that I heard the word 'loser' from over her shoulder. So I leant forward against the glass of the still stationary train window, and banged my head so hard that I bruised it. That was Belmont Park: a parrot, a girl, a bruise on the side on my face. And a lesson in the art of choosing.

CHAPTER ELEVEN

Imagine that you're driving a car. It's dark, so your lights are on, and you get into that frame of mind when you really need to concentrate. You have to focus so hard that your head starts to hurt a little and your eyes ache as sharp splinters of light smash into your retina. And then imagine that obstacles are put in your way. Nothing huge, nothing obviously life threatening, but you know that you have to avoid them and that, if you clip the odd one then you'll be OK, but if you hit too many of them then the car will be going off the road, and you with it. You make 70 decisions on your journey, and then on each of the next three days, you have to make 70 more. They're never the same decisions, and the heater in your car is stuck on its highest setting which makes you sweat and feel that the lights get a little brighter until, by the fourth day, you feel that you'll never be able to concentrate again. If you think of that pressure, the constant need to make decisions, and the physical toll that takes, then you're thinking of what it's like to compete in a major golf tournament in America.

I've always been convinced that golf is the closest sport to gambling, and that good golfers have the minds to become successful punters. They could cope with the pressure, but more importantly they have the ability to assess a situation, and work out the best course of action. Having an overall vision and a staking plan is probably the most underestimated part of gambling, and course management likewise in golf. The ability not just to play the shots and hole the putts, but to know what is the right shot to hit at any given time and know what the potential reward is for the risk that you're taking. Players like Seve Ballesteros, the genius who would find himself stuck behind a tree and somehow conjure a way to move the ball onto the green, they're the ones who are always described as the great gamblers, but it's the players with the ability to make the most of their talent, the ones who know when to risk and when to play safe, that end up on top more often, and that best provide the template for how to gamble successfully. I know of at least one ex-professional who made a good if unspectacular living out of his course management skills who is now a very useful gambler. So I went to the Congressional Country Club just outside Washington DC, trying to find the winner and hoping to learn some lessons.

The US Open is the second golfing major of the season, preceded by the US Masters at Augusta, and followed by the Open Championship and the slightly undervalued USPGA. Majors are the standard by which the careers of golfers are defined, and that's why players like Tiger Woods and Phil Mickelson are obsessed with winning them while lesser golfers are happy to simply contend in one of the more prosaic US tour events. Golf and tennis are alike in having four events a year which set the standard, and a thriving series of tours which operate underneath the major championships, and provide worthy competition themselves.

The US Open is supposed to be different. Whereas many golf tournaments are won by a player shooting double figures under par, by four rounds in the 60s or at least something near it, par is meant to be a brilliant score at a US Open. In his definitive book on the subject, *US Open: Golf's Ultimate Challenge*, Robert Sommers, puts it very simply, and accurately:

> 'Not only does the USGA take the Open to the best courses, it sets them up to be much more testing than the players are accustomed to. In the philosophy of the USGA, a cham-pion golfer should be able to hit his driver both long and straight, so fairway widths are narrowed to between 30 and 35 yards, depending on the length and configuration of each hole, and bordered by rough up to five inches deep. The Open Champion is expected not only to hit the greens, but also to place his ball where he'll have a chance for a birdie. To test that ability to the full, the greens are kept firm and very fast.'

Sommers' style might be a little old fashioned, and the fairways are certainly narrower these days, but he makes the point neatly. This is not a tournament in which you get lucky; it's one that the great play-ers win. The other thing of which the USGA is rightly proud is that their tournament is an 'Open', and as such buys in whole heartedly to the American Dream. The theory is that 'Open' means just that: anyone can enter it and therefore anyone can win, but the bare facts are that this is a brutal test of golf, and it's not by accident that the best players in the world at any given time tend to flourish at this event more than any other. Every one of the courses which are used for this event, from Pebble Beach in California to Shinnecock Hills in Long Island, are set up to be as tough as possible. And this year's venue was extra special, if a little hard to get to.

The shorthand had it that this year's US Open was to be played at Congressional Country Club in Bethesda, Maryland. I'm sure that this is geographically true, but the course felt a world away from Bethesda's quaint and slightly scruffy main drag. If you drove to the tournament from Bethesda, then you ended up parked further away from the place that you'd started, and so the best approach was the take the metro and then get a green Peter Pan bus to the course from a metro stop called Grosvenor Strathmore.

From the urban looking Strathmore Park, with its red brick anonymity, you head eventually to Willowbank Drive, and past the Park 'n'Ride and Kiss 'n'Ride, and you start to move out of the town. You head down Tuckerman, where it's still pretty built up, then across Luxembourg and eventually past the Sandy Spring Bank and Balducci's Market at the Potomac Mall. It's there where you start to see shops that are called things like Yves Delorme, and Pierre Deux, and Renaissance Fine Art, and you know that you may just be moving somewhere slightly different. You turn right down Democracy Boulevard and the houses start to get bigger, as do the gaps between them. You can glimpse swimming pools and tennis courts through the trees, you go past the equally exclusive Avenel Club which used to host the Kemper Open. Eventually you come onto the wide avenue that runs alongside the course, and you're there.

I probably shouldn't have been too shocked, but the make-up of the crowd at Congressional was interesting. Remember, this is the tournament that calls itself 'Open' and plays heavily on that fact. We were a metro and a bus ride away from Washington DC, a city that, until the turn of the century had a black population of over 50 per cent. And yet, for all that people would like to believe otherwise, this was securely white middle-class territory. No great surprise in such a white middle-class game, but the fact that the tournament had been so poorly publicised in the city itself made me wonder if this was just how people wanted it. It certainly provided temporary jobs for the guys that I shared a bus with back from the course each day, the ones who joked about how people from Baltimore call cigarettes fugs, and people from Jacksonville describe them as lucys. But they didn't care about golf. They didn't feel any sense of pride in what was going on, they were more concerned about what the Redskins did next season, and indeed, given the potential for a lockout, if there'd be an NFL next season.

Ernie Els had won at Congressional the last time that the US Open visited, but the time before the tournament had thrown up a fairy story. The US Open at Congressional in 1964 took place in the middle of a drought, and the weekend featured weather conditions which would turn the tournament into one of the most unkind in golf history. A young Californian with curly hair called Tommy Jacobs led after the first round after a 64, and barely noticed on the leaderboard was Ken Venturi, who had gone through two rounds of qualifiers to get into the tournament, and who had come close to giving up the game in the early part of that year.

Even in the qualifying tournament itself, he'd started so badly that he had said to his playing partners that he was going to 'pack it in'. He'd been dissuaded, qualified, and now here he was. These were the days in which they used to play the final two rounds of the US Open on the same day, a Saturday, and as the weekend dawned Venturi suddenly caught fire and played the front nine of Congressional in just 30 shots. That flung him up the leaderboard as others started to fade, and suddenly, in temperatures of well over 100°F., Venturi was thrust into the spotlight. His swing had been remodelled by the legendary American Byron Nelson, and he'd been helped out by the patronage of a man called Ed Lowery, who as a ten-year-old had caddied for the only amateur ever to win a major championship, Francis Ouimet, in 1913. This tournament was in his bones, and golf, more almost than any other sport, loves its links to the past.

The 90 per cent humidity and the soaring temperatures were challenging the whole field, and as Jacobs struggled and Arnold Palmer's putting stroke started to let him down, Venturi was left with a great chance of winning. A letter that he received from his parish priest before the final two rounds stayed with him, and he says that under the most extreme pressure, it helped give him the patience to cope and the wisdom to play his own game. He continued to select the right shots to play, make the right decisions at the right times, but then his body started to give up. On Saturday afternoon, before the final round, Venturi was so dehydrated that he was seen by a doctor and advised not to carry on. He was in the danger zone, and the salt tablets and tea and lemon that he'd asked for, as well as copious amounts of water, weren't getting the fluid back into his body rapidly enough. Sommers tells the story of Raymond Floyd, Venturi's playing partner, going to speak to Venturi's wife Conni and telling her, 'he's sick.' But Venturi, with more salt tablets and a bag of ice cubes, did go out and play that afternoon, and the others cracked before he did. When Venturi holed his final putt, Floyd bent down and picked the ball out of the hole for him, and gave it to his playing partner with tears streaming down his cheeks. A man that I can only remember as a somewhat grizzled and cynical old pro in his later years was immensely touched by what he'd witnessed. And anyone reading the story of Venturi knows just what it takes to win a US Open at Congressional. This would be quite a test.

As it turned out, Venturi's US Open win came just in time. Later that year, he would be diagnosed with a disease in his hands that meant that he would never be the same player again. That strange fate that seems to govern sport, with an illogicality that sends fear into the heart of any gambler, had struck again. Venturi hadn't won in any way that could be predicted, he'd somehow won because he was meant to. And, after a career as a popular commentator, he would be back at Congressional this year to present the trophy to the winner. The problem for me was trying to work out just who that might be.

If you were using Venturi as a guide, then the man to turn to was probably the Spaniard Sergio Garcia. He had come close to quitting the game, but had decided to qualify for the tournament as the zest returned to his golf and the spring to his step. Garcia had come close in majors before, and was being tipped to go well on a course that would reward his brilliant iron play. The question, as ever, with Sergio, was whether his putting would hold up under pressure. The other thing to remember about Venturi was that he had blown a four-shot lead in the first major of the season, the US Masters, back in 1956, and there was a player in the field this year who had his own Masters demons to banish.

It sounds ridiculous now, but I barely considered Rory McIlroy as a potential winner at Congressional. He had thrown away a four-shot lead in the final round of the US Masters, and his implosion had been so absolute, that it was impossible to believe that a 22-year-old could cope so readily with what had been thrown at him at Augusta. By the end of the broadcast of the Masters, watching McIlroy was unbearable, and I wasn't the only one who sat at home and urged whoever was directing the TV coverage to stop showing the car crash. In the space of an hour, McIlroy had gone from being a confident young man and turned into a ten-year-old, lost and lonely. My mum wasn't the only person watching who wanted to give him a hug. If we were looking for clues, then perhaps we should have analysed more closely the way that McIlroy dealt with the interview he had to give just after he finished the 18th hole. He seemed gracious above all else, but also focused, and determined to learn the lessons from what had just happened. He had time on his side, and when you compared his reaction to that of a monosyllabic Tiger Woods, also beaten after he thought he might win, you at least felt proud that McIlroy had some class. What we didn't know then was just how much. I'd seen the youngster's inability to close out a major championship win as flakiness under pressure, when in reality it was just part of the learning curve, a series of painful steps on the way to greatness.

Woods had owned the US Open in the early part of the century, winning three times, most memorably at Torrey Pines in 2008 when he could barely walk. That was the last time that he'd won a major, and with injuries once again troubling him, he wouldn't be at Congressional. This was the first time since 1994 that Woods hadn't competed at the US Open, and yet his absence was everywhere. Sports reporting has become so postmodern in America that, in the days leading up to the event, we were treated to analysis of what Woods not being there would mean, and how strange it was that the media were still talking about him, even though he wasn't there. So sportscasters were reading out scripts that commented upon how curious those scripts were. Whatever those close to the sport might think, golf has some way to go before reaching its post-Tiger era.

Venturi's victory seems to prove the point that just about anyone lining up can win the US Open. One of the reasons that we love sport so much is that improbable stories happen, and yet we're always prepared to react to them, but rarely to try and predict them. It's far easier to pick a couple of players who'll be in contention, rather than go all out and look for something that's logic defying. The last ten major golf titles had been won by different players, but since Ernie Els won here at Congressional in 1997, the US Open had been won by a certain type of player. If you take the all-powerful Woods and his three wins out of the equation, then you're looking for someone who hits the ball very straight, putts well, and doesn't necessarily have a penchant for flair and imagination. Solid ball striking, rather than imagination, are what are needed in these events. Retief Goosen, Lee Janzen, Jim Furyk, Geoff Ogilvy, Lucas Glover. Brave men, players to have next to you in the trenches, but none that light up your television screen.

I wanted to answer the question of who it would be this time. I'd naively thought that golf would be the sport that, above all others, would reward a visit to the venue, and that a closer inspection of the players in practice would turn out to be a route to making a profit. I had images of watching the players on the practice range, of noticing that something was wrong, and of instantly being able to cross them off my list. And of walking the course and seeing just how sweetly someone was hitting the ball, and deciding on them as my outright winner, being proved gloriously and dramatically right on Sunday evening. All of that was fine in theory, but as I started to walk the course on Tuesday and Wednesday I realised that I don't really know anything about golf.

Don't get me wrong. I play a bit, badly, and it's a sport I love watching, especially live. I'd only ever been to Open Championships at windy courses in Scotland, where a day of standing in the rain would be rewarded with a whisky in the bar, so the experience of simply being at Congressional was one that I was cherishing. But as I followed player after player I realised that I had no idea who was playing well and who wasn't. I enjoyed watching the American Nick Watney up close, with a swing so loose and languid that it seems that he's going to drop the club every time he played a shot. He seemed to be hitting it straight, but I wasn't going to kid myself that I'd seen something. I'd fancied the Englishman Lee Westwood, as I thought that this course would suit the fact that he hits the ball so straight, but I was worried about his short game being up to the challenge, and as I watched him practising his chipping in the area sloping away from the clubhouse I didn't think that he looked particularly good. But I couldn't lie to myself and say that I was sure about what I was seeing. I watched McIlroy, who seemed to be enjoying himself, and Ian Poulter, who didn't, and the rest of the players seemed to pass by in a blur. I loved every minute, but I was learning nothing.

The most fun that I had was watching the local hero Fred Funk who had been one of the unlikeliest ever winners of a Players' Championship, a man who was fully aware of his responsibility to the crowd as he practised alongside someone that I quite fancied for the tournament, the pudding faced Texan Chad Campbell. Campbell has come close at major championships once or twice before, and seemed to have the kind of game that could work in a tough US Open. He looked uncomfortable as Funk messed around with the crowd. When Funk stood on the long par three second hole, he stood behind his ball and then turned the crowd and said: 'This is a par four, isn't it?' – he got a laugh, as the golf fans chuckled in the sycophantic way that they do, and Funk then played a horrible tee shot which fell into the bunker that's short and left of the hole. He turned again and said: 'Told you it was a par four' – I sensed that Campbell wasn't coping with any of this very well, he's one of those straight up and down US pros who likes to stay in his bubble and play in his bubble. The fact that he would be lining up with Funk early on Thursday was a worry, and I could at least put a line through his name.

And I watched Phil Mickleson practice. Mickleson was going through his round the clock putting routine, where he places balls all around the hole and then tries to hole each putt as he moves around and changes the angle. He wasn't getting too much further than ten past two before he missed one. There were those who feel that Mickleson was somehow due to win this US Open, as he'd finished second on five occasions, but he'd have to putt better than that, and I was happy to cross him out too.

With a few thoughts, but no real ideas, I decided to talk to the locals, and tried to find some people who played the course regularly.

The best way of doing this seemed to be to sit in the stands which were located next to just about every green, listen in on people's conversations, and work out if they were Congressional members. I became used to listening out for the right kind of conversation. Anything that covered real estate or the state of the markets hit paydirt, and, despite the fact that these people were rich enough to own the entire street that I live on, they were open and friendly and told me what they thought about Congressional.

All the members I spoke to expressed their surprise at just how easy the course seemed to be playing. They were used to the rough being a lot deeper and thicker than it looked today, and they felt that the USGA had made a mistake and misjudged the weather. There had been storms predicted in recent weeks which hadn't materialised, and no water meant that the rough had refused to grow, and so the course was looking exposed and nowhere as difficult as it ought to be. So many members told me this that I wondered if it was an example of Groupthink, and that somehow they'd all been talking to each other, so I went out to see for myself.

It's difficult to judge the state of a golf course when you haven't seen it before, and have nothing to relate to, but the rough didn't look very long, or particularly thick. I walked the course five times over two days, and made a point of checking how penal the rough seemed in the key areas, just off the fairway where drives would be landing and around the greens in the areas that wouldn't be protected by bunkers. I got down on my hands and knees on more than one occasion and looked closely at the rough, and I came very close to another security guard moment to echo Philadelphia when I decided to stretch out on my stomach on the fourth hole and study the grass intently. I got a quizzical look and a tap on the shoulder, but was politely allowed to continue with my day, provided that 'I didn't do that again.'

Covering any kind of mileage around the course was made more difficult by the humidity. When Venturi won in 1964 it had reached 90 per cent, and while it wasn't quite there yet, the forecasts for the weekend suggested that the air in the valley of the Potomac river would get heavier and heavier. The hot air blows in from the Gulf of Mexico and the mountains that lie on the other side of Montgomery County are just tall enough to keep it trapped. That means even on a day when it's not sunny, you can almost reach out and touch the air as you walk through it. It changes shape and smothers you for as long as you're out in it. The locals are used to it, and their reaction to the man with the English accent commenting on the weather was entirely predictable. 'You think this is bad,' went the refrain, 'just wait until it gets *really* humid.'

The US Open is meant to be tough, but the USGA became so obsessed about making courses ultra hard that we had the Shinnecock Hills farce of 2004, when the greens were ridiculously fast and the tournament became a lottery. Mike Davis took over the responsibility for setting up the courses, and made them a little easier, easy enough anyway to encourage aggressive play, which of course would make for better TV. And I'm all for that. Except that at Congressional they went way, way too far. Before the tournament, the USGA's agronomist, a man by the name of Stan Zontek, said on the eve of the first round that the preparations were behind and that he wasn't sure that they could make up for lost time. You could clearly see on Tuesday that there was brown on some of the greens and that this could be a disaster. Zontek said of the rough that: 'the golfers are going to love it.' The last two weeks had been staggeringly hot, and the greens were struggling to hold up, while the rough simply hadn't grown at all, hadn't needed cutting. That Zontek quote seemed to go largely unnoticed. He felt that the golfers would love conditions, and he should know.

I decided to check the prices on what the winning score might be, and wondered if bookmakers were presuming that this would be a difficult test. If the price was right, that would be one bet, but I was no nearer finding my idea of the winner, and so I kept walking.

Golf in America walks the line between powerful over sincerity and downright insincerity. And that tightrope seems to become narrower every year. It's strange how the reporting of a sport can affect the attitude of those spectating, and yet at Congressional you could hear it everywhere, the TV phraseology that was the hum of the golf course. The main culprit is a man called Jim Nantz. He's a fine commentator, and his love of the game is beyond doubt, but his deep voice is one that you most associate with a particular kind of golfing syrup that can become hard to bear.

The first point of note, and this habit has seeped through to the players themselves, is the need to prefix ordinary and fully understandable words with the word 'golf'. So any reference to the course becomes the 'golf course', and the ball becomes the 'golf ball'. The hole often turns into the 'golf hole' and so on. It hints at a reverence for the sport, a feeling that a hole may be a hole in normal life, but once it becomes a 'golf hole' then it is truly blessed. And to make things worse on the sugary sentimentality front, these days the US Open concludes on Father's Day in the USA, and that allows the gloopy emotion to come out in full force. There was something truly moving about the hug that Graeme McDowell gave his dad after pulling off his breakthrough win at Pebble Beach the year before, but that felt like an organic reaction, whereas in other years you can feel the dad being lined up, the emotion being pre-programmed, so that commentators could reach for their lines which affirm those basic principles of life, and somehow the golfing nation could be covered in honey. Give me Floyd's tears at Venturi's sacrifice any day.

I overheard spectators at Congressional apeing Nantz as if that was the way that you had to talk about golf. 'If Mickleson gets this up and down that will be some golf shot', 'This is one difficult golf hole', and my favourite of all, a man who watched an approach shot by an American journeyman called Ryan Moore and, wild eyed, turned to his friend and shouted, 'OH. MY. GOD.' It was such a lunatic reaction that I gave the man the benefit of the doubt and, as the players moved on, I asked him if Moore was a friend of his. He looked surprised and said: 'No. But it was some shot, wasn't it?' I kept my distance after that, and before you judge me too much for being cynical, that incident didn't happen during the tournament itself, but in one of Ryan Moore's practice rounds. Go figure.

You may think that I'm adopting a tone here about Americans, but the strange thing is that I love America. Really love it. In a movetheretomorrowificould way. Walking around this place, with its big men in bright shorts, its bandy-legged jocks in flip flops, and its stick thin women in sun visors, made me wonder why, and I started to think about why I get such a buzz every time I'm in New York, or California, and even Washington and Philadelphia. And then I got it. The reason that I love it is tightly tied in with what irritates me about the place. The reverential attitude towards golf, the overreactions to good shots by run-of-the-mill players, the need somehow to constantly establish that we're witnessing something special. All of that comes from an optimism, and a belief that the everyday can be extraordinary, and that on any given day anything might happen. And that's at the root of the American attitude to life, and I think that's why I love the place so much. A natural cynic, I'm drawn, it seems, to the optimists. There are plenty of shades of grey in between, but that's the fundamental difference between Brits and Americans, and you can see it in our approach to life, sport, to everything. The American perspective starts from a point of view of optimism, the British from a point of view of cynicism. Imagine, for a moment, that a friend of yours has just got a new job, a pay rise and a rise in responsibility. In America, I believe that more often than not the conversation would go like this:

'Have you heard that Andy's got a new job?'

'Has he?'

'Yeah, you remember he wanted that opportunity out in Florida? Well, he went for an interview, and they decided to give him a chance.'

'Oh brilliant, good for Andy – he's worked really hard for that, I hope it works out for him.'

Then imagine the same conversation in England:

'Have you heard that Andy's got a new job?'

'Has he?'

'Yeah, you remember he wanted that opportunity out in Basingstoke? Well, he went for an interview, and they decided to give him a chance.'

'He'll be a bit out of his depth, won't he? Anyway, how
did he get a job like that? He must know someone.'

Don't get me wrong, I'm not suggesting that cynical Americans don't
exist and that there's no such thing as an optimistic Briton, and I'm
also aware how important someone's location within a country is, but
I don't think it's an unreasonable observation, and is a fair starting
point when you assess the difference between the two countries.

It was time to stop philosophising, to remember why I was here,
to knuckle down and find a bet or two. It was Wednesday, and, having
spent some more time avoiding stewards and lying down to look at
the rough, I had already decided to back a winning score of four
under par or better at 5-4. That would be the headline bet, but the
name of the potential winner left me baffled. It's at this point before
any major championship that I usually decide to have a bet on the
American Brandt Snedeker. I'm convinced that Snedeker will win a
major one day, and I think I know why. My greatest ever golf bet
was one I had on Justin Leonard to win the Open Championship
back in 1995, when he had been relatively unfancied and a decent
price. Leonard won because of a phenomenal putting performance
on the final day at Royal Lytham and St Anne's, when he shot a 65
and blew the field away. So, since then, I've liked streak putters, players who might do nothing for a few weeks, even a season, and then
suddenly catch fire. Snedeker was one of those, and had already won
this season, beating Luke Donald in a playoff at a prestigious US tour
event called the Heritage. I worked out that I'd backed him for something like the last ten majors in the hope of him hitting form at the
right time, and he'd always disappointed. The problem with holding

on to an idea like that is that you never know when to stop, constantly in fear that *this* could be the major when he does it. You resolve never to back the player again and then cowardice and uncertainty drags you back in. I would find an alternative, but I was pretty sure that I'd also be backing Snedeker.

And then, after another day of prowling the fairways and trying to work out just what might happen over the next four days, I started to feel strange. My legs turned red and every step that I went suddenly became an effort. I worked out that the sun may have got to me, and went to the front of the queue for one of the water fountains, doing my best to shove my head underneath the rapidly diminishing trickle. That didn't work, and so I ended up filling bottle after bottle with water and pouring it over myself. I got some funny looks, but by that point I was beyond caring. There were people in the queue behind me and so, still an Englishman in my near-delirium, I filled the bottle, poured it over myself, went to the back of the queue and then repeated the dose, over and over. I would happily have done that for the rest of the afternoon, but then a kind old lady, who I didn't really deserve, suggested that maybe it wasn't working and that maybe I should head for one of the medical tents.

I think that she helped me get there, although I'm not sure as I can't really remember the walk, but I do remember waking up in cool, tented surroundings, with a beautiful blonde woman looking down at me. It turned out that the super professional on-site doctors had been a bit short of business, and so when I arrived, soaked through and unintelligible, they all pounced on me wanting to help. For some reason, the female doctor from California was at the front of the queue, with the others waiting a few steps behind her, twitching and on the front foot. I may have felt terrible, but I was being treated by a young Christie Brinkley, and so I was beginning to cope.

She asked if I'd been out in the sun, a question that a 100 per cent me would have scorned with a 'no, I got here on a sledge', but in this semi-conscious state I murmured that I had and that it had probably been a bit much for me. The consultation involved her being kind to me, me agreeing with everything that she said, and then her and her colleagues feverishly consulting just out of earshot. I started to wonder if there was something fundamentally wrong, such was their level of debate, but I think that I was their first case of the week and so merited the best that they had. She finally sat down next to me and told me in a sombre voice that they'd give me some painkillers and some antihistamines and that the best thing was probably for me to drink water and sit down in a dark place for a while. I asked if that dark place could be in this tent for a bit and she said: 'Sure.' And she led me by the hand to a corner of the tent and said that I had as long as I wanted. I managed to resist the temptation to awkwardly flirt with her, and silently made my exit, feeling refreshed, but no closer to finding the winner.

On my way home, I met an extraordinary man in a diner in Bethesda. The food wasn't that good, and unless you like sloppy eggs, unsmiling service and coffee that tasted only slightly of coffee then it really wouldn't be the place for you. He was a few pounds overweight, and wore a cap at an angle, and when he heard my accent he told me that he was a soccer fan, Manchester United in fact. This wasn't a great surprise after seeing the number of Manchester United shirts that there are all over Maryland, but he knew his stuff and started waxing lyrical, with genuinely misty eyes, about George Best. I wondered why the story touched him so much and then he told me that he had the same problem as George, but that he'd conquered it, 22 years and counting now. He showed me the coin that he had been given by Alcoholics Anonymous, which was proudly emblazoned with the number 22 and said that 23 would be coming in a month, God willing. He spoke calmly and intelligently, in a measured twelve steps way, and the often repeated message that he left me about addiction was: 'You have to surrender in order to win.' I was still a little delirious, and on reflection realised that I'd probably surrendered a long time ago.

What followed was a feverish evening in my hotel that was located at the end of the main strip in Bethesda. The air conditioning was broken, and that, combined with the effects of the sun earlier on, made me feel like something from an Edvard Munch painting. I veered between sitting bolt upright in bed and then falling into an unhelpful sleep in an armchair, and wasn't helped by the occasional reading of a book about addiction that I'd picked up locally. Throughout this journey, I became a little obsessed with reading accounts of other people's failings and how they'd got through them. Some authors, like Augusten Burroughs, write disarmingly well about where they went wrong and how they set about putting things right, while reading others feels like rolling around in their vomit.

I was engrossed in a depressing volume written by a woman called Nancy Makin about how she had lost 530 pounds in weight. (Yes, I did a double take at the figures as well.) It wasn't ideal 3 a.m. reading in that I found that the story of her tragic gluttony made me hungry and the supposedly uplifting bit towards the end made me sad. Her overeating had been down to boredom and loneliness, and she described how: 'My incarceration crept up on me over years, built not in a day, but in millions of moments, one upon the next, as if each were a single brick in some ominous structure of my own design.' She only escaped and started on the road back to normality when some friends got hold of a second-hand computer and gave her something else to focus on and so she started to engage in syrupy email conversations rather than pancakes. Her summing up of her condition, though, hit me like a lightning bolt at around 6 a.m. as the sun started to rise over Bethesda:

'Food is the obese person's tool to stuff feelings. We eat to avoid a hellish reality: the thought that we are worthless, for whatever reason. Food, for a moment, becomes the non-judgemental friend that will soothe that harsh reality. It's the obese person's heroin, but instead of track marks, we sport stretch marks.'

I'd definitely gambled during those six months of a different hell for the same reason. Avoiding a hellish reality, in my case the fact that Emma didn't want me any more, was definitely a large part of it. Wallowing in self-pity, and not wanting to see friends, and filling the holes in my day not with mountains of food but with a series of bets that were never going to win.

I must have gone to sleep, dreaming of doughnuts, and after all that realisation and self-loathing, coupled with sunstroke, I was freaked out. I thought back to what I'd seen on the practice days and hurriedly wondered if I had time to make up my mind, but then I noticed that the morning had nearly gone. I'd desperately wanted to get there at 6 a.m., in good time to see the first players tee off, but I'd made a mess of that. For the first time in my adult life, I'd allowed a major golf championship to start without me picking a winner.

That was no problem, I thought, maybe I could watch for a while and then come up with something at halfway. Although, by halfway, the tournament was as good as over. Rory McIlroy was sensational for those first two days, and near perfect in the end on all four. There were gasps around the course as the red number next to his name went higher and higher, and his score got better and better. After what had happened in the Masters, there were plenty of people offering the opinion that he would fall apart again, so I played the role of Brit, one with which I'm not massively comfortable, and confidently told them that he'd be fine. The numbers were looking great for my bet on the winning score too. A thunderstorm on the Thursday night had softened up the greens, which meant that now the course was unprotected by the rough and the greens soft and receptive to shots. Players could keep the ball in play, they could stop it near to the hole, and they could take the course apart.

On television, playing in a major golf tournament looks serene. You see shots of the crowd, of course you do, and when a player hits a wayward shot and his ball ends up where the crowd is, then you see them standing mighty close. But that's as close as they seem to get to reality: the rest of it is all empty fairways and silence punctuated by the odd roar from elsewhere. Well, the first thing to say is that those pictures of the players don't come out of the ether, and nor does the sound of the club striking the ball. When a player is deemed worthy of following, then every shot that he plays is framed by a cameraman and an assistant standing behind him, and a sound man standing holding a long furry microphone. The on-course commentary doesn't come from the heavens either, and the major groups will have a guy from NBC, a reporter from Sky and a few others all populating the fairway. When you add to that the radio commentators and the security guards and the rules officials then you have quite a group. It's not just Lee and Luke and Martin enjoying a round as if it were a Sunday morning back home.

The microphone picks up the noise of the club hitting the ball, the swooooosh as the player makes contact that adds to the drama on TV, and it will also pick up some of the lunatic shouts from the gallery, that seem, and certainly are, pre-planned. Any golf fan will tell you that it annoys them, but one of the secret joys of watching a big tournament from America in the old days were the cries of: 'get in the hole' or 'way to go' that interrupted the pompous tones of Peter Alliss. To hear *that* noise, in *those* accents, was as otherworldly as the Denver Broncos against the Cleveland Browns, and to a 15-year-old watching Jack Nicklaus win the Masters at the age of 46, it seemed like a noise from somewhere that you'd never go. Well, the getinthehole merchants have died away, and if the jocks that throng the fairways *do* say that, it's done with a sense of irony, and followed by a gale of laughter. The cries are much more imaginative now, my favourite being the man standing next to Martin Kaymer on Thursday when he sensibly chipped out of the rough on the fifth hole: 'Manage the course, Martin. Manage the course.' I even heard one American fan, a large man with a beard, say: 'I hate that prick Westwood. I'm gonna slam the door of the john just as he takes a shot.' He then went to the toilet and did just that, but mercifully Westwood stayed on line.

There's pressure on the top players because of who they are, but there's pressure on the unknowns too, of a different kind. It's hard to be a Donald or a Westwood or a Watson, but it must be harder to be a Tryon, a Barr, a Wilcox. These guys play at an unsexy time of day, when television couldn't possibly be interested, and you often see them hitting shots with no gallery at all. It's one thing being distracted by ambient noise, another to play in the knowledge that no one really cares how you perform.

Sitting by the sixth green on that first day, the crowd in the grandstand were waiting for a big name to appear, or at least for a low score to appear on the scoreboards that follow every group. For one excruciating hour, I watched Chappell, Kim and Rock followed through by Mills, Harto and Pinckney, then Irwin, Nelson and Gealy came through and Deforest, Williams and Heffernan finished things off. Robert Rock would end that first day being something of a story, but at that point no one knew or cared who these people were. They'd applaud a good shot, but the circumstances made it absolutely clear to the players that they were simply bit parts, making up the numbers to give the tournament the sense of openness and lack of privilege that is inferred by its name. But they had little chance.

Nor did anyone. McIlroy shot an opening round 65 and then backed it up with a glorious 66 in his second and nobody could get near him. I struck up a conversation with a man whose job it was to clear the players and the officials from the course in case of a thunderstorm. When the electrical storm finally arrived on Friday we cowered together under a metal bridge. A guy with a beard who'd had a bit too much too drink held up an umbrella against the rain that was sweeping onto us and told me that McIlroy wouldn't win, that he would fall and that YE Yang would catch him. I spelt it out with my new found Britishness: 'Listen mate, if he shoots par, par, over the weekend he wins. End of story.' And I believed what I was saying. McIlroy was six shots clear and, unlike Augusta, no one behind him seemed to be playing well enough to challenge. The Korean YE Yang was closest, but I'd followed him round on that second day and been amazed at how badly he was striking the ball. Shots into the green were wayward, and it was only his remarkable short game that had kept him going. If McIlroy wasn't going to win, I couldn't see how Yang would either.

Events at Augusta meant that there would always be doubters, and before the third round, a blogger on the Betfair Forum wrote an excellent and considered piece about why McIlroy probably *would* win, but might not. Included in the reasoning were the facts that he'd blown up before, that the course, easy though he'd made it look, *was* tough, and that he was going from playing in a threeball to a twob-all, which would bring his game under more scrutiny, and heighten the pressure as a result. I agreed with pretty much everything that the blogger wrote. McIlroy was the obvious winner, but there was a chance that someone would come from behind and put pressure on him, and there were some awfully big prices out there about some exceptional golfers. Lee Westwood, Matt Kuchar, Sergio Garcia. I, of course, went for Snedeker: a player who'd proved already that he could attack and come from behind and win, and one who I still believed had the game to win a major, particularly one like this. He was available at 45-1 to win and 14-1 to win without McIlroy, and sitting as he was at two under par, he seemed in the perfect position to strike. He would be my second bet of the tournament, although for once I was happy to hope for the unlikely rather than the near impos-sible, and so I backed him at 14-1 to finish second to McIlroy.

So, even though I'd missed the chance to back him beforehand, here I was again, throwing my money at Snedeker. And, of course, I was wrong to do it. Having played exceptionally for two days, Snedeker continued to strike the ball well, but seemed incapable of holing a putt. He'd finish creditably, but it was the Australian Jason Day who came through the field to finish second as Yang's poor ball striking finally caught up with him. I'd been right about the Korean, but wrong about the identity of the man who would catch him.

All of that lying down in the rough had been worth it though. All the locals I'd spoken to about the course beforehand were right. You only need one player to finish better than four under to win the bet, but in the end many of the statistics were record breaking. McIlroy ended on 16 under par, with 19 other players under par, the second most in the history of the US Open. Jason Day's second place total of eight under par would have been good enough to either win or tie the winning score in all but six US Opens since 1948. I needed one player to finish four under or better, and in the end the drought followed by the thunderstorms, and the inability of the USGA to react to them, meant that ten players were better than that mark, and the bet was won comfortably. Snedeker finished on three under, tied for eleventh place, and Lee Westwood once again earned a top-three finish, but his short game looked short of top class. For all that, though, even I have to accept that Westwood is a likelier major champion of the future than my old friend Snedeker.

McIlroy didn't stay in Washington for long. The day after his win, he fulfilled a sponsor's commitment at Willowbend Country Club on Cape Cod. The newspapers were all calling him a kid, a phenomenon, a Celtic Tiger, and yet he was out playing golf again before the ink on the headlines was dry. As he did that, I decided to put the unrealistic atmosphere of the golf course behind me and head to the centre of the political world, which was both 20 minutes and a world away. I wanted to indulge another punting passion of mine, or at least try to. Since I read a copy of *Time* magazine in a bored moment on a train in my teens, I've been a little obsessed with American Presidential elections, and have had my moments in terms of predicting them. I've had the odd nightmare, like being hugely confident that John Kerry would beat George Bush, but have always enjoyed trying to work it out, and had been successful with a decent-sized bet on Barack Obama to be the next president. As always with me, it hadn't been enough to celebrate Obama's win as a potential changing of the world order. I had to be able to say that I had a few quid on him at 8-1, months before the Democratic selection process started.

The American politics thing means that I love the TV show *The West Wing*, and in an alternate life, with a vastly bigger brain, a different nationality and 50 times the charisma, I'd have loved to be Josh Lyman, the suave and funny Deputy Chief of Staff played by Bradley Whitford. There's one scene in particular that I'd always wanted to replicate, and I thought that this was my chance, the only one that I'd ever get. I don't know why it always appealed to me so much, but in the scene in question, Lyman goes for a late drink with a beautiful lobbyist, and orders a martini with two olives. His date finds that funny, and the two olives thing becomes a mini motif of their relationship. The bar is a hotel bar, the Marriott, and I felt suitably suave and intelligent as I sauntered into the real thing, fashionably late on that Monday night. I'd arranged to meet a friend of a friend of a friend, a lobbyist, and I hoped that she'd be suitably beautiful and impressed by my order, all ironic and aware.

The first thing that happened was that my phone buzzed. A text from the lobbyist saying that she couldn't come. I'd hoped to discuss the following year's election, and see what she thought of my theory that the Texas governor, Rick Perry, had a big chance at a double figure price of wresting the presidency from Obama. Instead of that, I was suddenly alone, and so I ordered my two-olive martini. When the barmaid brought it, I smiled what I thought was a sophisticated smile and wondered aloud how many times she'd had that order. She smiled back and said: 'What, do you mean today?' It was time to leave Washington behind, political fantasy unfulfilled, golfing bet won, and dignity just about intact.

CHAPTER TWELVE

In terms of the events that had cost me so dearly back in 2009, that was it. The US Open had been the final link in that regrettable chain, and I hadn't done badly. I hadn't come anywhere near winning back the five-figure sum that I'd lost, my miscalculation in Hamburg had seen to that, but I reached the end of the summer feeling happy. I suppose that before I started I would have accepted being in profit by a penny as it wasn't about the money any more, it was a case of proving a point. To myself, if no one else. And I'd done better than a penny. Cheltenham week and Li Na had been the highlights by a long way, and I walked away from Congressional £6,400 in profit, regretting the French Cup Final and the Klitschko fight in particular, feeling disciplined but also restricted by the staking plan that I'd set out. Then again, I suppose that's the point of a staking plan.

I wasn't quite finished, though. The idea had always been to end this on the Sussex Downs, in bright sunshine on a Saturday, and the colourful cavalry charge that had drawn me into gambling in the first place. My first ever bet, placed on my behalf by a boy at my school who looked older than me, had been on the Stewards' Cup at Goodwood in 1986. I was 15 years old then, and I suppose that I've been hooked ever since. My fancy that year was a horse called Green Ruby, and I couldn't tell you now why I liked it back then, but it won at 20-1, and I sat that evening with a dirty looking £20 note in my hand, grinning from ear to ear. I often wonder how things might have turned out if the horse had lost. Would I have realised straightaway how stupid gambling was as a pursuit and given it up as a bad job? I'll never know, but Green Ruby and that race set me off on the trail that I'm still following now.

Ever since that day, I've tried to find the winner of the Stewards' Cup. Never missing a year, always insistent on a study of form or a search for inspiration the night before, whatever else I'm supposed to be doing. I've missed bits of weddings and been late for various jobs all because I've wanted to read about or watch that race. And the really stupid thing about it is that I'm awful at finding the winner. The Stewards' Cup is a dash over six furlongs, the draw has always had a massive influence on what happens, and for all the logic and hard work I've tried to apply, it's all come down to luck. Since Green Ruby, in the space of 25 years, only twice more have I found the winner: Superior Premium in 1998, at 18-1, and Evens and Odds, a year ago, at 33-1. The prices mean that, had I backed everything to a level stake, then I'd actually be up on the Stewards' Cup in that 25-year period, so I suppose that I shouldn't be too downhearted, even though it feels at times like a pointless pursuit.

So, the final step along the road would be a bet on the race that started it all off for me. But this time I wouldn't slavishly study form, or follow a tip, I'd try something different – something to do with a book that I'd read, and something that brought everything together in my head, as I wondered how my story would end.

If I'd really wanted it to have a happy ending then I should have just stopped. It would be a tale of someone who messed up, and then tried to put things right, in his own mind at least, by proving that he could travel to the events that had broken him and make some kind of profit. But I hadn't really proved anything. Li Na's win was an outrageous piece of luck, a nod and a wink from a friend who considered her as an afterthought. John Higgins may have shown an iron will, but when he was down and out in that semi-final against Mark Williams I'd lost all confidence, and for all of his amazing stick-ability, there had still been an element of luck. Strangely, I didn't feel that I'd been that lucky at Cheltenham, just that I'd shown gambling discipline for the first time in my life and put in the hours. And it had paid off.

I read two books along the way that had a huge impact on me. One of them, *The Art of Choosing*, jumped out of me from a bookshelf near Penn Station as I tried to put into context just what had happened on Belmont Stakes day. The other was recommended a long time ago by a friend and colleague of mine, Lydia Hislop. Lydia works, among other things, as a presenter on Racing UK, and loves horses and horseracing with a passion. She's seen as a divisive figure in the sport, but that's only because she says what she thinks. There are figures like her in every major sport and yet very few on racing broadcasts. The ability to tell the truth, even if it's not what people want to hear, is something that should be prized, and not dismissed. But too often jockeys and trainers cold shoulder her on the basis that she doesn't know what it's like to ride a horse in a big race, and therefore can't possibly comment on it. I think that's nonsense, and I know a lot of people within the sport who actually think that she's right a large percentage of the time but don't dare say it. And, more importantly than anything, she's a punter, so I like her.

Anyway, Lydia isn't one for wasting words and one day she walked up to me at Cheltenham and said: 'You should read a book called *The Wisdom of Crowds*, I think that it will help with your book.' She was right, and all I can say to you, particularly if you're a gambler, is go out and read it. I'll explain a bit, but could never do it justice. The fundamental principle of James Surowiecki's work comes from an experiment that was carried out by a British scientist called Francis Galton at the start of the last century. Galton believed that society could only be driven forward by the few, and that the vast majority of people were actually pretty stupid. He was at a country fair one day, and decided to conduct an experiment that centred on a large group of people, around 800, who were trying to guess the weight of an ox. The crowd was what he regarded as average, consisting of 'many non-experts', and more intriguingly, people who in his mind were 'like those clerks and others who have no expert knowledge of horses, but who bet on races, guided by newspapers, friends and their own fancies.' Ring any bells?

Galton was trying to prove how stupid the crowd was, but in the process he discovered the opposite. He took each person's guess, and worked out the average. The crowd was one pound out, and therefore, had democratically come astonishingly close to the correct answer. The intelligence of the crowd had been established, and Galton had managed to prove the opposite of what he'd intended.

Surowiecki makes the case for this collective wisdom compellingly, and has an explanation for it as well, which is that most of us have limited decision-making powers, and 'instead of finding the best possible decision, we will often accept one that seems good enough.' When we go racing, we presume that the best thing to do is ask a handful of experts what their opinion is, and follow that, whereas if we ask a crowd, no matter how large, then it will contain the experts anyway, and the good and bad choices will even each other out, leaving us with, if you like, a central core of wisdom which will be a more honest version of the truth.

If Surowiecki is right, then this is pretty hard for the average gambler to take. Perhaps sustaining a profit over a long period has nothing to do with how right or wrong your individual opinions on a sporting event are, but more of a long-term numbers game. This theory gives those who rely on value alone a huge boost, and lends you to believe that when you sit down with your newspaper on a Saturday morning and try and pick out some kind of accumulator bet on the day's races, you're actually wasting your time. The reality, of course, is that you're not, and you're doing it in the main because you *enjoy* doing it, and feel that one day you will get it right and it will return a handsome payment. And there is, of course, a chance that it will, though if your methodology is flawed you are lessening that chance. You, of course, may not care, with the process of making the selections as important to you as the end result. And I'm not going to argue with you. If you punt for fun, and keep it to that, then good luck to you.

I couldn't help but wonder, though, how Surowiecki's theories might help find the winner of my favourite race. As I've already said, there are layers and layers of subtlety in his arguments, but I liked the central idea of a crowd reaching a more intelligent answer than an individual. Given that I'd only ever backed the winner of the race three times in my lifetime, a crowd couldn't do any worse than me alone. The question was which question to ask.

The key factor in the Stewards' Cup has always been seen to be the draw. That's why such an enjoyable fuss is made every year over the stall that'll be allocated to each horse. This year, with the race sponsored by Blue Square, it was the manager of Stockport County (and very keen punter) Dietmar Hamann who had the task of picking the horses' names out of a barrel in front of Goodwood's weighing room. As each horse's name comes out, the assembled connections select which stall number they want. And so the draw continues, and the sun beats down, and by the end of the lengthy process no one looks like they care any more, least of all Hamann.

There's a theory, though, that the draw has been less important in recent years. High numbers, that is those horses drawn furthest away from the grandstand, seemed to throw up the winner more often than not, the theory being that the ground underfoot on that part of the course had taken less punishment and therefore would give a horse a better chance of winning. In recent years, however, the winners had come down the middle of the course, with the last four victorious horses being drawn in stalls 11, 14, 10 and 11. The high and low bias that used to prevail seemed to be a thing of the past.

I wanted to choose my own crowd, and it would make its decision from a list of numbers that it wouldn't understand. The crowd had to make a judgement call simply based on the evidence that was in front of it, not with any knowledge of what it was actually deciding. It would be pointless to simply ask a group of people to tell me which horse that they thought would win the Stewards' Cup, as they would use all sorts of different methods to reach that conclusion. Some would pick a name that they liked, others would go for a particular jockey, and the rest might try and apply different levels of logic to reach their decision, some doing it with no knowledge of racing, others with a good deal. Numbers would be simpler, and, of course, the crowd would not be allowed to talk to each other, because that way Groupthink lies.

As far as selecting the numbers for my list, I was torn between using the draw of the previous winners, and their prices. There's a theory that says with all that is built into the price of a horse, probability and presumption, looking at the prices of previous winners of a race could be one of the best guides to future success, and one of the few relatively untapped areas left to the serious gambler. Prices, though, are so familiar, even to those who don't gamble regularly, that I felt that a list of those would give away the subject matter to my crowd. Maybe I was being too sensitive, but the moment that someone saw numbers like 16, 33, and 66 on a list, they just might cotton on. And I didn't want that. So the draw it was.

I knew that I had to go back a suitable length of time, but it couldn't be too long, as people would lose interest in a mammoth list of numbers, and so I decided that, for an experiment that paid homage to *The Wisdom of Crowds*, without following it to the scientific letter, I would send out a list of numbers which contained the draw number of the first four home in the Stewards' Cup between, and including, my last two wins in the race. From Superior Premium in 1998 to Evens and Odds in 2010. So a list of people who are important to me received the following email the week before the race.

Dear All

Sorry for bothering you on a Friday with a strange email, but I need your help if you have a spare minute or two. As most of you know, I'm currently in the final stages of writing a book, and after a slightly mad journey, there's one final chapter on which I need your help. It's going to seem a bit weird, but I'm doing an experiment based on a book/theory called *The Wisdom of Crowds*, and as people who have either helped me with the book, been involved in the events during it, or are just friends whose judgement I trust, I'd like you all to be part of it.

This is what I'd like you to do. Below you'll find a series of numbers, which may or may not be in a particular order. What I'd like you to do is clear your mind, take a look at the list of numbers for no longer than a minute and then write down the number that comes into your head after looking at the list. You don't have to look for patterns necessarily, but I'm sure that one will jump out at you. There's no right or wrong answer, and all that you have to do is email me a number. If you have time, and could print off the list before looking at it, that would be great.

To make it work properly, there are a couple of rules. Your choice needs to be independent so please don't reply to all, and if you're sitting in an office near each other then please don't talk to each other about your choice as that introduces a group element which kind of ruins the experiment... Oh, and a note for the horse racing people on this list. If you think about it too much, then you'll know pretty quickly what the numbers relate to, so please don't overthink it and just send me back the number that comes into your head organically!

The cumulative result of all of this will turn into a bet at the weekend, and that will be the final bet of my book. So my fate is kind of in your hands…

Thanks for helping, and sorry again for the email, I know that it can be a pain to get insane emails like this, but I'd really appreciate your help,

All the best

Dave

The list of numbers goes like this:

28
25
29
23
8
10
28
6
28
24
4

19
19
30
23
7
29
9
22
16
27
29
28
3
1
24
28
6
19
17
20
27
19
26
22
28
11
7
25

13
14
3
1
7
10
16
11
13
11
10
17
14

That was it. I would wait to see how many replies I got and take both the mean and the median from the list. Those two numbers would be faithfully applied to the draw for this year's race, and that would be it. A decision based not on any of my feelings about which horse might win, but purely on a set of statistics, conjured up by me, and answered by a crowd. On the list of people to whom I sent the email was what I considered to be a cross section. There were those who had helped me along the way, from the worlds of golf, football, racing, tennis and American football. There were punters, and those who've never had a bet. Each person who loves sport was counterbalanced by one who doesn't much care for it, and every racing fan by one who professes complete ambivalence to it. There were those whose judgement I trusted, those who make me laugh and those who are close to me. Somehow, I wanted my friends to carry me over the line.

At this point, maybe you could join in and do what it says on the email. Don't worry if you don't want to, or don't have time. The race has gone now, and it's not going to be much use. But what I found fascinating was that, when the emails started coming back, one number appeared more than twice as much as any other. So go on, have a look at that list and see if anything jumps out. I'll tell you what it was in the next paragraph in an attempt to build up suspense. The numbers that came back were mostly high, and that, of course, makes sense given the prevalence of numbers over 20 in the list, with high draws having been preferable over the years. The average of the responses that I received ended up being 23, and so that would be one of my numbers.

The one that appeared twice as much as any other was 28. It would be odd if that was the one that jumped out at you as well. I agonised over whether to be pure and strict about the experiment, or whether I should take into account that this year the stall numbers for the Stewards' Cup had been switched round to make things easier for spectators. So what had been 1 was now 28 and what had been 28 was now 1. Confused? So, I suspect, were the spectators. In the end, it felt like the right thing to do. Having thrown a series of numbers at people which related to one aspect of a race it would be ridiculous to not take account of the fact that those numbers now meant something different. And so, revolving around an axis of 14, the stalls that I would go for would be numbers 1 and 7. That meant that the two horses that would carry my money on this final leg would be Mac's Power (drawn in stall one), trained by James Fanshawe and ridden by Pat Cosgrave, and Fathsta (drawn in stall seven), trained by David Simcock and ridden by a jockey who was having a breakthrough season, Silvestre De Souza. I won't dwell long on form or figures, as they were absent from my calculations, but Mac's Power would go off as second favourite for the race at 13-2, while Fathsta was considered a live outsider and priced at 16-1.

All that remained was to work out just how much I should have on them both. I've always staked more on the Stewards' Cup than on any other race, and my feeling was that I should be gung ho and romantic, daredevil and dramatic, and split my winnings so far down the middle, chucking half on each horse. And that's definitely what I would have done in a previous life. But, boringly and sensibly, I stuck with the staking plan. That had both cost me and saved me throughout the journey, and I wasn't going to desert it now. Besides, if this 'Wisdom of Crowds' thing didn't pay off, then at least I'd walk away from the six months in profit. So, it was £310 on Mac's Power to win and £125 on Fathsta to win. All I had to do now was sit back and see what would happen next.

I decided that the best place to go and watch the Stewards' Cup was from the start. You can catch a bus from the gate at Goodwood that takes you along the racecourse and up through the woods, down to the tranquillity of the end of the course. From there, the horses crash out of the stalls and head down a straight six furlongs, with the screaming grandstands on their left. When you watch the race from the start, you're aware of just how peaceful it is, and as you watch the next 50 seconds or so, you see each enclosure rise up in turn as the noise gets louder and the finish closer. Most of that Mexican wave would have backed Hoof It, the strong favourite for the race, who was considered by some to be far too good for this field, and capable of moving up in class. He would be carrying more weight than any other horse in the race, but most good judges felt that he could do it, and he was certainly a worthy favourite. Down at the start, I saw De Souza quietly give Fathsta a pat on the neck, and Cosgrave do something similar with Mac's Power. In those moments before a big race, some of the jockeys chat loudly, and others look into the distance and have a few final thoughts on the job in hand. They're all in it together, but know that only one of them will be on board the winner.

As the horses went into the stalls I wished myself luck for one final time, I paused for breath, and then the clanking noise of the stalls opening meant that they were off and running. I turned and let my eyes follow them as they made their way from the peace and down towards the noise and the passion. It was Mac's Power and Fathsta for me, and for those of you who don't know what happened, this is how the commentator Richard Hoiles described the race:

'And they're off, and racing. And from the stalls the major-ity of them heading over towards the near side. Hoof It is certainly one of those. Pastoral Player having a slight change of mind, but he is going to come down the centre of the racecourse. So Nasri leads Tiddliwinks, High Standing stayed over on the far side, meanwhile down the centre Evens and Odds and Fitz Flyer show up there with Tax Free, Victoire De Lyphar is being strongly ridden to chase the pace. So far that far-side group are just a little behind the leaders as they make their journey down through the first couple of furlongs. So Nasri on the stand side with Tiddliwinks. Also in that group is Doc of the Bay and High Standing. Mean-while down the centre, Evens and Odds leads over there with

Fitz Flyer, Tax Free, Hoof It's prominent on the far left, also coming through is Global City with Secret Asset. Fathsta behind them, with Quest for Success, Jimmy Styles, Ancient Cross as they make their journey... now still, with a good furlong and a half to run, Tiddliwinks under the near side, out in the centre is Nasri, the yellow cap of Evens and Odds, Tax Free, Hoof It on the far side is right front rank with the leaders at the moment. Hoof It in the pink jacket, from Tax Free, still staying on is Nasri on the near side, and Mac's Power is coming home strongly, but Hoof It under this ten-stone burden, is a Group horse in a Handicap and will win the Stewards' Cup. What a performance, under that weight. Hoof It has won by as much as three lengths.'

So there it was. The favourite was so good that the outcome was never really in question. The result meant that Chubby Chandler's sporting influence was getting bigger and bigger. He was now the manager of the first three major golf champions of the year, and the owner of the Stewards' Cup winner. Mac's Power ran a blinder to finish third, and I'd briefly been excited at the late surge that he made up the rail (those words 'Mac's Power is coming home strongly' will live with me for a long time), but he would never have caught Hoof It. The winner showed so much speed that his jockey Kieran Fallon was able to shift him from his draw in stall 18 onto the side where the low numbered horses were running and he bolted up the rail to win easily. The draw, for once, was largely irrelevant. In behind Hoof It, the second placed horse, Tax Free, had come from stall 13, and Mac's Power, of course, from number 1. Nasri, in fourth, had been drawn in stall 27. Fastha hadn't been quick enough and had faded away after looking to have a chance at halfway, and so I had to take it on the chin. My final two bets were losers.

But as I looked down towards the finish line and saw the beaten horses file back to the stables, I didn't feel like a loser, and it was the first time in a long time that I'd been able to say that. You're not going to get any Damascene nonsense from me, any sense that somehow I'm a different person who might be happier without gambling, or who has worked out how to do it. This book isn't about addiction, although the story it tells would have never have happened without it. I'm not pretending for a minute that this has been anything close to a study of gambling addiction, but hopefully it has shone a light into some of the corners of a world with which many of you won't be familiar. And, of course, there'll be those of you who've maybe nodded a bit here and there and recognised the madness. I think I behaved like an addict for a six-month period and I did it for a reason. Everything that I have done since has been to put that right.

I suppose that there should be a part of this, the final chapter, in which I try and sum up all of the things that I've learned. I think that I am a better gambler than I was when I started. I know I'll never be perfect, no matter how many essential oils I smell or however many Pilates classes I attend. The title of the book was always just that, a title. I've also learned that *not* placing a bet is as good as having one. That's the kind of discipline that you need to make a success of it. I'd always been irritated, as a few punters are, by the habit of Kevin Pullein in the *Racing Post* of saying at the end of a long column:

'Recommendation: No Bet'. Now, though, I see the sense of it, and realise that he is probably cleverer than us all. The option to keep our money in our pockets is one that we should all exercise a lot more.

I've definitely learned that there's no shame in changing your mind about a strongly held opinion, and also that you should bet on what you think is going to happen, rather than a version of it. That's why I now accept in black and white that Brandt Snedeker is probably destined not to win a golf major, and that I'm not going to get rich backing him. I'll leave him behind, and look for someone else to hang my hat on. I'll also forever regret my decision to back Wladimir Klitschko to beat David Haye inside the distance, rather than just beat him, as I don't think that I've ever been more certain of anything in my life, and yet lost money on the event.

I've learnt to listen to those who know, like Steve Davis and John Parrott, like Chris Bradnam and Tom Segal, like James Eastham and Martin Dixon, and to those who have an exceptional instinct, like Simon Reed and my nameless mate who tipped Pour Moi for the Derby. They gave me the biggest thrill of the year, in those never to be forgotten ten minutes.

There's no question as well that the process of writing down your thoughts on your own gambling is an excellent way to avoid disaster. This has obviously been compulsory for me this year, and is optional the rest of the time, but it's a tactic that I'm keen to adopt, a habit within a habit. I'd always been told that writing down every bet that you place and then going back over your diary at least once a week is a good thing to do and I'd never bothered, but trust me, everything that you do, right and wrong, needs to be recorded. For me, for the time being, it's in this book; for you it should be somewhere slightly more reliable than on the back of a wet fag packet. It will make you wince when you do something particularly capricious, reckless or ill thought out, and also lead to an odd kind of betting remorse, which compares to that mixture of pain and shame that you feel after being drunk at a party. It goes something like: 'Did I do that? Jesus. I did? Said that? To her? And then I... ? Oh God.'

The next day you'll find yourself letting out an involuntary noise and then possibly punching yourself in the face. If you respond to social humiliation like that then you should do exactly the same when you back a 5-1-on shot and it loses. Write it down, snap a few pens in half, and then read it over and over. After you've recorded a few mistakes in black and white, you won't do it again.

The point of this experiment was to rid me of a whole lot of demons, but also to cover every single angle that I could before placing a bet. We all think that we do this, but at the same time make the mistake of seeing things at face value and no deeper. You don't have to travel to the US Open to get an idea of the winner, you can do all that putting yourself in a virtual position by the side of the green. Be aware of the weather and look for an angle beyond the obvious. Reading an article about the USGA's horticulturist proved far more profitable for me than any research I did on players, and, although wall-to-wall coverage means that there are fewer undiscovered nuggets out there, I still think that we can find them, and with them, gain an edge. Once you have got as close as you can to the action, pitchside or court-side or wherever it may be, then ask yourself before placing the bet whether you know exactly what you think will happen, and why. And if you can't answer that, then keep hold of your money. I also learned just how hard it is to cover so many different angles at so many different events, and have to admit to myself that I badly ran out of mental energy on the day of that Klitshcko fight. I got seriously lazy, and paid the price. Another example of when the sensible thing to do is to keep hold of your money.

I learned that you have to have the courage to bet against the crowd when the price has been driven down or up by reasons with which you don't agree. Don't sit there and think that just because a price is short, someone must know something. Often they don't. It's your money after all. You should stand or fall by the courage of your own convictions. That doesn't mean that you should ignore tipsters, though. Like many punters, I have enormous faith in Tom Segal of the *Racing Post*. He makes betting on horseracing enjoyable, makes you feel as if you have a way in to a sport that can often seem impossible. James Eastham and his French football knowledge is also something that I like to have onside, as are the golfing opinions of Steve Palmer in the *Racing Post*, and its football tipsters Mark Langdon and Dan Childs, both of whom get a lot more right than they do wrong. Knowing who you want to listen to is very definitely a good thing.

A while ago, when I was sitting in a cafe, a man with a ponytail and an attitude was sitting with a girl who was blatantly out of his league, yet he was trying his luck. Maybe I was just jealous, as it's not the kind of thing that I would do. He threw a couple of vaguely impressive quotations at her, and then came up with what he must have thought was the winner, as he solemnly intoned: 'Talking to a scholar for a night is better than reading for ten years.'

The disturbing thing about the conversation seemed to be that our hero felt that he was the scholar in this relationship, and his indication was that we would all be better (god knows, his voice was loud enough), for having listened to him. People with voices as booming as his often cultivate them because otherwise nobody would take them seriously, and having been subjected to his views on life for the good part of an hour, I left, but curiously I took the proverb with me.

Anyway, armed with this apparent drivel, I got to thinking about scholars, and wondered just how many of them we really have in the gambling world. There are many, but there are also a lot of people who talk a good game, but who I wouldn't want to listen to for ten minutes, let alone ten years. The kind of people, as previously discussed, who shout the word 'value' at you without having a real understanding of what it means. I love the concept of value in betting, and think that it's core to the whole caper, but I often hate the use of the word, as it's become a panacea to deal with muddy thinking. And thinking muddily, as we've already established, is a one-way ticket to the madhouse.

The other scholar that I haven't mentioned is the professional gambler Patrick Veitch. His book *Enemy Number One* is a decent read and highly recommended for its content and for the lessons that it can teach us. I could parrot his opinions on how to analyse horse races, but I suggest that you go out and buy the book if you want to do that. However, there's one section that fascinated me, and surprised me so much that I had to re-read the page. The approach detailed by Veitch is studious and methodical, it's about such a slavish attention to detail that you're bound to have an edge on every other gambler and many bookmakers, as you have worked so hard. But amidst all of that, there's a bet on a horse called Enfilade at Chester, and he summarises it:

'A win in a Chester Handicap for Enfilade was uplifting, all the more so because there wasn't a single strong reason for the bet. I just felt the horse was a big price and finally found the confidence to have a full bet on my own instinctive judgement without needing a long list of reasons to back me up. I looked upon it as a turning point.'

The fact that a man like Veitch admits, in print, that instinct even has a part to play in gambling is interesting, all the more so that he regards the incident as a turning point after a bad run. What had been missing from his armoury was instinctiveness, that feeling when you just know that a bet is right. I find it immensely reassuring that somebody who I had always presumed was just way more disciplined and better and braver and richer than me would think in this way. Something that I consider as a flaw in myself is actually an essential weapon in his war with the bookmakers. It convinced me absolutely that the right kind of instinct is key, and it's something that we should all seek to heighten.

And that kind of instinct isn't something that's unique to gamblers. Remember, I believe that everyone is a gambler anyway; it's just that the majority of people refuse to admit it. The instinct that you have about buying a house, putting money away in an ISA, getting a girl's phone number. It's the same one that leads me to fancy a horse for a race. I'd proved that at Cheltenham, the instinct about Carlito Brigante proving far more useful than all the hours of dull research that I did about the Champion Hurdle. I've always lived my life instinctively, and that got me thinking about Emma. As I'd crumbled and fallen into six months of throwing my money away, I'd always presumed that she had been the one, and that I would now be half a person. And yet now I realised that I'd been wrong. My instinct had meant that I'd met her in the first place, and that we'd fallen into what we believed was love. After she'd gone, all that I'd done was remember the good stuff about her. The way she made me laugh and the way she looked when she was happy. But what I hadn't realised in the dream state which took me over was that she was completely wrong for me, and we were different in many more ways than we were similar. I should never have been so arrogant to trust my instinct over what was staring me in the face.

I saw her, just once, a few weeks after that Stewards' Cup. She still looked the same, still had the same air of confidence, chin jutting against the world. She saw me and looked surprised, and we had an awkward moment, exchanged a few words that aren't worth repeating. I was surprised at how warm she was towards me, and as I walked away I felt strange. Not because I missed her, or because she made my heart leap, but because she didn't. I was over that love affair, if not necessarily the habit that had caused it all to go wrong in the first place. I smiled as my stride quickened and I moved further away from her. For the first time in two years I felt free. And, after what had happened, that's all that I could ask for. Carried, like all of us, on the wind. Held back by imperfections, driven on by possibility, but free.

ACKNOWLEDGEMENTS

There are three different groups of people who deserve thanks. Those who helped me get into the events that I covered, both literally and intellectually; those who offered a helping hand along the way by dispensing much-needed expertise; and a third group of people who may not even have known they were helping, but who with a cheery bit of encouragement allowed me to scale what at times felt like an impossible summit. So, here goes:

None of the American journeys in the book would have been possible without the help of Jon Sheiman in New York and Pete Kowalski of the USGA. Gabriele Marcotti gave geographical advice and a great deal more, although I fear that he will have to wait a while before his beloved Eagles win the big one.

The Ryder Cup team of Richard Kaufman, John Hawksworth, Gary Moran, Bob Bubka, Paul Eales, Gordon Brand Junior, Peter Baker, Ron Jones and Matty Adams made a potentially gruelling event a lot of fun, and were generous with their time and patience.

Dom Wright went way beyond the call of duty at the Crucible Theatre and allowed me access to a world in which the participants couldn't have been more helpful. My thanks to Jason Woodward, Greg Duke, Matthew Knight, Phil Yates, Ivan Hirschowitz, John Parrott, Neal Foulds, Terry Griffiths and, of course, Steve Davis.

At Cheltenham I'm lucky enough to be surrounded by friends and experts in equal measure. The insights of Rory Delargy and David Cleary were invaluable, as was Julia Fairbank's ability to analyse the way that a horse moves while keeping me sane at the same time. The words of wisdom of Chris Barnett and Martin Kelly are also much appreciated, and thanks go to Alex Steedman, Paul Jacobs, Kieran Packman, Martin Dixon, Chris Foulerton and Shaun Crook. I had no right to expect Simon Claisse to be as patient with me as he was, and Andy Clifton, Rebecca Morgan and Peter McNeile must also be sick of the sight of me. My thanks to all.

I'm fortunate to count James Eastham as both a friend and a source of information on French football, and knowing that both he and Nico Thiriot were on the end of the phone was a great comfort. Robbie Thomson, Matt Spiro and David Astorga all did their best to get me a place at the Stade de France at the last minute, and Matt was generous with his knowledge of Paris and its troubles. Also a great help with their knowledge and opinions on football were Stewart Robson, Gary O'Reilly, Matt Jackson, Iain Dowie and Paul Walsh, while Jonathan Wilson offered wise counsel as he always does.

I've described my admiration for Eurosport's tennis team in the book, but specific thanks go to Simon Reed, Chris Bradnam and Sam Smith, all of whom manage to pull off the trick of being excellent broadcasters and unfailingly pleasant people. Thanks also to Stephanie Taplin, who included giving me tickets among her many other jobs. And to Andrew Castle, Mats Wilander and Russell Fuller for their time and insight. Paris is always made fun by the presence of Eddie Hayes, Richard Hogqvist, Ollie Compton and Jeremy Wintrebert.

I wish that I could thank Roy Jones Junior for talking to me in Hamburg, but I was both too much in awe of him and too sure of myself even to ask. Can I thank him for standing in the same lift of me and saying hello? Tobias Drews, Ingo Rohrbach and Benno Stricker were a great help, and Mike Costello and Bob Mee were their usual generous selves. Thanks to all of them for making that evening seem somewhere near sane.

The process of writing this book could have made my working life extremely difficult, but the support and ability of the following people not to punch me in the face will be forever remembered: Simon Carr, Paul Charalambous, Frank Callaghan, Tom Skippings, Lorna Gibbs, Jo and James Robinson, John Mackay, Charlotte Healy, Jon Stockdale, Keron Steele, Stuart Brown, Maxwell Liu, Joe Dyer, Nick Moody, Steve Clune, David Stewart, Marcus Buckland, Issy Clarke, Ian Darke, Carlos Pena, Shelley Garton, Victoria Harris, Emma Booth, Ian Hinkley-Smith and, of course, those irrepressible and ill-advised gamblers Chris McKee and Shane Stitt.

Bruce Millington and Kevin Pullein from the *Racing Post* both offered advice and encouragement, and all of the writers from the *Post* deserve a mention. There isn't space for that, so a simple thank you for your contributions to my favourite newspaper, endlessly knowledgeable, brave and opinionated. Long may it flourish.

This book would forever have been an idea and little more had it not been for the encouragement and guidance of my agent David Luxton and the imagination and intelligence of my editor Charlotte Atyeo. To them, and to all at Bloomsbury, many, many thanks.

LF 4/12.

And finally, the people who've been at the centre of this project, the ones who have helped and encouraged every step of the way. Whether it was a word of advice, a kind comment, or a kick up the backside, I can honestly say that without you I would never have done it and I hope that I can repay the favour one day. In no particular order, Alan Dudman, Lorna Fowler, Ollie Bellwood, Simon Foat, Jamie Pacheco, Lydia Hislop, Steve Mellish, Claire McDonnell, Steve Tebb, Ollie Kneen, Miral Hamani, Douglas Dean, Jacqui Oatley, Ben Lyttleton, James Butterfield, Holly McEnaney, Dan Roebuck, Shelley Alexander, Maria Moeller, Steve Ellis, Mark Clark, Daniel Pearce, Andy Bodfish, Guy Havord and Liam Hanley. I can never thank any of you enough, and the same goes for my mum and all of my family, who have given me love, encouragement and wisdom.

I would also like to acknowledge material quoted from the following sources: page v, *The Finkler Question* by Howard Jacobson (Bloomsbury), reproduced with permission; page 35, *Dry* by Augusten Burroughs (Atlantic Books); page 40–41, *Fast Company* by Jon Bradshaw (High Stakes Publishing), reproduced with permission; page 67, *The Italian Job* by Gabriele Marcotti and Gianluca Vialli (Bantam), reprinted by permission of The Random House Group; page 68, *Bury Me in My Jersey* by Tom McAllister (Villard); page 225–6, *The Art of Choosing* by Sheena Iyengar (Twelve); page 231, *US Open: Golf's Ultimate Challenge* by Robert Sommers (Stanley Paul), reprinted by permission of The Random House Group; page 249, *How I Lost More Than a Quarter Ton and Gained a Life* by Nancy Makin (Dutton); page 270–1, Richard Hoiles' commentary on the Stewards' Cup 2011, reproduced with permission; page 277, *Enemy Number One* by Patrick Veitch (Racing Post), reproduced with permission.